Votes for Women
1860–1928 THIRD EDITION

Paula Bartley

D1351027

HODDER
EDUCATION
PART OF HACHETTE LIVRE UK

For Dóra and Jonathan Dudley

I would like to thank the series editor, Dr Robert Pearce, for the care he has taken in editing this book. His kind, yet rigorous, criticism has certainly made it much better. Thanks also to Jane Tyler at Hodder for her meticulous editing, and her patience. The incisive comments made by the examiners from various boards were very helpful and I would like to thank them too. My greatest thanks are to my husband, Jonathan Dudley, for his constant support and encouragement.

Study guides updated, 2008, by Sally Waller (AQA) and Angela Leonard (Edexcel).

The publishers would like to thank the following individuals, institutions and companies for permission to reproduce copyright illustrations in this book: © Bettmann/CORBIS, page 175; Courtesy of *The Courier, Dundee* © D.C. Thomson & Co., Ltd/Dundee City Council, page 112; W.K. Haselden, *Daily Mirror*, 13th March 1914 and the British Cartoon Archive, University of Kent, page 124; W.K. Haselden, *Daily Mirror*, 16th November 1923 and the British Cartoon Archive, University of Kent, page 164; © Hulton-Deutsch Collection/CORBIS, page 46; © Imperial War Museum, page 145; Mary Evans Picture Library, pages 41, 45; Mary Evans/ The Women's Library, pages 70, 166; Courtesy of The Mitchell Library, Glasgow, page 142; © Museum of London, pages 32, 48, 49, 52, 60, 72, 86, 116, 117; © Museum of London, UK/The Bridgeman Art Library, page 149; © Oldham Local Studies and Archives, page 37; Private Collection/The Bridgeman Art Library, page 13; Reproduced with permission of Punch Ltd., www.punch.co.uk, page 16.

The publishers would like to thank the following for permission to reproduce material in this book: AQA Material is reproduced by permission of the Assessment and Qualifications Alliance, extracts used on page 159; Edexcel Limited for extracts used on pages 33, 97, 133.
The publishers would like to acknowledge use of the following extracts: Allen Lane for an extract from *The Pankhurst's* by Martin Pugh, 2000; Fontana for an extract from Women at War, 1914–1918 by Arthur Marwick, 1977; Oxford University Press for an extract from *The March of Women* by Martin Pugh, 2000; Routledge for an extract from *The Women's Suffrage Movement* by Elizabeth Crawford, 1999; Time Warner Books UK for an extract from *My Own Story* by Emmeline Pankhurst, 1914.

Every effort has been made to trace all copyright holders, but if any have been inadvertently overlooked the Publishers will be pleased to make the necessary arrangements at the first opportunity.

Hodder Headline's policy is to use papers that are natural, renewable and recyclable products and made from wood grown in sustainable forests. The logging and manufacturing processes are expected to conform to the environmental regulations of the country of origin.

Orders: please contact Bookpoint Ltd, 130 Milton Park, Abingdon, Oxon OX14 4SB. Telephone: (44) 01235 827720. Fax: (44) 01235 400454. Lines are open 9.00–5.00, Monday to Saturday, with a 24-hour message answering service. Visit our website at www.hoddereducation.co.uk

© Paula Bartley 2007
First published in 2007 by
Hodder Education, part of Hachette Livre UK
338 Euston Road
London NW1 3BH

Impression number   5 4 3
Year   2011 2010 2009 2008

Cover photo © Museum of London/Heritage-Images
Illustrations by Gray Publishing
Typeset in Baskerville 10/12pt and produced by Gray Publishing, Tunbridge Wells
Printed in Malta

A catalogue record for this title is available from the British Library

ISBN: 978 0340 926 857

Contents

Dedication   **v**

Chapter 1 Change and Continuity in the Position of Women 1860–1918   **1**
1 Introduction   2
2 Education   2
3 Work   4
4 Marriage and Divorce   5
5 Sexual Morality   7
6 Politics   8

Chapter 2 Votes for Women: The Debate   **11**
1 The Case for Votes for Women   11
2 The Case Against Votes for Women   23
3 Suffrage and Anti-suffrage Arguments   29
Study Guide   31

Chapter 3 Suffragists and Suffragettes   **35**
1 The Origins of Women's Suffrage   36
2 Disunity in the Suffrage Movement   38
3 The National Union of Women's Suffrage Societies and its Offshoots 1897–1914   43
4 The Women's Social and Political Union 1903–14   48
5 Key Debate: Suffragette Membership   53
6 Disunity in the Suffragette Movement   58
7 Other Suffrage Societies   61
8 The Opposition to Votes for Women   63
9 The Key Debate   64
Study Guide   66

Chapter 4 The Suffrage Campaigns 1860–1914   **68**
1 Introduction   69
2 Peaceful Methods of Campaigning   69
3 Parliament and Women's Suffrage   76
4 Increasing Militancy   82
5 The Key Debate   92
Study Guide   96

Chapter 5 Men and Votes for Women   **99**
1 Introduction   100
2 The Political Parties   100
3 The Liberal Government 1906–14   110
4 The Alternative Establishment   118
5 Male Organisations   125
6 Research and Men's Support of Votes for Women   128
Study Guide   131

Chapter 6 Women, Suffrage and the First World War

| | | 135 |

1 The Suffrage Movement and the War 136
2 Women's War Work and the Vote 143
3 War, Suffrage and the Government 147
4 The Key Debate 152
Study Guide 155

Chapter 7 Life after Suffrage

| | | 161 |

1 Introduction 161
2 Effects on Parliament 162
3 Effects on the Women's Movement 168
4 Effects on Women's Work 169
5 Effects on Marriage and the Family 172
6 Effects on Sexual Morality 173
Study Guide 177

Glossary 179

Index 185

Dedication

Keith Randell (1943–2002)

The *Access to History* series was conceived and developed by Keith, who created a series to 'cater for students as they are, not as we might wish them to be'. He leaves a living legacy of a series that for over 20 years has provided a trusted, stimulating and well-loved accompaniment to post-16 study. Our aim with these new editions is to continue to offer students the best possible support for their studies.

1 Change and Continuity in the Position of Women 1860–1918

POINTS TO CONSIDER

This book examines the suffrage movement between 1860 and 1918. It considers the arguments put forward by those who supported and those who were opposed to votes for women. It introduces the key figures and the key organisations involved in the women's suffrage movement before analysing the various ways in which women and men campaigned for the vote. Women's contributions to the First World War are also examined. This first chapter introduces the main achievements made by women during this period and, in so doing, places the campaign for the vote within a wider historical context. The key areas examined are:

• Education
• Work
• Marriage and divorce
• Sexual morality
• Politics

Key dates

1857	Divorce Act
1860	Nursing School for Women established at St Thomas' Hospital, London
1864	First Contagious Diseases Act
1865	Elizabeth Garrett Anderson became first woman to qualify as a doctor
1869	Single women able to vote in town elections Girton College founded
1870	Education Act
1870	Married Women's Property Act
1875	First woman Poor Law Guardian elected
1878	Domestic Science compulsory for girls in Board Schools London University admits women
1879	Somerville and Lady Margaret Hall, Oxford, founded
1881	Elementary schooling compulsory between the ages of 5 and 13
1882	Married Women's Property Act
1883	Royal Holloway College, London, founded
1884	Matrimonial Causes Act
1885	Criminal Law Amendment Act

1886	Contagious Diseases Acts repealed
	Maintenance of Wives Act
	Custody of Infants Act
1888	Single women allowed to vote in county elections
1891	Free elementary schooling
1893	First female factory inspector appointed
1894	Married women allowed to vote in local elections
1895	Summary Jurisdiction Act
1902	Education Act
1907	All women allowed to vote in local elections
1947	Cambridge awarded degrees to women
1994	Marital rape made illegal

1 | Introduction

Britain today is a representative **democracy**. A general election is held at least every 5 years when all citizens over the age of 18 have the chance to vote for a Member of Parliament (MP) who will represent them in the House of Commons. It is the rule of the people by the people, often believed to be the best way to govern, since people have the right to chose who will represent them. For some people living in nineteenth-century Britain democracy was a long-cherished ideal, born out of struggle with authority and only slowly achieved. Britain did not become a full democracy until 1928.

Women were the last group of people to obtain the vote. In 1918, women over the age of 30, who were **householders** or wives of householders, who paid rent of more than £5 a year or were graduates of a British university, gained the vote. But it was another 10 years before women achieved the vote on equal terms with men who, at the time, could vote if they were over 21. Eventually, in 1928, all women over the age of 21, regardless of their marital status or financial position, were **enfranchised**.

Even so, women only gained the vote after a long, and at times highly controversial, campaign. This book tells the story of the **suffragists** and the **suffragettes** who fought hard for this objective. Yet, although this book is about women's suffrage, the vote was just one of a number of demands put forward by those who campaigned for social change.

2 | Education

Feminists believed that education was the key to unlock the closed doors into the masculine world of politics. In the 1860s, when the campaign for **suffrage** began in earnest, the majority of women from all social classes generally lacked a formal education. By 1918 there had been some remarkable changes, though not all as a response to pressure from women and not always beneficial to them. As Dorothy Thomson, a political historian, has pointed out, 'generalisations about a whole gender

Key terms

Democracy
An electoral system in which every adult has the vote.

Householders
Those who lived at a permanent address and paid taxes on their home.

Enfranchised
Given the vote.

Suffragists
Women who sought the vote using peaceful methods.

Suffragettes
Women who sought the vote using violent methods.

Feminist
Someone who believes that women and men should be treated equally.

Suffrage
The vote.

Key question
What were the key shifts in educational provision for girls between 1860 and 1918?

Key terms

Working class
A collective term for those people and their families who earned a living as manual workers.

Factory schools
From 1833 cotton manufacturers had to provide half-time schooling for children who worked in their factories.

Pauper children
Children who had no family and lived in workhouses.

Workhouse schools
From 1834 workhouses had to provide schooling for the children who lived there.

Charity schools
Schools set up by individuals or religious groups.

Education Act of 1870
This established School Boards that had the authority to build schools from money collected from local taxes. Women were allowed to vote for and serve on School Boards.

Education Act of 1902
Abolished School Boards and set up Local Education Authorities (LEAs), which were given the power to establish secondary schools. Women were not allowed to vote or serve on these.

have to be treated with great caution'. Educational developments affected working-class and middle-class girls and women quite differently; and while it is thought to have limited the working class, new educational provision opened up opportunities for middle-class women.

The education of working-class girls

Until 1870 girls who were **working class** were educated in a variety of ways. Young factory workers attended **factory schools**, whereas **pauper children** went to **workhouse schools**. The remainder of the female population, if formally educated at all, were taught in small fee-paying schools run by older women or in **charity schools** for poor children.

When the **Education Act of 1870**, which allowed local authorities to build schools for children between the ages of 5 and 13, was passed, state schools replaced this informal system. The period from 1870 onwards saw the construction of a British education system that by the end of the nineteenth century had made schooling free and compulsory for all children up to the age of 13. This new state-funded system of education gave some chances for working-class girls to become numerate and literate – by the end of the nineteenth century 97 per cent of all children could read and write – but it offered too narrow a curriculum, too rigid a teaching method and too large a class size to have any great effect on work opportunities for young women.

All too often, the school syllabus included cookery, needlework and housewifery at the expense of other subjects. Indeed, in 1878 domestic science became a compulsory subject for girls, but not for boys. It has been suggested that state schools trained rather than educated their pupils. By preparing girls either for domestic service or for the role of wife and mother, they reaffirmed, rather than challenged, women's roles in society. Change, for the young working-class schoolgirl, did not therefore necessarily mean progress. However, a further **Education Act of 1902** permitted local authorities to build secondary schools. This gave working-class girls the opportunity to continue their education after the age of 13 if their parents could do without their wage.

The education of middle-class girls

In mid-nineteenth-century Britain the majority of girls of the middle and upper classes did not go to school but were educated at home by a governess or by a member of their family. Some attended small family-type schools but the nature of their education remained virtually identical to that of those taught at home. Middle-class and upper-class girls were educated to be the wives and mothers of men from the same social class as themselves. It was unthinkable that they would go out to work for a living. By 1918 this situation had changed to some extent when a number of new schools were opened for the daughters of middle- and upper-class families. These schools offered an

academic curriculum consisting of science, economics and
mathematics.

Higher education for women

Feminists worked hard to achieve access for women into higher
education. By 1860 two London colleges, Queen's and
Bedford, had tutored a number of leading feminists (such as
Barbara Bodichon), yet the rest of higher education remained
resolutely male. All women, whatever their intelligence or
capability, were denied access to Oxford and Cambridge
universities and medical schools. This prompted some feminists
to campaign for women to be admitted to medical training and
into the universities. They also promoted the training of teachers.
By the end of the nineteenth century both London and
Manchester universities accepted women, various women's
colleges had been founded at Oxford and Cambridge (even
though Cambridge did not award degrees to women until 1947)
and women's teacher training colleges were established. In turn
these women went to teach in the newly opened secondary
schools for girls.

A Working Women's College in London was founded in the
1860s but opportunities for working-class women generally
remained limited. Furthermore, with an increasing emphasis
placed on teacher training, the old pupil–teacher scheme
(whereby bright working-class girls learned to become
teachers by working in a classroom alongside a fully
qualified professional) fell into disrepute and was soon
abandoned.

Barbara Bodichon
1827–91; a women's
rights activist in the
early suffrage
movement. She
helped to found
Girton College,
Cambridge.

Key figure

3 | Work

There were great differences in the working patterns of middle-
class and working-class women. Indeed, there were two distinct
types of work for women in this period: one for the working class
and another for the middle class.

Key question
How did women's
work change over this
period?

Working-class women

Apart from a brief interlude during the First World War (see
pages 143–6), when women worked in **munitions factories** or
else took over the jobs of men, domestic service continued to be
the most common occupation for working-class women. One in
three was a domestic servant at some time in her life. Cotton was
Britain's most important export throughout most of the
nineteenth century, so it is not surprising that textile work
remained the second most important job for women. However,
this work was concentrated in the cotton towns of northern
England and in parts of Scotland. In the rest of the British
Isles women were employed in a variety of unskilled and low-
paid jobs.

Yet there were a number of new developments. The growth
of banking and commerce, the invention of the typewriter and
the telephone all created new opportunities for women. By 1914

Munitions factories
Factories that
produced guns,
bullets, shells and
other weapons.

Key term

approximately 20 per cent of clerical workers were female. Nevertheless, despite some attempts to improve wages and working conditions, working-class women remained at the bottom of the economic scale. Equality with men was a long way off as most women workers continued to earn about 65 per cent of a male wage.

Middle-class women

In 1860 it was expected that middle-class women – single or married – should remain at home, look after their families and engage in charitable works. If they were forced to work for money, as many were, the occupation of governess was open to them. By 1914, however, middle-class women had created new professions and had made a few inroads into a number of previously male-dominated ones. A School for Nursing, for instance, was established in 1860 at St Thomas' Hospital, London, by **Florence Nightingale** and attracted middle-class women. In 1881, according to the census, there were 35,715 trained nurses. Women also trained as doctors: the first woman doctor to practise medicine was **Elizabeth Garrett Anderson**. In addition, they gained the right to become architects, factory and workhouse inspectors and to enter the civil service. By far the greatest number, however, became teachers. Even so, there were still a number of professions, such as the law, banking and the stock exchange, which remained closed to women.

Until the First World War, the sexual division of labour, whereby women and men were designated to do different jobs, remained almost insuperable. During this war, which lasted from 1914 to 1918, the nature of women's work altered dramatically when women took over many jobs traditionally held by men. But this turned out to be a temporary measure since most women returned to their traditional jobs when the war ended.

Key figures

Florence Nightingale
1820–1910; nurse who found fame when she reduced the death rate among wounded soldiers in the Crimea. She founded a nurse training school.

Elizabeth Garrett Anderson
1836–1917; the first English woman to qualify as a doctor in 1865.

Key question
What were the main obstacles preventing women from achieving equality in marriage in this period?

4 | Marriage and Divorce

Pressure from feminists was largely responsible for persuading Parliament to make a number of significant changes in the legal position of both working-class and middle-class married women in the nineteenth and early twentieth centuries. When the suffrage movement began in the 1860s, women very much remained the unequal partner in marriage, so not surprisingly feminists of the time campaigned to end a number of the grosser legal injustices. Property rights, marital rights and divorce were their major concerns.

Property rights

Once married, women were considered the property of their husbands. Husbands owned the home and the wealth of their wives, whether or not they were still living together. In the notorious case of the Norton family, George Norton took all the money earned by his wife Caroline after they had separated. On the other hand, husbands were responsible for their wives' debts and so, in return, Caroline Norton ran up bills that her husband was forced to pay. Feminists like **Elizabeth Wolstenholme Elmy** worked hard to change the law. Eventually the **Married Women's Property Acts** of 1870 and 1882 gave, if not equal status to women, then a stepping stone to future reform.

Marital rights

There were other improvements too. The Matrimonial Causes Act in 1884 went some way towards ending marital injustice by denying husbands the right to lock up their wives because they refused to have sex with them. In 1891 this Act was reinforced by the Court of Appeal that upheld a complaint by a Mrs Jackson, who had been locked up by her husband. Mrs Jackson had refused to live with Mr Jackson so he had grabbed his wife outside her church, forced her into his carriage, took her to his home and locked her up. Fortunately for Mrs Jackson, her friends led a campaign for her release and, after a long legal struggle, the courts decided that Mr Jackson had no legal right to force his wife to live with him. Mrs Jackson may have won her case, but she suffered from considerable hostility from local people for refusing to live with her husband. Moreover, despite the efforts of a number of feminists, wife-battering and marital rape remained legal in the nineteenth century. In fact, marital rape was not made illegal until 1994.

Divorce rights

Divorce law exhibited similar inequalities. Before 1857 it was extremely difficult and very expensive to obtain a divorce in England. Only very rich – and determined – men were generally able to afford the high costs of divorce. The 1857 Divorce Act reformed the divorce law, but it benefited men rather than women. Men were able to divorce their wives for adultery, whereas women had to prove bigamy, sodomy, bestiality, cruelty or long-term desertion to gain a divorce. This, argued nineteenth-century feminists, consolidated the **sexual double standard** because it laid down different grounds for divorce. Moreover, once divorced, women found it difficult to obtain maintenance and custody of their children. There were some improvements in the latter part of the nineteenth century. For example:

- The Matrimonial Causes Act (1884) allowed maintenance to separated women whose husbands had been convicted of assault.
- The Maintenance of Wives Act (1886) gave magistrates power to give maintenance to deserted women.
- The Custody of Infants Act (1886) gave separated mothers the right to keep their children.
- The Summary Jurisdiction Act (1895) gave battered women the right to obtain a divorce.

Nevertheless marital equality with men was not achieved by the time women won the vote.

Key figure

Elizabeth Wolstenholme Elmy 1833–1918; a leader of various campaigns to improve the lives of women. She was involved in education, marriage and suffrage reforms.

Key terms

Married Women's Property Acts
The 1870 Act gave women the right to keep their earnings, their personal property, and money under £200 left to them in someone's will. The 1882 Act gave women control of the money they brought into marriage and acquired afterwards.

Sexual double standard
The moral standard whereby it was acceptable for men, but not women, to have sex outside marriage.

5 | Sexual Morality

Key question
To what extent was the challenge to the sexual double standard successful?

In the nineteenth and early twentieth centuries a number of women were dismayed by the sexual double standard whereby women had to remain virginal before marriage and faithful inside it. On the other hand, a blind eye was turned if men had sex with more than one partner. One of women's greatest victories was the repeal of the Contagious Diseases Acts (CDAs). These Acts, the first of which had been passed in 1864, allowed police in a number of **garrison towns** and naval ports the right to arrest women suspected of being common prostitutes and require them to be medically examined for sexually transmitted diseases. If found infected, women could be detained for treatment. This, according to feminists, was unfair because it blamed prostitutes for the spread of sexually transmitted diseases, not the men who used their services. Under the leadership of **Josephine Butler**, the **Ladies' National Association** led a campaign to repeal these Acts and eventually succeeded 22 years after they had been passed.

The success of this campaign prompted feminists to launch a crusade against the sexual exploitation of young girls. In 1885 they achieved a victory when the **Criminal Law Amendment Act**, which raised the age of sexual consent to 16, was passed. Feminists and others founded the National Vigilance Association to ensure that this Act was put into practice and to promote equal high moral standards between the sexes. Edwardian feminists, such as Christabel Pankhurst, took up the social purity cause and demanded that men improve their moral code by remaining chaste outside marriage. Although feminists achieved a small victory in repealing the CDAs, the campaign to raise moral standards can be considered to have failed miserably. Today sex before marriage is accepted by the majority of people living in Britain, a fact that would have dismayed these early reformers.

Key terms

Garrison towns
Towns with an army stationed there.

Ladies' National Association
An organisation for women founded in 1869 to repeal unjust laws for prostitutes. Today it is known as the Josephine Butler Society and continues to campaign against the exploitation of prostitutes.

Criminal Law Amendment Act
Raised the age of sexual consent to 16. It also made homosexuality illegal and brought in stricter laws against prostitution.

Key figure

Josephine Butler
1828–1906; fought against child prostitution and led the campaign to raise the age of sexual consent to 16. She was President of the North of England Council for the Higher Education of Women.

6 | Politics

Women who campaigned for political change faced heavy criticism because they criticised the '**separate spheres**' philosophy. According to Victorian and Edwardian sentiment, God made men and women biologically different, and so it made sense that they performed distinct roles. Women were the only sex able to become pregnant, have babies and breast-feed, so it was thought appropriate for them to remain within the 'private sphere' of the home. Not surprisingly, women were also believed to be better qualified for the domestic jobs of cooking, cleaning and child-rearing because home was their natural domain. In contrast, men's historic hunting role made them innately suited to the 'public sphere' of politics, making speeches, writing leaflets and, of course, voting. In claiming a share of the 'public sphere' for women, feminists therefore challenged the fundamental principles of society.

National politics

Women may not have achieved the British parliamentary vote until 1918, but there were other political achievements. On 1 January 1881, 700 British women were able to vote at the House of Keys in the Isle of Man, 37 years before women in mainland Britain were granted the same privilege. The Manx, as the people who live in the Isle of Man are known, had kept their own institutions, independent of Britain, and governed themselves through the Tynwald Court, which had an Upper Chamber and an elected House of Keys.

Elsewhere in Britain, women were engaged in politics through their party organisations. The **Women's Liberal Federation** was an autonomous, women-only organisation that offered invaluable training to feminists. Delegates at annual meetings claimed the right to define party policy and concerned themselves with suffrage and with radical social policies, such as health, housing and education. Similarly, the **Independent Labour Party** attracted large numbers of women activists who spoke at meetings, wrote articles in newspapers and helped to develop party policy. Women also joined the women's section of the Conservative **Primrose League**, but tended to play more of a secondary role than their Liberal and Labour counterparts.

Local politics

It is sometimes forgotten that some women achieved the vote in local government long before they won the right to vote in national elections:

- Single or widowed **rate-paying** women were given the right to vote for town councils in 1869.
- Single and widowed rate-paying women were granted the right to vote for county councillors in 1888.

Key question
What opportunities existed for women in politics in the nineteenth century?

Key terms

Separate spheres
An idea that there were two spheres in society. Men belonged to the public sphere, whereas women belonged to the private sphere. Each sphere was seen to be different but equal.

Women's Liberal Federation
Founded in 1886 by female Liberals to promote votes for women.

Independent Labour Party
Founded in 1893 to promote the interests of the working class. It had a women's section.

Primrose League
Founded in 1883 to spread Conservative ideas. A woman's section was formed in 1885.

Rate-paying
Paying local taxes.

- Married women who were householder occupiers received the vote in local elections in 1894.
- Women rate-payers were allowed to participate in all aspects of local government in 1907.

As well as voting in local elections, women worked for change in their local areas. For example, some middle-class women in London's poorest areas 'worked all hours to get property repaired and fumigated, drains rebuilt, infant mortality reduced, and open spaces inserted into the slums'. Women also encouraged authorities to build public lavatories, baths and parks for the inhabitants of working-class districts.

Women's work as Poor Law Guardians

Key term

Poor Law Guardian A locally elected official who supervised the workhouses in the area.

In 1875 the first woman **Poor Law Guardian** was elected and by 1900 there were approximately 1000 women Guardians, many of whom, like Emmeline Pankhurst, tried to mitigate the worst excesses of workhouse life (see page 17). As a Poor Law Guardian in Manchester, Mrs Pankhurst found 'old folks sitting on backless forms or benches. They had no privacy, no possessions, not even a locker. The old women were without pockets in their gowns so they were obliged to keep any poor little treasures they had in their bosoms. Soon after I took office we gave the old people comfortable Windsor chairs to sit in, and in a number of ways we managed to make their existence more endurable'.

Agatha Stacey, a Birmingham Poor Law Guardian, was so concerned about the poor in the local workhouse that she helped to found homes for the homeless, single mothers and those with special learning needs. A number of female Poor Law Guardians were prominent figures in Poor Law administration nationally and used their influence to initiate reforms elsewhere.

Women's work in education

When the 1870 Education Act was passed women were eligible to vote for and to serve on the newly created School Boards. These School Boards had responsibility for the education of children in state schools from the age of 5 years and upwards. Some women sought election because they wanted to make a public statement that women were capable of governing. Others, such as the suffragist Lydia Becker (see pages 37–9), tried to put their feminist ideas into practice by encouraging boys as well as girls to do cooking and needlework. However, when Local Education Authorities replaced School Boards in the Education Act of 1902, women were declared ineligible for election. Five years later, in 1907, they regained this privilege.

Towards the vote

During the period 1860–1918 women experienced a number of significant improvements to their lives. However, blatant inequalities remained and it was these that stirred the campaigning spirits of the suffragists and the suffragettes. And so, by the time of **Edward VII**'s coronation in 1901, the vote had become their major focus of attention.

Some women believed that an all-male Parliament would only go so far to improve the lives of women and wanted the vote because they believed it would lead to better laws. In their view the vote would improve educational and job opportunities for women, and lead to more equality in marriage and better behaviour by men. It took women 58 years of campaigning to succeed. They began their struggle in 1860 but did not gain the vote until 1918.

Edward VII
1841–1910;
ascended the
throne in 1901.

Key figure

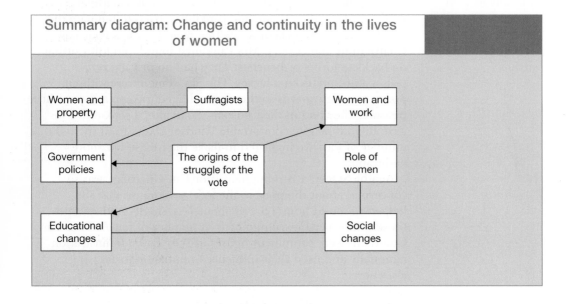

Summary diagram: Change and continuity in the lives of women

2 Votes for Women: The Debate

POINTS TO CONSIDER

It is sometimes supposed that those who supported votes for women regarded the vote as an end in itself. This is not so. Campaigners wanted the vote to end women's economic and social subordination and to brighten their future lives. At the same time, many people disagreed with women's suffrage. This chapter examines the main arguments of both those who supported and those who opposed votes for women, and will account for the similarities and differences between them under the following headings:

- The case for votes for women
- The case against votes for women
- Suffrage and anti-suffrage arguments

Key dates

1832	Great Reform Act
1867	Second Reform Act
1869	Secret ballot
	Propertied women given the right to vote in municipal elections
1869–1918	Women gained the vote in the USA
1881	Women gained the vote in Isle of Man
1883	Corrupt Practices Act
1884	Third Reform Act
1893	Women gained the vote in New Zealand
1893–1909	Women gained the vote in Australia
1906	Women gained the vote in Finland
1907	Women gained the vote in Norway

1 | The Case for Votes for Women

The issue of votes for women created a great deal of discussion. Not surprisingly, given the broad political composition of the suffrage movement and the length of time it went on for, there emerged several different arguments in support of votes for women.

Growth of democracy

Parliamentary democracy and the vote

The vote had an important symbolic significance: it was the hallmark of citizenship in a country governed by a Parliament. Suffragists were disappointed when women were consistently omitted from each of the franchise reform Acts of 1832, 1867 and 1884 and were thus denied full citizenship status.

- The **Great Reform Act of 1832** swept away many of the abuses of the parliamentary system, but the new vote was confined merely to men. Suffragists argued that, for the first time in legal and political history, women were explicitly excluded from voting because those who framed the Act had deliberately used the term 'male' rather than 'person'.
- The attainment of **household suffrage** in the **boroughs** in the **Second Reform Act of 1867** threw the exclusion of women from the democratic process into even sharper relief. Although not all men were enfranchised – the residence qualification meant that domestic servants, the armed forces and sons and other men living at home were excluded – approximately one and a half million more men were granted the vote.
- The **Third Reform Act of 1884** added approximately six million men to the voting register. This reform enfranchised two-thirds of adult males, but all women, as well as criminals and patients in lunatic asylums, remained voteless.

Suffragists considered it inappropriate to claim that Britain was a true democracy when the majority of the population was disenfranchised because they were female. They argued that no government, least of all one that saw itself as democratic, should want to preside over what was essentially an undemocratic system. By the end of the nineteenth century Britain's politics were criticised for being both unjust and unbalanced.

Women's involvement in party and local politics

The successful participation of a small number of women in both party and local politics reinforced women's claim to the parliamentary vote.

- The three franchise reform Acts of the nineteenth century, combined with the **secret ballot** and the **Corrupt Practices Act**, created a need for sophisticated party machines to organise the new mass electorate. Various women's organisations were set up within the main parties with the dual purpose of shaping women's opinion and canvassing votes in support of MPs. Women helped men to get elected, so it appeared illogical for them not to be able to vote.
- In 1869, single women and widowed rate-payers were given the right to vote in local elections and, once again, it seemed absurd for them to be denied the parliamentary vote. Women made a significant contribution to local politics by helping provide better education and by improving the lives of paupers in workhouses (see page 9).

(see page 9).

Key question
Why did suffrage campaigners claim that Britain was not a democracy?

Key terms

Great Reform Act of 1832
This gave the vote to approximately one in seven men.

Household suffrage
Male heads of households permitted to vote.

Borough
A town represented by an MP in the House of Commons.

Second Reform Act of 1867
This gave the vote to approximately one in three men.

Third Reform Act of 1884
This gave the vote to approximately two in three men.

Secret ballot
A system where the choice of voters is kept confidential. Until 1872 voters had to declare their vote in public.

Corrupt Practices Act
This limited the use of people being paid to persuade others to vote for their candidate.

Key date
Propertied women given the vote in municipal elections: 1869

Key figures

Louisa Twining
1820–1912;
granddaughter of
the head of the tea
and coffee
merchants, Twining.
She set up the
Workhouse Visiting
Society in attempt to
improve conditions
for paupers in
workhouses.

**Angela Burdett-
Coutts**
1814–1906;
granddaughter of a
wealthy banker,
Thomas Coutts. In
1837 she became
the richest woman
in England but gave
much of her money
to charity. In 1883
she helped to set up
the National Society
for the Prevention of
Cruelty to Children.

Key terms

Suffrage Atelier
An organisation
founded in 1909 to
encourage artists to
draw or paint
material in support
of votes for women.

**Proprietor of white
slaves**
A man who bought
and sold women for
prostitution.

- Moreover, as much of education and Poor Law legislation was centrally directed, it seemed to be an odd perversity that women laboured under laws they had not helped to frame.
- It was considered unfair that a few distinguished women, who had already made a significant contribution to the country's good, should be disenfranchised, while illiterate and uneducated men were free to vote. Women such as **Louisa Twining**, **Angela Burdett-Coutts** and Florence Nightingale were cited by suffragists as examples of women who would contribute much of value – for both men and women – to future parliaments if they had the right to vote.

The poster published by the **Suffrage Atelier**, below, illustrates this well. On the one hand, the poster shows a number of women from different walks of life, all of whom have contributed in some way to the welfare of the country, in either a public or a private capacity. It implies that women would have much to offer to national politics if they had the vote. On the other hand, the cartoon shows men who were criminal, mad, immoral (**'proprietor of white slaves'**), disabled or dissolute allowed to vote. (Prisoners and those in lunatic asylums were denied the vote while inside institutions, but were allowed to vote once they had left them.) The implication here is that these men would have very little to offer the country. By showing images of worthy women in contrast with unworthy men, the poster highlights the absurdity of women not being able to vote. Many people in the nineteenth and early twentieth centuries were also prejudiced against disabled people, who they called cripples. In showing an able-bodied woman alongside a man who was disabled the artist reflected the bigoted opinions of some people of the time.

'What a Woman may be', published by the Suffrage Atelier, 1912. How useful is this source to a historian investigating the causes of women's suffrage?

World-wide democracy

Suffragists, and later suffragettes, pointed to the fact that a number of countries had already enfranchised women – the Isle of Man, New Zealand, Finland, Norway, various states in Australia and America – without calamitous results. The granting of the vote to all women in the Isle of Man, Australia and New Zealand was especially significant since these three countries shared a similar social and political culture with Britain. Suffragists used these successes to demonstrate that British women should be enfranchised too.

- They argued that votes for women elsewhere cast a shadow on the country that was supposedly the 'mother of democracy'. Suffragists presumed that Britain would lead other nations in enfranchising women and the fact that other countries had done so challenged British democratic supremacy.
- British suffragists claimed that votes for women in the various US states had led to a calm and orderly election process. Women in Britain would also exercise the vote responsibly and, as with the USA, would clean up political life. For example, in the USA male politicians had to avoid personal scandal such as divorce or drunkenness in case women voted them out of office.
- With their respectably high turn-out at the polls, both Australia and New Zealand confirmed suffrage arguments that women wanted the vote, even if they did not campaign actively for it.

These successes were encouraging for British suffragists since it gave them positive signals that theirs was not a lone struggle against insuperable odds.

It was assumed that Britain should provide a role model for other countries to copy. If women were granted the vote in Britain, other countries might be encouraged to treat their women better. The following extract from a speech made by Clive Eastwick MP in the debate in the House of Commons on the Women's Disabilities Bill on 3 May 1871 indicates that the ideas that Britain should lead by example were widely held:

> There was a special reason why this country should be the first to adopt the enfranchisement of women. That reason was the immense influence which the example of England must exert upon the 200 millions of Asiatics in India, among whom, with a few brilliant exceptions, women have been degraded to a state little better than slavery. How could we expect that Indian women would be emancipated from the imprisonment of the *zenanah* [harem] or be admitted to the full privileges of education, so long as we continued to proclaim the inferiority of women in this country?

Key question
Why was international suffrage important?

Key dates

Women gained the vote in the USA: 1869–1918

Women gained the vote in Isle of Man: 1881

Women gained the vote in New Zealand: 1893

Women gained the vote in Australia: 1893–1909

Women gained the vote in Finland: 1906

Women gained the vote in Norway: 1907

Women's Social and Political Union Founded in 1903 by Emmeline Pankhurst to campaign for votes for women. Known as suffragettes, they used violent methods.

National Union of Women's Suffrage Societies Founded in 1897. Known as suffragists, they favoured peaceful methods.

Key question
Why did suffragists use history as a reason for granting votes for women?

Richard Pankhurst 1834–98; a leading Liberal barrister who believed in the abolition of the House of Lords, Irish Home Rule, universal suffrage and free education. He drafted the first bill for women's suffrage to be presented to Parliament in 1866. He married Emmeline Pankhurst and later joined the Independent Labour Party.

The vote and race

A number of women active in the late nineteenth-century suffrage campaign believed (wrongly) that the Anglo-Saxon race, that is the northern European, white race, was superior to all others. As a result, they wanted the vote for British women (who were generally white at this time) in order to safeguard white supremacy throughout the world. They feared that when black males in the USA were enfranchised in the 1860s it sent out the racial message that black men were capable of exercising political judgement whereas the majority of the white race – that is women – were not. Over 30 years later, the leadership of the **Women's Social and Political Union** (WSPU) reiterated this. In an editorial for *Votes for Women*, Christabel Pankhurst argued that British women were the rightful heirs to democracy. She felt that it was disgraceful that 'they should have their inheritance withheld, while men of other races are suddenly and almost without preparation leaping into possession of constitutional power'.

Nevertheless, both the **National Union of Women's Suffrage Societies** (NUWSS) and the WSPU constantly emphasised the need for women all over the world to unite in their campaign for the vote. Indeed the WSPU made it clear that for their members the unity of women overrode differences in colour, race or religion.

The rights of women

Restoration of an old right

Historians agree that suffragists active in the 1860s believed the vote to be the restoration of an old right rather than the exercise of a new one. Suffragists argued that women had in the past played a significant role in parliamentary politics and drew on many historical examples to support their claim.

- Abbesses, they argued, had owned vast tracts of land in the medieval period and attended and participated in the early Parliaments. In particular, the abbesses of Barking and Winchester, who headed two of the most prestigious abbeys in medieval England, had been involved in policy making at the highest level.
- Even when the English Reformation (by closing abbeys and convents) put paid to religious women's formal involvement in parliamentary affairs, women continued to influence politics. In the sixteenth century, suffragists insisted, women freeholders were still able to vote at parliamentary elections.

In 1867 large numbers of women householders reclaimed this old privilege and tried to register for the vote. Despite the fact that many successfully placed themselves on the electoral roll, most were rejected. This led to an appeal in the courts where over 5000 Manchester women, defended by **Richard Pankhurst**, claimed the right to vote. The judges disagreed with this claim and held that 'every woman is personally incapable' of voting. And so, after 1868, because the suffragists lost the legal case for women's suffrage, the argument that women were legally entitled to vote lost its persuasive appeal.

Property rights and the vote

Since male suffrage was based on property qualifications, both suffragists and suffragettes thought it particularly unfair that women were not allowed to vote. Women, as well as men, owned property, so to deny the vote to women seemed blatantly unjust. This argument gained considerable ground after each extension of the franchise gave the vote to more and more men on the basis of property.

- When the property qualification for the male vote was lowered in 1867 and again in 1884, more and more wealthy women saw men less well off than themselves obtain the vote. Some women owned and controlled vast acres of land, enjoyed fortunes derived from industry and were both householders and taxpayers. Even so, they did not have the same rights as men of their class because they were unable to vote.
- After 1884, 30,000 Englishwomen farmers watched many of their male agricultural workers use their newly acquired vote

Key question
What were the links between property and the vote?

THE DIGNITY OF THE FRANCHISE.

QUALIFIED VOTER. "AH, YOU MAY PAY RATES AN' TAXES, AN' YOU MAY 'AVE RESPONSERBILITIES AN' ALL; BUT WHEN IT COMES TO *VOTIN'*, YOU MUST LEAVE IT TO *US MEN!*"

'The dignity of the franchise' published by *Punch*, 10 May 1905. How useful is this source to a historian investigating support for women's suffrage?

while they remained disenfranchised. Suffragists insisted that women who owned land and property should have the same political rights as men who owned land and property.

The cartoon on page 16 illustrates this clearly. It was first produced by *Punch*, a satirical magazine, but was later used by the WSPU as propaganda in support of votes for women. The man entering the polling station is obviously working class and is portrayed, by his physical appearance, his body language and his speech, as inferior to the upright, respectable and middle-class woman left outside. This cartoon confirmed the women's suffrage argument that illiterate and uneducated men were enfranchised, and probably should not have been, whereas educated and literate women were denied the vote.

Furthermore, taxation and representation were linked in the British parliamentary system as it was held that those who put money into the national purse should be able to control its spending. From at least the 1860s onwards those who campaigned for women's suffrage complained that even when women paid taxes they had no control over how those taxes were spent. In 1909 a **Women's Tax Resistance League** was set up as a channel for the bitterness these women felt.

Benefits of the vote

Vote brought benefits to men and disadvantages to women

Of course, it was not just the vote as a symbol of citizenship that mattered, but the use to which it could be put. At the beginning of the nineteenth century the vote was less significant in parliamentary politics because so many of the population were denied the vote anyway. The government, voted in by such a small electorate, did not worry too much about national popularity. However, by the end of the nineteenth century governments took more notice of its electorate. Suffragists therefore insisted that under a representative government, the interests of any non-represented group were liable to be neglected. The group that held political power, which was men, made laws favourable to themselves and neglected the interests of those without power, including women. This reasoning was borne out by experience: as more and more men were enfranchised, so laws were enacted that reflected the wishes of the various classes of male voter. For example:

- After 1832 the government passed a series of laws including the **Poor Law Amendment Act** (1834) that represented the particular interests of the newly enfranchised middle-class male. It was hoped that the new Poor Law would reduce the burden of local taxation that would benefit the middle classes who paid more taxes.
- After 1867, when many working-class men were granted the vote, important educational and trade union reforms were introduced that benefited the working class.

In contrast, it was believed that women faced hardship because their views remained unrepresented. As **John Stuart Mill** pointed

---

Key terms

Women's Tax Resistance League
An organisation that supported women who refused to pay taxes because they could not vote.

Poor Law Amendment Act
Encouraged local authorities to build workhouses for their unemployed poor rather than to help in other ways.

Key question
Why did the vote help men?

Key figure

John Stuart Mill
1806–73; a Liberal philosopher and writer; MP for Westminster 1865–8. He campaigned for women's suffrage and wrote, with his wife Harriet Taylor, an important book on women's rights called *On the Subjection of Women*.

out, 'women do not need political rights in order that they may govern, but in order that they may not be misgoverned'. Indeed the male electorate was seen to use their exclusive power to make laws, such as the Contagious Diseases Acts (see page 7), which adversely affected, and were strongly resented by, women. Moreover, whereas early **Victorian** governments adhered much more to the principle of *laissez-faire*, it was apparent by the **Edwardian** era that this principle was dead and that Parliament, as the governing body of the country, had the power to change the way people worked and lived.

Once women had obtained the vote, suffragists and suffragettes argued, governments would be forced to take women's issues seriously. Both groups considered the vote to be a defence against the tyranny of men over women and believed that women would be better off with it. But even though the vote was seen as a means to the end of greater social justice, that end varied considerably. For some it meant the improvement of women's financial situation, for another group it meant the improvement of women's marital position, while for others it meant the improvement of women's condition in all areas of life.

The vote and working-class women

Feminist historians, such as Jill Liddington and Jill Norris writing in the 1970s, tend to focus on the fact that suffragists wanted the vote to improve the pay and employment opportunities of working women.

- In 1872 suffragists alleged that, in England alone, nearly three million unmarried women and 800,000 married women received wages far below those of men of the same class. Forty years later, suffragettes were making similar complaints. Male working-class wages had risen throughout the late nineteenth and early twentieth centuries, suffrage campaigners insisted, because men were able to pressurise Parliament into passing laws favourable to them. In contrast, women accomplished less, largely because they were without the vote.

- Women not only earned less than half the male wage, but were barred from a number of occupations. Throughout the nineteenth century governments had excluded women from certain types of work, restricted their hours and regulated their working conditions. For example, the government banned women from working underground in coal mines in 1842 and tried to stop women from working as **pit-brow women** in 1887 and 1911. Many suffragists objected to this 'protective' legislation because it either deprived women of jobs or made them compete unfairly with men for work, resulting in the further lowering of female wages. In the Edwardian period, suffragettes put forward similar arguments and believed that the vote would help to bring about equal pay for equal work.

Key question
How would the vote improve marriage laws?

The vote and marriage laws

Throughout the nineteenth century suffragists wanted the vote as a legal protection against avaricious or cruel husbands. Before the Married Women's Property Acts were passed (see page 6) the **common law** would not permit women to keep their own property and money after marriage. Even after 1882 the British marriage laws were considered the most barbarous in Europe:

- Husbands still had the right to beat their wives and compel them to return if they left home (see page 6).
- Children over 7 years of age were legally the property of their fathers, who were able to take them away from their mothers if they wished.

By the beginning of the twentieth century, when many of these legal injustices had been removed, both suffragists and suffragettes turned to issues of sex and morality.

Key question
How would the vote improve men's sexual behaviour?

The vote and sexual morality

Until the work of feminist historians in the 1970s, most history texts ignored the emphasis placed on sex and morality by the suffragists and suffragettes. The few historians who did mention it ridiculed the suffragettes. For instance, the suffragette slogan 'Votes for Women and **Chastity for Men**' is seen as an amusing peculiarity by George Dangerfield in the 1930s and Roger Fulford in the 1950s and as an example of spinsterish eccentricity by Andrew Rosen in the 1970s. However, the relationship between sexuality and the vote has enjoyed a long history in the annals of women's suffrage. Both the suffragists and the suffragettes placed women's franchise within the wider context of sexual politics and took the question of sexuality very earnestly indeed. For some suffrage campaigners such as Millicent Fawcett (see pages 46–7) and Christabel Pankhurst (see page 52) the vote was as much about improving men's sexual morality as it was about improving women's working conditions.

The majority of suffragists did not wish to discuss female sexuality, fearing that it would offend Victorian prudery and so lessen support for the cause. However, a number wanted the vote to clean up public life and to ensure that men and women adhered to the same moral principles. Men, as well as women, should not have sex outside marriage. In this sense, the women's suffrage movement was seen as much as a moral movement as a political one.

- Indeed, some suffragists believed in a female moral superiority, whereby women were the keepers of virtue and men the lustful destroyers of chastity. Lydia Becker (see pages 37–8), one of the founders of the suffragist movement, insisted that the vote was 'a protection for women from the uncontrolled dominion of the savage passions of men'.
- Over 30 years later, Emmeline Pankhurst confidently assumed that votes for women were necessary to eliminate the sexual double standard whereby it was acceptable for men, but not women, to engage in pre-marital sex. When Emmeline Pankhurst was a Poor Law Guardian she had been distressed by

Key terms

Common law
Law which is based on legal judgments made by judges hearing court cases, as opposed to statutory law which is made by Parliament.

Chastity for men
A view that men should be chaste, that is abstain from sex outside marriage.

the number of single mothers who were in the workhouse because men refused to marry them or pay them maintenance. Throughout her life, she constantly made references to the abhorrent selfishness of male sexual activity.

- Her daughter Christabel even insisted that sexually transmitted diseases would be eliminated once women had the vote (she claimed 75 per cent of men were infected with gonorrhoea and 25 per cent with syphilis). In her pamphlet *The Great Scourge* she argued that female inequality was the fundamental cause of sexually transmitted diseases. Once women were educated and gained better jobs, she argued, they would not be dependent on men for money. They would then be able to say a firm no to men who wanted sex with them outside marriage, thus reducing the risk of sexually transmitted diseases.
- Christabel Pankhurst promoted a two-fold political programme of chastity for men and votes for women. Indeed, she fervently believed that once women were enfranchised laws could be passed to transform male sexual behaviour:

... the canker of venereal disease [sexually transmitted diseases] is eating away the vitals of the nation, and the only cure is Votes for Women. ... The real cure of the great plague is – Votes for Women, which will give to women more self-reliance and a stronger economic position and chastity for men ... Apart from the deplorable moral effect of the fact that women are voteless, there is this to be noticed – that the law of the land, as made and administered by men, protects and encourages the immorality of men, and the sex exploitation of women.

This extract from her pamphlet, which might read a little strangely to modern eyes, needs to be placed within the historical context. People in Victorian and Edwardian Britain were anxious about the increase of sexually transmitted disease and its far-reaching effects, not only on the health of the individual, but also on that of the nation. Nevertheless, it is fair to argue that Christabel Pankhurst expressed a minority view when she associated sexually transmitted diseases with votes for women.

The vote and prostitution

The vote was seen as a device that could be used to curb unfair legislation against prostitutes and ultimately to end prostitution. In particular, Victorian suffragists were critical of the Contagious Diseases Acts because the Acts blamed prostitutes for sexually transmitted diseases, not the men who paid for their services. Feminists, under the leadership of Josephine Butler's Ladies' National Association (LNA) (see page 7), opposed these Acts and supported votes for women to end this legal injustice.

Some went even further. Millicent Fawcett not only supported the LNA campaigns, but believed that the vote would also end prostitution. As president of both the NUWSS and the

Key question
Why was prostitution an issue for suffragists and suffragettes?

Key term

National Union of Women Workers
Founded in 1895, mainly to support women who worked in charity organisations, this organisation was initially concerned with the elimination of prostitution. It is still in existence and is called the National Council of Women. One of its aims is to encourage women to take an active part in public life.

National Union of Women Workers, Fawcett was well placed to see a direct connection between women's lack of franchise and the existence of prostitution. This link was also confirmed by a leading member of the NUWSS in the early years of the twentieth century:

> We wish for it [the vote] because there exists a terrible trade of procuring young girls for immoral purposes. The girl is first entrapped and seduced, and when once she has fallen, it is very difficult for her to return afterwards to her home, or to be received among respectable girls in workshops or in domestic service. She becomes a prostitute … we believe the time has come when women must claim their right to help … and the first step to this lies in their enfranchisement, for without this they have no real power in the matter. It would be much more difficult for this cruel and wicked traffic to be carried on if it were recognised by the law that women were of the same value and had the same standing in the State as men.

It was believed that women became prostitutes because they did not earn enough to support themselves. Armed with the vote, women could press for higher wages and better jobs, thus eliminating the need to earn money from prostitution. Christabel Pankhurst went further and argued that prostitution was based on male vice, which could only be eradicated once women had the vote. Once women were enfranchised governments would be forced to listen to the women who wanted to pass laws curbing men's sexual behaviour. Of course, the ideas of Christabel Pankhurst have been proved wrong since prostitution continues.

Wording of a leaflet published in the latter part of the nineteenth century.

WHY WOMEN WANT THE VOTE

BECAUSE no race or class or sex can have its interest properly safeguarded in the legislature of a country unless it is represented by direct suffrage.

BECAUSE while men who are voters can get their economic grievances listened to, non-voters are disregarded.

BECAUSE politics and economics go hand in hand. And so long as woman has no political status she will be the 'bottom dog' as a wage-earner.

BECAUSE the legislature in the past has not made laws which are equal between men and women: and these laws will not be altered till women get the vote.

BECAUSE all the more important and lucrative positions are barred to them, and opportunities of public service are denied.

BECAUSE wherever women have become voters, reform has proceeded more rapidly than before, and even at home our municipal government, in which the women have a certain share, is in advance and not behind our Parliamentary attitude on many important questions.

BECAUSE women will be better comrades to their husbands, better mothers to their children, and better housekeepers of the home.

Suffragist and suffragette arguments: conclusions

It used to be assumed that whereas the suffragists wanted the vote as a means to an end, the suffragettes wanted the vote as an end in itself, but this interpretation has recently been revised. The literature produced by both groups suggests that they wanted the vote to end the economic, social and moral exploitation of women. However, there were some differences in practice. For example, large numbers of suffragists were reluctant to associate sexual morality with the vote because they felt this would do harm to the suffrage cause. In contrast, the leading suffragettes had few such qualms: Christabel Pankhurst, for instance, promoted votes for women and chastity for men simultaneously.

Suffragists and suffragettes developed numerous justifications for women's franchise, but what is remarkable is the consistency of those arguments over time. Indeed, there were no specifically 'suffragist' and 'suffragette' justifications. Both groups claimed the right for women to vote on the same terms as men in parliamentary elections. However, as the nineteenth century progressed, the meaning of this demand changed. If the first women's suffrage bill (see page 77) had been passed in 1870 it would have been decidedly élitist, as only a very few rich women would have been enfranchised. By 1900, when the property qualification for men was much lower, more and more women would have been eligible to vote if the terms had been the same. What did change was the confidence with which the case was argued: whereas early suffragists argued their points very tentatively, the Edwardian suffragists and suffragettes, more secure in the justice of their cause, produced the most startling propaganda (see pages 116–17).

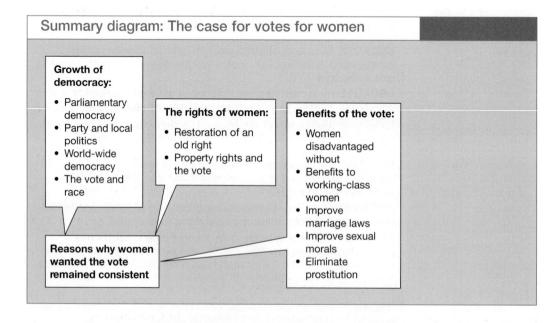

Summary diagram: The case for votes for women

Growth of democracy:
- Parliamentary democracy
- Party and local politics
- World-wide democracy
- The vote and race

The rights of women:
- Restoration of an old right
- Property rights and the vote

Benefits of the vote:
- Women disadvantaged without
- Benefits to working-class women
- Improve marriage laws
- Improve sexual morals
- Eliminate prostitution

Reasons why women wanted the vote remained consistent

2 | The Case Against Votes for Women

Key question
What were the main arguments of those who were opposed to votes for women?

Key figures

Mary Kingsley
1861–1900; a famous explorer of Africa who lived with local tribes and defended aspects of African life that shocked British people. She wrote a number of best-selling books about her travels.

Gertrude Bell
1868–1926; a traveller, archaeologist and government official who helped to create the modern state of Iraq. She spoke several languages including Arabic, Persian and Turkish. During the First World War she went to Basra in Iraq to advise the British Army and after the war ended she helped Faisal to become the first king of Iraq in 1921.

Frederick Pethick-Lawrence
1871–1961; a lawyer and politician who campaigned for votes for women. He edited the paper *Votes for Women* (see page 57).

Key question
Why were women thought unsuitable for the vote?

Those who opposed women's suffrage (often called the 'Antis') marshalled equally numerous arguments against votes for women. At first the Antis found it easy to discredit women's suffrage by commenting on the psychological differences between the sexes and the inappropriateness of women taking part in politics. Over the years they were forced to sharpen up their arguments as those in favour of the female franchise refuted each of their objections and public opinion changed. Until the work of Brian Harrison in the 1970s, historians have generally ignored this opposition movement, possibly because it was considered unfashionable – and perhaps politically incorrect – to examine those who were hostile to what is now considered a perfectly reasonable demand.

To most of us in the twenty-first century the ideas of the opponents of women's suffrage may seem wildly unconvincing. But we have to remember that, at the time, these ideas were more representative of popular opinion than those of the female suffragists. It is also important to remember that the Antis were not all men: a number of eminent women (such as **Mary Kingsley** and **Gertrude Bell**) spoke out against votes for women. The Antis' arguments were varied but generally centred on the perceived physical, emotional and intellectual differences between men and women. As **Frederick Pethick-Lawrence**, a strong supporter of women's suffrage, remarked about the Antis:

> Men, it was said, were governed by reason, women by emotion. If once the franchise were thrown open to women, they would … force an emotional policy on the country … In particular it was said that on sex matters women were narrower and harder than men; and that if they were given power they would impose impossibly strict standards of morality … A further fear was that women … would lose their special charm and attraction … .

Men's right to rule

As Brian Harrison pointed out, those opposed to votes for women were often people with an inherent dislike of change and with no wish to alter the political *status quo*. For them, any extension of the franchise, either male or female, would damage Britain because it would destabilise the existing political structure. A few Antis were opposed to any increase in democracy because they feared that an 'uneducated, politically inexperienced and irrational class' would gain ascendancy over Parliament. Indeed, opponents of women's suffrage believed that a small political élite (i.e. themselves) were destined to – and should – rule over the mass of the population.

The inferiority of women

For a lot of Antis it was self-evident that women should not vote simply because they were women. In their opinion women were so obviously inferior to men that it would be too ridiculous to enfranchise them. As more than one Anti claimed: 'Votes for Women? We shall be asked next to give votes to our horses and dogs'. By the end of the nineteenth century a better organised women's suffrage movement had emerged and its cogent and persuasive arguments had gained converts to the cause. This put the Antis on the defensive, forcing them to make more rational arguments against votes for women. For example, **Mrs Humphrey Ward**, a leading Anti of the late nineteenth and early twentieth centuries, maintained that women were different from, but not unequal to men.

The vote and physical strength

Many Antis stressed the relationship between the right to vote and the responsibility to fight for one's country. Women, it was alleged, were not capable of full citizenship because they were not available for the **defence of the realm**. As the notorious anti-suffragist **Lord Curzon** stated in 1912, 'What is the good of talking about the equality of the sexes? The first whiz of the bullet, the first boom of the cannon and where is the equality of the sexes then?'

One leading female anti-suffragist argued that women should not have the vote because political power rested in the end on physical force, to which women were not capable of contributing. This argument against votes for women remained remarkably consistent between 1860 and 1914, but it was one that had several strands:

- Antis argued that since Britain ruled a vast empire it needed a strong army to govern. Women could not fight, and because they could never fulfil this vital obligation of citizenship, they should be denied the right to vote. In addition many believed that countries, such as India and the Caribbean islands, over which Britain ruled, would not give British authority the same respect if she were governed by women (the fact that Queen Victoria was the head of state seemed not to bother them). Afro-Caribbean and Indian men, it was believed, would not accept being ruled by a country whose government was elected by women. It was also feared that colonised countries would demand their own enfranchisement, which would inevitably lead to demands for independence.
- The second strand rested on fears that votes for women would lead to **pacifism**, as women would be reluctant to wage wars against foreign enemies. As a consequence Britain might go into decline and face invasion because women generally favoured peace rather than war. People were concerned that Germany, which was building a strong military force, might quickly subdue Britain.
- The third strand rested on the belief that domestic political power needed a show of armed strength to support it. Women would be unable to govern because of their inability to

Key figures

Mrs Humphrey Ward
1851–1920; born Mary Augusta Arnold, she was the granddaughter of the famous educationalist Dr Arnold of Rugby. Mary Ward wrote at least 25 novels and helped to found the Women's National Anti-Suffrage League (see page 63).

Lord Curzon
1859–1925; Viceroy of India from 1895 to 1905 and Foreign Secretary from 1919 to 1924. In 1908 he founded the Women's National Anti-Suffrage League (see page 63).

Key terms

Defence of the realm
The protection of Britain from enemy forces.

Pacifism
A belief that war and violence are wrong and that all quarrels can be settled peacefully.

enforce the laws they had made; this would inevitably lead to **anarchy**, a brutal **civil war** and ultimately the end of British civilisation.

Psychological differences

The vote and female biology

Key question
Why were women considered to be biologically unfit to vote?

Men and women were perceived, by the Antis, as very different from each other physically, psychologically and intellectually. Victorian scientific theory legitimised this belief by suggesting that the differences rested on a biological basis. Women were seen to be intellectually inferior to men because their brains weighed less on a set of measuring scales.

Moreover, medical opinion claimed that women were guided by their wombs – which were seen to be particularly unstable at puberty, menstruation, pregnancy and menopause – rather than by their brains. At least one medical expert compared giving birth to having an epileptic fit. In 1873 an article in *The Lancet* said that labour comprised 'a series of convulsions indistinguishable from epilepsy'. It followed that women were more prone to insanity. This was a view shared by many non-medical men, and indeed women. According to one female Anti, writing in 1909, 'The point of **hysterical** emotion and unreason is always nearer with women … their nerve force is slighter, their self-restraint less.' Women, at the mercy of their reproductive cycle, were seen as fickle, childish, capricious and bad-tempered, making it easy for Antis to argue women were unlikely to make rational judgements about political issues or events.

Certainly some politicians believed that women were naturally less logical than men. In a House of Commons debate on women's suffrage in 1871, one MP commented that because men were led by reason and women were led by instinct it was foolish to grant votes for women: it would mean a House of Commons dominated by emotion at the expense of logic. These opinions continued to be held in the twentieth century. During a debate on votes for women in 1912, Viscount Helmsley insisted that suffragette violence confirmed that 'the mental equilibrium of the female sex is not as stable as the mental equilibrium of the male sex'.

Generally, Antis dwelt on the defects of temperament and intellect of women and argued that, as women were likely to regard politics in personal terms, they would become absorbed with the trivial and the domestic rather than with the more important parliamentary politics which dealt with international as well as national affairs.

The vote and separate spheres

Key question
How did men's and women's roles differ?

The sexes, it was argued, occupied two separate spheres. Politics was considered to be part of the public sphere belonging to men. Antis believed that it was God's wish that men should rule and women be governed. Biblical references to Adam and Eve were made: Eve was formed from the spare rib of Adam and so was subject to his rule. It was the responsibility of the male head of

Key terms

Anarchy
Disorder; lack of government.

Civil war
A war between people of the same country.

The Lancet
A medical journal that was influential and esteemed at the time; still published today.

Hysterical
Today, the word means mad, wild, uncontrolled or frenzied. Derived from '*hystera*', the Greek word for womb.

household to defend his family, to go out to work and to run the political system. Mrs Humphrey Ward maintained in 1889 that certain government departments should be the exclusive preserve of men:

> To men belong the struggle of debate and legislation in Parliament; the hard and exhausting labour implied in the administration of the national resources and powers; the conduct of England's relations towards the external world; the working of the army and navy; all the heavy, laborious, fundamental industries of the State, such as those of mines, metals, and railways; the lead and supervision of English commerce, the management of our vast English finance, the service of that merchant fleet on which our food supply depends. In all these spheres women's direct participation is made impossible … Therefore it is not just to give to women direct power of deciding questions of Parliamentary policy, of war, of foreign or colonial affairs, of commerce and finance equal to that possessed by men.

In contrast, women's role was firmly located within the private sphere of the home. Mrs Parker Smith, married to an MP and President of a Scottish Women's Liberal Unionist Association, did not agree with votes for women: she believed that women could never play a full part in public life because of their role as wives and mothers. Family life would be destroyed if women gained the vote, she believed, because women would set about challenging the authority of the male. And as the family was perceived to be the bedrock of society, it followed that society would be destroyed.

The vote and femininity

The Antis often spoke of politics being too dirty a game for women. **Hustings** were considered unfit places for women because men were often bribed with drink, making polling a raucous and disorderly event. Certainly, before the introduction of the secret ballot, elections were often the excuse for a riotous party. Women were considered far too delicate to enter the fray of this particular form of politics. Antis even argued that sensible men sent their wives and families away from home during elections because they feared for their safety. To involve women in the tumult of politics would be unseemly and to solicit their votes distinctly improper – the very process could defile their natural modesty. As the Liberal Prime Minister **Gladstone** stated, it would 'trespass upon their delicacy, their purity, their refinement and the elevation of their whole nature'. Not surprisingly it was argued that the courtesies that women received from men would cease if women gained the vote since having the vote would rob them of their feminine charms.

Some Antis certainly viewed the campaign for women's suffrage as the brainchild of a few crazy, dissatisfied **spinsters**. They drew attention to the small numbers of women who either belonged to suffrage societies or engaged in suffrage activities. They were firmly convinced that the majority of women did not want the vote and were by nature devoid of any direct interest in the affairs of state. Most women, they understood, wished to remain at home looking after their husbands and children, and 'the House of Commons had no right to force upon women a privilege which only a very limited number of their sex asked for'.

Men's influence over women

Women indirectly represented by men

Antis argued that it was unnecessary for women to be enfranchised because they were already indirectly represented by the men in their family. In the first part of the nineteenth century, they claimed, Parliament represented communities rather than individuals, so a landowner represented his village community, a mine owner his mining community – and a husband the interests of his wife and children. 'Women', said one MP in 1870, 'should be satisfied with the great power they now possess indirectly'. In addition, some women exerted a subtle and indirect control on national affairs as the wives and mothers of powerful men. Both **Disraeli** and Gladstone, for example, discussed government secrets with their wives.

Women influenced by men

Fears were expressed that women were incapable of forming their own opinions and were overly influenced by the men in their lives. Husbands and fathers, in particular, expected their wives and daughters to agree with their political views: opponents suggested that if women were enfranchised this would have the effect of giving two or more votes to men with close female relatives. It was also feared that Roman Catholic women would be too easily persuaded by Catholic priests who used the pulpit and the confessional for political as well as religious purposes.

Women would vote as women

Antis insisted that the moral and social order would collapse if women were enfranchised: they would not listen to men. On the assumption that electors voted according to their own self-interest, women were expected to vote for issues relevant to their own gender roles. Antis argued that women would vote as women rather than as individuals and would seek to legislate for social reform and against male interests. For example, it was feared that women might vote for **temperance reform** and ban the sale of alcohol. And as women would predominate in an electorate (in 1929, when women voted in the first **universal suffrage** election, they constituted 52.7 per cent of the electorate) they would conceivably succeed.

Key question
How, in theory, did men look after the interests of women?

Key figure

Benjamin Disraeli
1804–81; a Conservative Prime Minister (1868, 1874–86) who believed in political and social reform.

Key question
How did men affect women's political views?

Key question
Why would votes for women lead to the collapse of order?

Key terms

Temperance reform
Reform of the alcohol laws.

Universal suffrage
Votes for all adult men and women.

Women's influence outside parliament

By the beginning of the twentieth century not all Antis considered that women were basically inferior. A number of Antis distinguished between local government (with its focus on social welfare) and national government (with its focus on international and diplomatic affairs). Mrs Humphrey Ward, for example, thought it appropriate for women to engage in local politics: it was housekeeping on a grander scale and so did not undermine the principles of the separate spheres. She argued that women should elevate the tone of public office through their religious, educational and charitable work rather than busy themselves with national politics.

The leaflet below, which was published in the early twentieth century, while recognising that women played an important part in local government, argued that Parliament should remain the province of men.

Key question
Why was it considered appropriate for women to participate in local politics?

AGAINST WOMAN SUFFRAGE
by Grace Saxon Mills

Because women already have the municipal vote, and are eligible for membership of most local authorities. These bodies deal with questions of housing, education, care of children, workhouses and so forth, all of which are peculiarly within a woman's sphere. Parliament, however, has to deal mainly with the administration of a vast Empire, the maintenance of the Army and Navy, and with questions of peace and war, which lie outside the legitimate sphere of woman's influence.

Because women are not capable of full citizenship, for the simple reason that they are not available for purposes of national and Imperial defence. All government rests ultimately on force, to which women, owing to physical, moral and social reasons, are not capable of contributing.

Because there is little doubt that the vast majority of women have no desire for the vote.

Because the acquirement of the parliamentary vote would logically involve admission to Parliament itself, and to all Government offices. It is scarcely possible to imagine a woman being Minister for War, and yet the principles of the Suffragettes involve that and many similar absurdities.

Because the United Kingdom is not an isolated state, but the administrative and governing centre of a system of colonies and also of dependencies. The effect of introducing a large female element into the Imperial electorate would undoubtedly be to weaken the centre of power in the eyes of these dependent millions.

Because past legislation in Parliament shows that the interests of women are perfectly safe in the hands of men.

Because Woman Suffrage is based on the idea of the equality of the sexes, and tends to establish those competitive relations which will destroy chivalrous consideration.

Because women have at present a vast indirect influence through their menfolk on the politics of this country.

Because the physical nature of women unfits them for direct competition with men.

Summary diagram: The case against votes for women

Men's right to rule:
- The inferiority of women
- The vote and physical strength

Psychological differences:
- The vote and female biology
- The vote and separate spheres
- The vote and decorum
- The vote and femininity

Men's influence over women:
- Women indirectly represented by men
- Women influenced by men
- Women would vote as women

Women's influence outside Parliament

Arguments used by those opposed to votes for women

Key question
How similar were the beliefs of those in favour of votes for women and those against?

3 | Suffrage and Anti-suffrage Arguments

Those who supported and those who opposed women's suffrage often shared similar ideals. Such similarities are perhaps not surprising, as after all the suffragists, the suffragettes and their opponents inhabited the same cultural world and historical period. And it is sometimes said that one has to have common areas of agreement in order to disagree!

- First, neither side had any desire to undermine women's domestic role. Both the suffragists and suffragettes did not want the vote to undermine women's role in the home. Indeed, they reiterated their commitment to the separate spheres philosophy whereby women and men held distinct roles within society. In their view, democracy needed a woman's touch. Millicent Fawcett (see pages 46–7) held that women 'wanted the home-side represented in politics … woman at her best stood for mercy, pity, peace, purity and love'. As the historian Sandra Holton writing in the 1980s has pointed out, suffrage activists believed women to have the necessary mothering qualities needed for a state increasingly committed to social reform and improving the lives of its citizens. Those who supported female suffrage believed that women's unique capabilities would improve government; but the Antis, who also believed that women's talents originated in the home, believed that they should remain there.
- Secondly, most of those involved in the suffrage debate believed that votes for women was the means to an end. They all agreed that the vote would bring about a social revolution, but whereas the suffrage campaigners welcomed such change it struck fear into the opposition. Suffragists and suffragettes looked forward to the day when women would be able to end

the exploitation of their sex by changing the law and increasing educational and employment opportunities for women. For them, the vote would herald a new dawn of equality. In contrast, the Antis feared the reforming zeal of enfranchised women because it would undermine the authority of the male.

- Thirdly, the suffragists, the suffragettes and their opponents recognised women's contribution to local government. Those who supported women's suffrage used this to convince people of women's ability to engage in national politics, whereas the Antis used the same argument to demonstrate that women had already fulfilled their political potential. In fact, some Antis considered local government to be women's proper sphere because it concerned education, health and housing.

- Finally, both suffrage campaigners and the Antis were conscious of Britain's role as an imperial power and used this to argue either for or against votes for women. At times both used white supremacist arguments: the suffragists believing that white women should gain the vote before black men; the Antis believing that black men would not accept the authority of women whatever their colour.

Both sides advanced powerful arguments, but it is fair to say that, at first, the Antis seemed to be winning. The campaign for votes for women was treated as a joke by large numbers of people in Britain. Early suffragists had to be particularly careful in their speeches and their leaflets to advance a rational defence, whereas all the Antis had to do to gain support was to laugh at them.

By 1914, however, many of the ideas of the Antis appeared ludicrously old-fashioned and it was evident that the argument in favour of votes for women had, more or less, been won. Both sides, however, considered that their own particular assertions were correct and, therefore, the debate could not be decided intellectually. Suffrage campaigners may have won the debate but those who opposed them drew on the fact that most women remained indifferent to the franchise, some were opposed and very few campaigned for it. Certainly, although most MPs now favoured women's suffrage, government still had to be convinced that the cause was genuinely popular. As one MP put it, the government 'could not consent to make a revolution for a handful of fanatics'. Instead, political pressure would play a decisive role in the case for and against women's suffrage: hence suffrage actions began to speak louder than words.

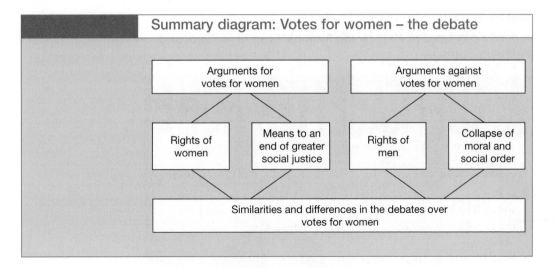

Summary diagram: Votes for women – the debate

Arguments for votes for women

Arguments against votes for women

Rights of women

Means to an end of greater social justice

Rights of men

Collapse of moral and social order

Similarities and differences in the debates over votes for women

Study Guide: AS Questions

In the style of Edexcel

Study the following source material and then answer the questions that follow.

Source 1

From a letter sent to Lloyd George, June 1912, by Gladys Gladstone Solomon.

'Dear Sir

As a typical woman householder and rate and tax payer I beg you – a typical man – to take upon your stronger shoulders the burden of responsibility for the safety of the Empire, the Army and Navy, Trade, Shipping, Mining, Railways etc. I am too thankful to pay my taxes in return for your protection, if only you will leave me to look after my home and child.'

Source 2

A poster produced in 1900 by the National League for Opposing Women's Suffrage.

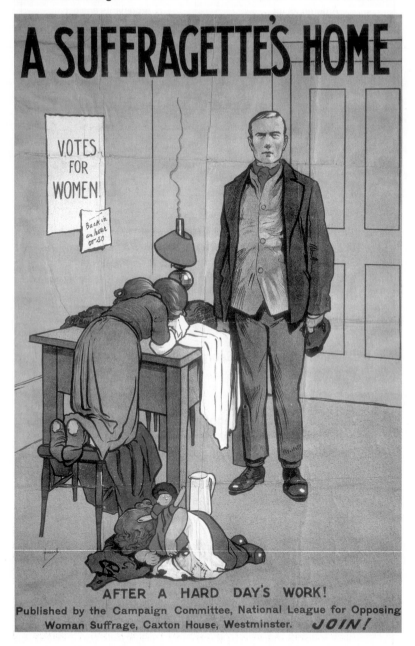

Source 3

From a speech made by Elizabeth Robins, 1862–1952, at the Waldorf Hotel on 4 May 1909.

'I believe that only through political equality will we hope to see a true understanding and a happier relationship between the sexes. Changes in society have increased separation between men and women in practically all the interests of life. In the world of industry, of business, of thought – even in society, the growing tendency has been to divide the world into two separate camps. Men who are 'doing things' have less time to give to us because they see women as having no share in the various aspects of the game of life. Instead of still further dividing us, women's suffrage is in reality the bridge across the chasm between men and women.'

Source 4

From Elizabeth Crawford, The Women's Suffrage Movement, 1999.

'It was the use to which a vote might be put that became the rationale given – that the interests of women would never be protected until they were in charge of their own destiny. It is clear that the vote was a symbolic proof of self-worth and that without full citizenship women were unprotected.'

(a) **Study Sources 1, 2 and 3**

How far do the sources suggest that the suffrage movement had a negative impact on women's lives? (20 marks)

(b) **Use Sources 3 and 4 and your own knowledge**

'It was the use to which a vote might be put that became the rationale given – that the interests of women would never be protected until they were in charge of their own destiny.' Do you agree with this view put forward by Elizabeth Crawford? Explain your answer, using these two sources and your own knowledge. (40 marks)

Source: adapted from Edexcel, January 2005

Exam tips

The cross-references are intended to take you straight to the material that will help you to answer the questions.

(a) For this question you just need to focus on the sources. The strong message of Source 2 is that women involved in the suffrage movement neglected their families and homes to attend meetings, and this is corroborated by what is implied in Source 1 – that freedom from having to consider those matters that men take on their 'stronger shoulders' allows the writer to care for her own family more effectively. Remember that you will need to use the evidence of Sources 1 and 2 to show that these messages are present in the sources. Source 2 also shows the nature of opposition to women in their struggle for the vote and consequently the impact on their lives, as after all women faced public disapproval if they supported the enfranchisement of women. The woman quoted in Source 1 also believes that the suffrage movement has had a negative impact. Source 3 suggests that women's suffrage would act as a 'bridge across the chasm between men and women' and would bring positive rewards to women.

Don't forget too that you need to address the sources as evidence in themselves. For example, the cartoon was a piece of propaganda produced by the Antis, and the letter by a woman unsympathetic to the campaigns. Both Sources 1 and 2 wanted to stress the negative effect that involvement in the campaign had on women's lives because they were opposed to female suffrage. The writer of Source 3, Elizabeth Robins, was a famous actress, a distinguished dramatist, and a member of the Actresses' Franchise League and the WSPU. She toured England making recruitment speeches on behalf of the WSPU and wrote several plays and novels about women's suffrage. In this speech she wanted to show that the vote would have a positive future impact on women's lives.

To achieve the high marks you could show how, taken together, the sources give valuable insights into how women were themselves divided about the impact that the campaign had on their lives. The cartoon and letter show the negative effects, whereas Robins emphasises the positive.

(b) Remember to incorporate the sources into your own knowledge. You need to show a developed analysis of the evidence, linked to and extended from your own knowledge. You should use the sources as a starting point for your analysis and then explore the issues raised by the sources – deepening and extending the range of points from your own knowledge.

- For example, Elizabeth Robins suggests that the vote would lead to 'true understanding and a happier relationship between the sexes' and an end to the 'separate spheres'. Certainly, both the suffragists and the suffragettes believed that the vote would improve marriage laws, improve sexual morality and give women greater opportunities (see pages 19–21).
- Elizabeth Crawford confirms the ideas put forward by Robins. In her view, suffrage campaigners believed that 'the interests of women would never be protected until they were in charge of their own destiny'. Suffrage campaigners believed that women were disadvantaged without the vote. They argued that the vote would bring political, economic and social benefits to women (see pages 17–18).
- However, in order to produce a balanced argument you must consider the opposing view also put forward by Crawford. The vote was not just seen as a means to an end but as a democratic right (see pages 12–15) and a 'symbolic proof of self-worth'. For example, women of property felt aggrieved that others whom they thought less worthy were enfranchised before them.

3 Suffragists and Suffragettes

POINTS TO CONSIDER

Two of the most well-known women's suffragist groups are the National Union of Women's Suffrage Societies (NUWSS), known as the suffragists, and the Women's Social and Political Union (WSPU), known as the suffragettes, but there were other suffragist groups too. This chapter will consider whether the women's suffrage movement was more diverse than these groups suggest. It will examine the various suffragist organisations under the following headings:

- The origins of women's suffrage
- Disunity in the suffragist movement
- The National Union of Women's Suffrage Societies and its offshoots 1897–1914
- The Women's Social and Political Union 1903–14
- Suffragette membership
- Disunity in the suffragette movement
- Other suffrage societies
- The opposition to votes for women

Key dates

1867	Second Reform Bill
	Manchester National Society for Women's Suffrage founded
	London National Society for Women's Suffrage founded
1868	National Society for Women's Suffrage (NSWS) founded
1877	National Society for Women's Suffrage reunited
1888	Central National Society for Women's Suffrage founded
	Central Committee of National Society for Women's Suffrage (remained NSWS) founded
1889	Women's Franchise League founded
1892	Women's Emancipation Union founded
1894	Local Government Act enfranchised some women
1897	National Union of Women's Suffrage Societies (NUWSS) founded

1903   Lancashire and Cheshire Women Textile and
          Other Workers, Representative Committee
          (LCWT) founded
          WSPU founded
1907   Women's Freedom League founded
          NUWSS adopted new constitution
          Millicent Fawcett became President of NUWSS
1908   Irish Women's Franchise League founded
          Women's National Anti-Suffrage League founded
          Conservative and Unionist Women's Suffrage
            Association founded
1912   Pethick-Lawrences resigned from the WSPU
1913   East London Federation of Suffragettes founded
1914   Sylvia Pankhurst resigned from the WSPU

1 | The Origins of Women's Suffrage

In 1860, when this book begins, there were no women's suffrage societies campaigning for votes for women whatsoever, but by 1914 there were approximately 56 different societies with a combined membership of 300,000. It is difficult to trace the origins of the women's suffrage movement which operated in late Victorian and Edwardian Britain since, like most political crusades, it had somewhat confused and erratic beginnings. The suffrage movement began slowly with several people in different towns thinking and agitating around similar issues, in this case the vote.

Key dates

Second Reform Bill: 1867

Manchester National Society for Women's Suffrage founded: 1867

London National Society for Women's Suffrage founded: 1867

The importance of 1867

Historians agree that the year 1867 was a significant landmark in suffragist history. In response to a promise by J.S. Mill (see page 17) that he would introduce a women's suffrage amendment to Disraeli's 1867 Reform Bill, some of the most notable feminist campaigners of the nineteenth century – Barbara Bodichon, **Emily Davies** and Elizabeth Garrett Anderson (see page 5) – drafted a petition to Parliament demanding the enfranchisement of all householders regardless of sex. Davies and Garrett carried the petition, signed by almost 1500 women, to the House of Commons, where two of the handful of sympathetic MPs, J.S. Mill and Henry Fawcett, presented it.

In 1867 too, the Manchester National Society for Women's Suffrage was formed by Lydia Becker (see pages 37–8), followed shortly after by similar organisations in Birmingham, Bristol, Edinburgh, Belfast and later Dublin. Each of these groups was independent, but it soon became obvious that there would be benefits in having a federal union.

Key question
Why was 1867 important?

Key figure

Emily Davies
1830–1921; campaigned for higher education for women and helped to found Girton College, part of Cambridge University. She was vice-president of the London National Society for Women's Suffrage.

Profile: Lydia Becker 1827–90

1827 – Born in Manchester
1862 – Awarded gold medal by Horticultural Society
1864 – Published *Botany for Novices*
1865 – Began Ladies' Literary Society
1867 – Founded MNSWS; wrote article entitled 'Female Suffrage'
1868 – Treasurer of Married Women's Property Committee; encouraged regional societies to unite into a national one, which became the NSWS
1870 – Elected to Manchester School Board; founded and edited *Women's Suffrage* journal
1874 – Published pamphlet 'Rights and Duties of Women in Local Government'
1877 – Reunited suffrage movement
1881 – Secretary of NSWS
1887 – President of NSWS; helped to set up committee of the parliamentary supporters of women's suffrage
1890 – Died of diphtheria in Switzerland

Lydia Becker was the eldest of 15 children born to Mary and Hannibal Becker, a chemical manufacturer. In her late thirties she attended a lecture given by Barbara Bodichon on female suffrage. Inspired by the lecture, Becker wrote a passionately, yet logically argued, article for *The Contemporary Review* on the need for votes for women. It was to be the beginning of her suffrage career.

Her major contribution to the suffrage movement was in:

- helping to found the first women's suffrage society
- directing suffrage policy
- founding the first women's suffrage journal
- uniting the suffrage movement after a series of splits
- establishing a committee of MPs in support of votes for women.

In 1867 Becker founded the Manchester National Society for Women's Suffrage which, in 1868, through her encouragement, amalgamated with other regional societies to unite into a national one (NSWS). She was not a great orator but she spoke clearly and logically, undertaking lecture tours when it was considered improper for ladies to speak in public. Becker's strength was as an organiser. She led a campaign that encouraged women to put their names on the electoral register (the electoral roll). She spoke personally to about 7000 women in an attempt to persuade them. In 1867 she accompanied **Lily Maxwell** to the election polls.

Following years of disagreements and splits, Becker managed to unite the suffrage movement for a brief period in 1877 when she established the Central Committee of the National Society. But this was a fragile consensus and the movement split again. In 1887 Becker was elected President of the reunited NSWS and she retained this post until her death 3 years later.

Becker founded the ***Women's Suffrage Journal*** and edited it until her death. This journal provided information about the

---

Key figure

Lily Maxwell
A widow who ran a small business and paid rates. In 1867 she became the first woman to vote in a general election, but her vote was eventually disqualified because she was a woman.

Key term

Women's Suffrage Journal
Published between 1870 and 1890 and edited by Lydia Becker. It enjoyed a small circulation: in 1875 the print order was for 400 copies.

disadvantages suffered by women in education, in the law and the home as well as in politics. She wrote numerous journal articles and organised support for bills sent to Parliament on the need for votes for women.

As well as her interest in suffrage, Becker was involved in other female campaigns: against the Contagious Diseases Acts, as treasurer of the Married Women's Property Committee, and as a member of Manchester School Board. Becker, as with other suffragists, believed that being deprived of the vote was only one of a number of injustices faced by women.

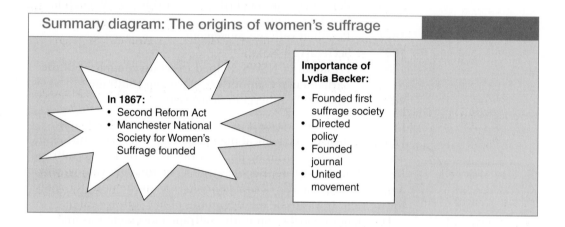

Summary diagram: The origins of women's suffrage

In 1867:
• Second Reform Act
• Manchester National Society for Women's Suffrage founded

Importance of Lydia Becker:
• Founded first suffrage society
• Directed policy
• Founded journal
• United movement

2 | Disunity in the Suffrage Movement

In 1868, encouraged by Lydia Becker, all the regional societies amalgamated to become the National Society for Women's Suffrage (NSWS). This, according to most historians, was the moment when organised national action began.

The unity envisaged by Becker was not to last. The early women's suffrage movement was characterised by political disagreements as the suffragists differed over the best way to achieve their objective. Consequently, the campaign for votes for women had an unusually complex and chequered history. There were three main areas of disagreement over policy and one over style. Each of these disagreements led to divisions in the suffrage movement and new organisations being founded.

> **Key date**
> National Society for Women's Suffrage (NSWS) founded: 1868

Suffragists and the Contagious Diseases Acts 1871: division over policy

In 1871 a division occurred between London and the rest of the country in response to the campaigns by the Ladies' National Association (LNA) against the Contagious Diseases Acts (CDAs) (see page 7):

> **Key question**
> Why did suffragists disagree over the Contagious Diseases Acts?

• On the one hand, members living outside London considered the LNA and the women's suffrage movement to be part of the same struggle against female oppression. In their opinion, the

CDAs were part of a male conspiracy by a male Parliament; such laws would not have been passed if women had voting power.
- On the other hand, members in London wished to keep women's suffrage distinct from the LNA. Talking about sex and sexually transmitted diseases was thought to be unseemly and suffragists feared it might create unnecessary enemies for the suffrage cause.

As a consequence, the women's suffrage movement split into two groups: the London National Society for Women's Suffrage and the Central Committee of the National Society for Women's Suffrage. Eventually, in 1877 the two organisations reunited as the New Central Committee of the National Society for Women's Suffrage (known as the National Society for Women's Suffrage), with Lydia Becker becoming **secretary**.

Suffragists and the Liberal Party 1888: division over policy

At the end of 1888 yet another split occurred, precipitated by major disagreements over political strategy:

- A number of the younger and more radical suffragists wanted to affiliate to the Women's Liberal Federation, the women's section of the Liberal Party, because the Liberal Party was perceived to be sympathetic to votes for women.
- Others – mostly the older members like Millicent Fawcett – disagreed because they wanted to keep the suffrage organisation independent of party politics. They wanted to gain support for votes for women from people of all political persuasions, not just the Liberals.

Once again, the suffrage movement divided into two, rather confusingly named, groups: the Central National Society for Women's Suffrage (CNS) with **Jane Cobden** as one of the leading figures and the Central Committee of the National Society for Women's Suffrage (known as the NSWS) with Lydia Becker and Millicent Fawcett (see pages 46–7) as key people. Lydia Becker, who had devoted her entire life to the suffrage movement, regarded the CNS as left wing and extreme, probably because most of its members were Liberal supporters. The upshot of these splits meant that the women's suffrage societies were too fragmented and decentralised to be effective nationally.

Key term

Secretary
An official appointed by a society to keep its records and look after the business side of the organisation.

Key question

Why did suffragists disagree over the Liberal Party?

Key dates

NSWS reunited: 1877

Central National Society for Women's Suffrage founded: 1888

Central Committee of the National Society for Women's Suffrage (remained the NSWS) founded: 1888

Key figure

Jane Cobden
1851–1947; daughter of the leading Liberal Richard Cobden.

Suffragists and the nature of the franchise 1889: division over policy

The question of which women should be given the vote was a matter of deep contention within the suffrage movement. Some wanted women to have the vote on the same terms as men while others wanted to restrict the vote to single women. As a result members of the newly formed Central National Society (CNS) started to disagree with each other because the CNS wanted to restrict the vote to single women:

- On the one hand, the CNS insisted that it was better to have a small reform rather than no reform at all. (It was a view shared by Millicent Fawcett, who insisted that she would even accept a suffrage bill that would only give the vote to women with dark hair, or to those who were 6 feet tall. In her opinion it would only be a first step to wider reform.)
- On the other hand, the policy of only enfranchising single women was criticised because it sacrificed the rights of married women in order to achieve a limited goal. 'I think,' Richard Pankhurst argued, 'it would push back freedom for married women certainly twenty or five-and-twenty years', and so the Women's Franchise League (WFrL) was established.

The WFrL was the first women's suffrage society to include married women in their demands for the franchise. It had two main aims. First, 'to extend to women, whether unmarried, married or widowed, the right to vote at parliamentary, municipal, local and other elections' on the same terms as men, and secondly, to 'establish for all women equal civil and political rights with men'. From the very beginning, this new organisation, like the CNS before it, identified with the Liberal Party.

The WFrL was a small organisation: in early 1890, according to the suffrage historian Elizabeth Crawford, it had 140 members and £70 in the bank. Even though it was small, the WFrL was influential. It included many of the leading political activists of the period: **Jacob Bright**, Josephine Butler (leader of the campaign to abolish the CDAs), **Harriot Stanton Blatch** and the Pankhursts. The WFrL attracted top Liberal support. In November 1889, it hosted a well-attended meeting in London at which R.B. Haldane (a Liberal MP) was a keynote speaker.

Suffragists and campaign methods 1892: division over style

Even the tiny WFrL could not agree on policy and a year later another split occurred. In April 1892 the Pankhursts led a disturbance at a suffrage meeting organised by Lydia Becker in St James' Hall, London. At the time a parliamentary franchise bill, put forward as a **private member's bill** by the Conservative MP Albert Rollit, was being discussed in Parliament. Lydia Becker, who called the meeting in support of Rollit, championed this bill, which would enfranchise single, but not married women. Both Pankhursts heckled the speakers: they interrupted proceedings by

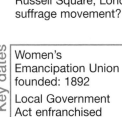

An 1891 print of a conference of the Women's Franchise League held in the Pankhursts' home in Russell Square, London. How useful is this source to a historian studying the early women's suffrage movement?

Key dates

Women's Emancipation Union founded: 1892

Local Government Act enfranchised some women: 1894

Key question
What was the effect of the 1894 Act on the campaign for women's suffrage?

Key figure

Ursula Bright
1835–1915; wife of leading Liberal MP, Jacob Bright. She was a founder member of the Central Committee of the National Society for Women's Suffrage and the WFrL. She was also a member of the Ladies' National Association and the Women's Liberal Federation.

shouting their objections to this limited franchise and demanding that married women be included. The effect of the Pankhursts' behaviour was to produce further splits within the suffrage movement. Elizabeth Wolstenholme Elmy (see page 6), critical of their disorderly behaviour, resigned from her position as secretary of the WFrL and set up the Women's Emancipation Union.

The WFrL and the 1894 Local Government Act
When Elmy resigned, **Ursula Bright**, a friend and colleague of Emmeline Pankhurst, was promoted to the post of secretary of the WFrL. Pankhurst and Bright – supported by their sympathetic husbands – worked hard to promote female equality and their efforts finally bore fruit in the 1894 Local Government Act. This Act enshrined the principle that all women, whether married or single, should be entitled to vote in local elections if they possessed the necessary property qualifications. Bright's husband, Jacob, spoke in Parliament in support of the Local Government Act, which Richard Pankhurst had written.

Not surprisingly, Emmeline Pankhurst and Ursula Bright were delighted with the success of the 1894 Act. In a triumphalist letter to her friend, Bright commented that the other two, rival, societies 'are simply mad at our success. They never calculated upon such a decisive victory … it will be impossible to carry a Parliamentary spinster's Bill if the married women are locally enfranchised.'

Bright's words were prophetic. From then on, it became impossible to exclude married women in the demand for the vote. In addition, the 1894 Local Government Act had the effect of destroying many of the old animosities between different suffrage societies. With married women safely enfranchised in local government, it seemed nonsensical, and possibly even churlish, to insist that only single women be given the vote. By the end of the nineteenth century, all suffrage societies were committed to campaign for women to be given the vote on the same terms as men. Thus, one of the disagreements between suffragists had been resolved and a few years later, in 1897, the NUWSS was formed to reunite the different groups (see pages 43–6).

The effect of disagreements on suffrage policy

It is important to remember that the continuous bickering and disagreements within the suffrage movement were good for the refinement of ideas and policy. Nonetheless, suffrage campaigners drew different conclusions from their experiences:

- A number of suffragists were convinced that it was important for women to bury their differences and unite in their struggle for the vote. These beliefs helped to shape the new organisational directions of the late nineteenth century.
- Others, like Emmeline Pankhurst, learned about the importance of disruptive action from their involvement with the WFrL. Their ideas were to shape twentieth-century suffrage politics. As Harriet Stanton Blatch commented, 'there rose from its ashes the militant work of the WSPU in England and the work of the Women's Political Union in America'.

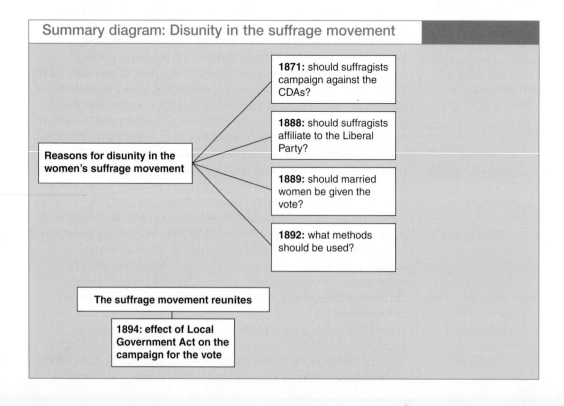

Summary diagram: Disunity in the suffrage movement

Reasons for disunity in the women's suffrage movement

1871: should suffragists campaign against the CDAs?

1888: should suffragists affiliate to the Liberal Party?

1889: should married women be given the vote?

1892: what methods should be used?

The suffrage movement reunites

1894: effect of Local Government Act on the campaign for the vote

3 | The National Union of Women's Suffrage Societies and its Offshoots 1897–1914

Key question
How was the suffrage movement reunited?

Key dates

National Union of Women's Suffrage Societies (NUWSS) founded: 1897

Millicent Fawcett became president of NUWSS: 1907

In the early 1890s, after the death of Lydia Becker, the suffrage movement seemed to suffer from a lack of coherent leadership. However, in this period the disagreements between the various suffrage groups diminished since all societies now agreed that both married and single women should get the vote. They also agreed on the need to work in unison.

- In 1896 a suffrage conference was held in Birmingham. Delegates from approximately 20 different suffrage societies met to discuss how to work together in the campaign for the vote.
- After the meeting a joint parliamentary **lobbying** committee was formed. This committee put pressure on MPs to support votes for women.
- In 1897, largely through the efforts of Millicent Fawcett, most of the various suffrage societies united once more under the federal structure of the National Union of Women's Suffrage Societies (NUWSS). This augured a renaissance of women's suffrage activity.

Organisation of the NUWSS

Organisational theory is often thought to be dreary and unexciting. However, without an effective organisation, women's suffrage was likely to continue to flounder. The structure of the NUWSS was well thought out: nobody wanted a repeat of the splits and divisions of the mid-nineteenth century. As a consequence, the NUWSS acted as conduit between the local suffrage societies and politicians. It co-ordinated rather than controlled the work of the various local suffrage societies and liaised between them and MPs in the House of Commons.

Each of the societies sent a representative to the NUWSS executive, but the decentralised structure allowed each section to remain responsible for its own decisions and activities. This loose federation meant that local groups could develop independent policies without alienating others and splitting the organisation. Various groups were brought together who might have otherwise misunderstood, disagreed with or distrusted each other. Unity was achieved, but it was unity at a cost. The NUWSS had no real authority over the various groups, no funds of its own to promote women's suffrage and no independent Executive Committee. In 1907 the NUWSS became a democratic and centralised organisation when it adopted a new constitution that provided for elected officers, an Executive Committee and an elected president.

Political parties and suffragists

Between 1860 and 1914 most of the leaders shared a family and friendship circle and held similar political convictions. Although the NUWSS claimed to be non-party political, many suffragists had links with the **Liberal Party** or were sympathetic to Liberal aims and had access to the Liberal political élite. Many were joint

Key terms

Lobbying
An organised attempt by people to influence law-makers.

Liberal Party
Founded in 1859. It believed in social reform. Under Gladstone it became committed to Home Rule for Ireland. In 1886 the Liberal Party split into Liberals and Liberal Unionists over this issue.

members of the Women's Liberal Federation and the NUWSS and were often the wives, mothers or daughters of prominent Liberal politicians. For example, Helen Taylor, daughter of Harriet Taylor and stepdaughter of J.S. Mill, Catherine Osler, sister-in-law of Joseph Chamberlain, the leading Liberal MP, Priscilla Bright McLaren and Millicent Fawcett all belonged to Liberal families.

Of course, not all suffragists were Liberal sympathisers. When the Liberal Party divided over **Home Rule**, many leading Liberals like Millicent Fawcett (see page 47) became **Liberal Unionists**. A few members of the **Conservative Party** formed their own organisation, led by Lady Betty Balfour, sister to Constance Lytton (see page 90) and sister-in-law of one-time prime minister Arthur Balfour (see page 103). Others, such as **Eva Gore-Booth**, Esther Roper and the Pankhursts (see pages 106–7), were attracted to the emerging **Labour Party**. Indeed, in 1912 the NUWSS, disillusioned with the Liberal Party, aligned themselves with the Labour Party (see pages 108–9).

Suffrage and class

The examples of suffrage personnel given above suggest that the early suffrage movement was predominantly an élite movement rather than a broad-based one. However, in their thought-provoking book *One Hand Tied Behind Us*, published in 1978, Jill Liddington and Jill Norris break the myth that the suffrage movement was completely dominated by middle-class women. Certainly, the membership of the NUWSS was socially mixed in the north of England. In some areas like Oldham it was predominantly middle class, whereas a few miles away in Clitheroe the membership was emphatically working class. One of the associations affiliated to the NUWSS, the North of England Society for Women's Suffrage, was committed to broadening the class composition of the suffrage movement and so put a great deal of effort into recruiting working-class women.

Nevertheless, there were certain tensions between the older middle-class members of the NUWSS and the newer working-class recruits of the North of England Society. In 1903 the Lancashire and Cheshire Women Textile and Other Workers' Representation Committee (LCWT) was founded specifically for working-class women. Although it was set up by the university-educated Esther Roper and the aristocratic Eva Gore-Booth, they encouraged working-class women to participate at a senior level: several textile workers and trade unionists took leading roles in the society. Not surprisingly, the LCWT worked closely with the Women's Co-operative Guild and the Manchester and Salford Women's Trade Union Council, of which Gore-Booth was co-secretary. Although the LCWT had broken away from the NUWSS, the two groups – unlike those of the nineteenth century – were not antagonistic towards each other. On the contrary, the LCWT received a lot of financial help from the NUWSS, with the result that it was able to campaign for women's suffrage in many textile towns in the north of England.

Key date
Conservative and Unionist Women's Suffrage Association founded: 1908

Key figure
Eva Gore-Booth 1870–1926; daughter of a wealthy Irish landowner. She helped to found a suffrage group for working-class women.

Key terms
Home Rule Self-government for Ireland. At the time Ireland was part of the UK.

Liberal Unionists Formed in 1886 after a split with the Liberal Party. They wanted Ireland to remain part of the UK.

Conservative Party 'Conservative' began to be used as a word for the Tory Party in the 1830s. They were against Home Rule and wanted the UK to remain united.

Labour Party Formed in 1906 as a socialist party committed to improving the lives of the working class.

Key dates

Lancashire and Cheshire Women Textile and Other Workers' Representation Committee (LCWT) founded: 1903

NUWSS adopted new constitution: 1907

Key term

Common Cause
Published between 1909 and 1920 as a journal of the NUWSS.

Growth of the NUWSS

The mid to late nineteenth century had witnessed a number of divisions within the women's suffrage movement that weakened it considerably. However, at the beginning of the twentieth century, the women's suffrage movement appeared to be united and strong. In 1907 the NUWSS elected its first president (Millicent Fawcett) and adopted a new constitution that gave its executive the power to make decisions, hire its own staff and control financial spending. The number of NUWSS branches rose from 33 in 1907 to 70 in 1910 and 478 in 1914. In 1909 it published its first newspaper, *Common Cause*. Membership figures grew accordingly: by 1914 the NUWSS had 52,000 members and attracted annual donations totalling £37,000. This unprecedented

Millicent Fawcett speaking at the Oxford Union, November 1908.

growth led to further restructuring. The NUWSS divided its regional groups into independent federations headed by their own committees. However, the suffragists were to face new challenges in the early twentieth century when a new organisation, the Women's Social and Political Union (WSPU), erupted onto the political scene.

Profile: Millicent Fawcett 1847–1929

1847 – Born in Aldburgh, Suffolk
1866 – Helped to organise petition asking for votes for women
1867 – Married Henry Fawcett
1868 – Joined the London Suffrage Committee; daughter Philippa born
1869 – First public speaking engagement
1870 – *Political Economy for Beginners* published
1874 – Joined the Central Committee for Women's Suffrage (CCWS)
1875 – Co-founder Newnham College, Cambridge
1877 – Joined the New Central Committee of National Society for Women's Suffrage (NSWS)
1884 – Helped to gain support for an amendment to include women in male suffrage bill
1885 – Founder of National Vigilance Association
1887 – Henry died
1888 – Helped to found Women's Liberal Unionist Association
1899 – Awarded honorary doctorate by University of St Andrews
1904 – Vice-president of International Women's Suffrage Alliance
1907 – President of NUWSS
1908 – First woman to speak at the Oxford Union
1918 – Vice-president of League of Nations Union
1929 – Died in London

Millicent Fawcett's involvement in the suffrage movement spanned at least two generations. Over this time she built up a formidable reputation, never wavering in her ideas about peaceful reform. By the 1870s she had become one of the very few women to speak regularly in public and was one of the foremost women in the suffrage campaign. She was the undisputed leader of the moderate section of the suffrage movement from the late nineteenth century until 1918 when women gained a limited franchise. Fawcett was not a naturally gifted speaker but she was a clear, logical thinker with a sense of humour so her speeches were warmly received. She quickly established a reputation as an exceptional organiser and conciliator: her role in ending the disagreements between various suffrage groups and in avoiding further dissension by creating the NUWSS was a significant one. She emerged as the natural leader of the NUWSS when it was established and in 1907 became its first president.

Fawcett is often perceived as a Liberal – after all she was married to a leading Liberal politician. However, she became a Liberal Unionist in 1886 because she was against Home Rule for Ireland. Certainly, Fawcett did not wish the suffrage organisation to be affiliated to the Liberal Party. When the suffrage movement split into two over this question (see page 39), she took the side of the Central National Committee of Women's Suffrage. And in 1912, wearied by Liberal unwillingness to grant votes to women, she, and the NUWSS, turned to the Labour Party for support.

Equally, she believed that suffrage should be independent of other women's issues. Even though Fawcett was a leading figure in the Repeal of the Contagious Diseases Act and close to Josephine Butler (see page 7), she did not wish the suffrage movement to align itself with it. In her view, the suffrage campaign would be disastrously affected if it were in any way associated with prostitution.

Like other suffragists, Fawcett was involved in various campaigns to promote equality for women in education, work and the law. In 1871 she co-founded Newnham College in Cambridge. She vigorously supported the work of Butler and was active in the campaigns against the white slave trade. In honour of her contributions she was elected president of the National Council of Women and vice-president of the **National Vigilance Association**. However, it is her contribution to votes for women that she is best remembered: as J.S. Mill wrote in 1869, 'the cause of women's suffrage has no more active, judicious and useful friends than Mr and Mrs Fawcett'.

Key term

National Vigilance Association Founded in 1885 to help to enforce the Criminal Law Amendment Act.

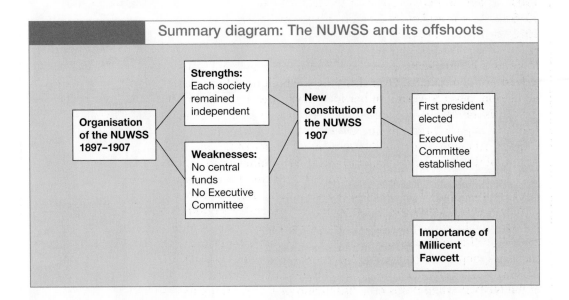

Summary diagram: The NUWSS and its offshoots

Organisation of the NUWSS 1897–1907

Strengths: Each society remained independent

Weaknesses: No central funds No Executive Committee

New constitution of the NUWSS 1907

First president elected

Executive Committee established

Importance of Millicent Fawcett

4 | The Women's Social and Political Union 1903–14

Key question
Why was the WSPU founded?

In 1903 Emmeline Pankhurst, who had been active in earlier suffrage campaigns, founded the Women's Social and Political Union (WSPU) at her house in Manchester. The women present at the meeting wanted to cast off the Liberal image of women's suffrage, to reverse the decades of suffrage defeat and turn the WSPU into a viable political machine that achieved results. In her autobiography, Emmeline Pankhurst stated that she wanted to keep the WSPU free from party affiliation, yet at first the WSPU was very sympathetic to the Labour Party and its early membership consisted of Labour Party activists.

Key date

WSPU founded: 1903

The structure of the WSPU

The WSPU has been accused of being an **autocratic**, man-hating organisation that was considerably less tolerant than its rival, the NUWSS. This is because:

Key question
Was the WSPU an autocratic organisation?

Key term

Autocratic
Dictatorial. Not allowing any discussion.

- from 1906, policies were decided by an unelected Central Committee with Sylvia Pankhurst as secretary, Emmeline Pethick-Lawrence as Treasurer and Annie Kenney (see page 54) as paid organiser

Emmeline, Christabel and Sylvia Pankhurst, October 1911.

Profile: Emmeline Pankhurst 1858–1928

1858 – Born
1879 – Married Richard Pankhurst
1880 – Elected to Committee of National Society for Women's Suffrage; Christabel born
1882 – Sylvia born
1884 – Henry Francis Robert (Frank) born
1885 – Adela born
1888 – Frank died
1889 – Henry Francis (Harry) born
1898 – Richard Pankhurst died
1903 – WSPU founded
1907 – Resigned from the Independent Labour Party: *Votes for Women* published
1908 – Imprisoned for the first time
1910 – Harry died
1912 – *Suffragette* published
1913 – Sentenced to 3 years in prison
1914 – Emmeline abandoned campaign for the vote
1915 – *Suffragette* newspaper changed its name to *Britannia*

Key term

Radical activist
Someone who campaigned for social and political reforms such as votes for women, improvements in working conditions and better housing for the working class.

Emmeline Pankhurst was a **radical activist** of some distinction: she was a Poor Law Guardian, a member of the Manchester School Board and a founding member of the Manchester Independent Labour Party, and was active in four different suffrage societies before she founded the WSPU.

In 1903, frustrated at the slow pace of the existing women's suffrage movement, she and her daughters founded the Women's Social and Political Union (WSPU). By 1914, the WSPU was notorious for its militant actions: breaking windows, destroying golf-courses and blowing up buildings. As leader of the WSPU, Pankhurst was held responsible for the crimes committed by its members, especially when she claimed that 'I have advised, I have incited, I have conspired … I accept the responsibility for it'. Not surprisingly, the government constantly summonsed, arrested, tried and imprisoned her. By 1914 Pankhurst was refusing to eat, drink or sleep when she was imprisoned. The government, fearful of public criticism, never force-fed her, releasing the leading suffragette from prison when her health was critical.

With the outbreak of the First World War Pankhurst ceased campaigning for the vote. After the war she continued, as she had done before the suffragette movement, to be involved in other forms of political action. In 1917 she co-founded the Women's Party (see page 163). In the early 1920s, and in her sixties, Pankhurst became a national figure in Canadian politics leading a campaign to prevent sexually transmitted diseases. When she eventually returned to England in 1926 she was adopted as Conservative candidate for the working-class district of Whitechapel.

- the Central Committee was assisted by a sub-committee which consisted mainly of family and friends of the Pankhursts. For example, **Mary Clarke** served on this sub-committee
- members did not participate in decision making, but were informed of new policies and strategies during the weekly Monday afternoon meetings held at the headquarters in Lincoln's Inn Field, London
- the Central Committee controlled all publications, all appointments to paid positions and of course the organisation's finances. The WSPU became a minefield of personal feuds, battles over methods and family tensions. At the centre of the storm were the Pankhursts: it was difficult, if not impossible, for members to oppose them.

Key figure
Mary Clarke 1863–1910; the younger sister of Emmeline Pankhurst. In 1907 she was appointed paid organiser of the WSPU. She was imprisoned in 1909 and 1910 for suffragette activity.

Critics of the structure of the WSPU

The WSPU's autocratic structure, its family-led group and its policy of forbidding debate seem to be strangely at odds with its demands for democracy. The WSPU was criticised for a number of reasons:

Key question
Why did people criticise the WSPU structure?

- It was considered hypocritical of the WSPU to condemn the Liberal government for its reluctance to widen the suffrage while failing to practise democracy itself. Democracy is usually based on discussion, freedom of expression and voting: the WSPU leaders certainly did not practise these. One suffragette commented that although Emmeline Pankhurst 'wishes women to have votes she will not allow them to have opinions'.
- It was believed that the vote should be sought through a democratic organisation that mirrored a future electoral system rather than one which clearly did not.
- It was thought that unquestioning obedience to a female **oligarchy** was inadequate preparation for the future female voter, who needed to evaluate the arguments of each political party.

Key term
Oligarchy Government by a small group of people.

The first historians to write about the suffrage movement also criticised Emmeline Pankhurst's decision to structure the organisation on such tight lines. Ray Strachey, the suffrage activist and historian, suggests that the WSPU 'entrusted all their decisions to their leaders ... These people alone decided what was to be done; the others obeyed, and enjoyed the surrender of their judgement, and the sensation of marching as an army under discipline.' The historian David Mitchell, writing in 1977, not only entitles the last chapter of his book *Queen Christabel*, 'Bitch Power', as an unflattering description of the suffragettes and their successors, but compares the WSPU with a German terrorist gang. Feminist historians, although using different terminology, subscribe to this interpretation: Jill Liddington and Jill Norris believe that the leadership of the WSPU exercised draconian control over its membership.

Key question
What arguments can
be used to justify the
WSPU's structure?

Key term

Constitution
Rules of an
organisation that
include its aims and
objectives, policies
and methods.

Arguments in favour of the WSPU's structure

Although the WSPU was undoubtedly dictatorial and had no
formal **constitution**, there are a number of points to take into
consideration before it is condemned out of hand. Indeed, later
historians of the suffragette movement are more apologetic of the
WSPU's lack of democracy. In particular, Paula Bartley's and June
Purvis's biographies of Emmeline Pankhurst, which were both
published in 2002, make the following points:

- Critics of the WSPU's structure were largely those in sympathy
  with the NUWSS, and because there was great rivalry between
  the two organisations they were not objective in their
  criticisms.
- Emmeline Pankhurst, the founder, had experienced the
  argumentative nineteenth-century suffrage movement and
  wanted to exert a firmer hold on 'her' organisation to prevent
  disagreements prohibiting action.
- The WSPU was not always undemocratic. Initially it favoured
  an informal approach to politics – there was no official
  membership list and any woman who wished to attend a
  meeting was welcome.
- Nobody was forced to belong to the organisation and members
  could always leave if they disagreed with the policies. Moreover,
  the suffragettes of the WSPU were not meek and mild
  individuals with no will of their own: these women were strong
  political activists who would not listen to or obey those with
  whom they disagreed or disapproved.
- The members of the WSPU certainly adored their leaders:
  Emmeline and Christabel maintained their position by sheer
  force of personality rather than by election, by charm rather
  than by fear.
- The WSPU educated its membership, encouraged their self-
  confidence and helped to develop political awareness. Many
  suffragettes told how they were taught the skills of public
  speaking and debate by WSPU leaders.
- Both Emmeline and Christabel Pankhurst made the point that
  a democratic organisation was probably inappropriate for their
  style of politics. Indeed, the WSPU became less democratic as
  its activities became more illegal. And as the WSPU
  increasingly operated within a hostile political climate, so
  military-style planning, command and action assumed greater
  importance than internal democracy. Time was a factor too.
  Certainly, Emmeline and Christabel Pankhurst's charismatic
  style of leadership meant they could make up policy on the
  hoof rather than wait for endless committees to debate and
  agree new decisions.
- Finally, although the London-based WSPU was undoubtedly
  undemocratic, this may not have been the case for the
  provincial branches and their regional offices. For the most
  part, branches and offices enjoyed considerable autonomy. A
  working-class branch of the WSPU organised by Sylvia, another

Profile: Christabel Pankhurst 1880–1958

1880 – Born in Manchester
1900 – Met Esther Roper and Eva Gore-Booth
1902 – Joined North of England Society for Women's Suffrage
1903 – Began law degree; joined WSPU
1905 – Arrested and imprisoned
1906 – Graduated with first-class law degree; moved to London; decided to oppose all party candidates at elections
1907 – Resigned from the Labour Party; *Votes for Women* published; arrested and imprisoned
1908 – Charged, along with others, with conduct likely to cause a breach of the peace and acted as lawyer in defence of the group; imprisoned
1912 – Fled to France to escape imprisonment; *Suffragette* published
1913 – *The Great Scourge and How to End It* published
1914 – Gave up suffragette activity to help with the war effort
1918 – Stood as MP for Smethwick
1936 – Made **DBE**
1939 – Moved to the USA
1958 – Died in the USA

In 1902 Christabel joined the North of England Society for Women's Suffrage (see page 44) and in 1903 joined the Women's Social and Political Union. She studied for a law degree and graduated top of her group of students with a first-class honours degree and a prize in international law. However, she was not allowed to practise law because she was a woman. She moved to London and lived with the Pethick-Lawrences between 1906 and 1912 where she directed WSPU policy.

Undoubtedly, Pankhurst initiated tactics designed to shock, in direct contrast to the NUWSS leader. She insisted that because suffragists had been unable to persuade Parliament, suffragettes needed to 'alarm' them since 'government moves only in response to pressure rather than persuasion'. She was imprisoned three times. In 1912, Christabel fled to France to escape further arrest and imprisonment and lived in Paris until the outbreak of war, controlling the movement in exile there.

Pankhurst was clearly the chief organiser and key strategist of the WSPU. She wrote leading articles in the *Suffragette* newspaper and spoke at many meetings in favour of militancy (see pages 78–91). Some of the policies she initiated were:

- beginning a new era of militancy
- deciding to oppose party candidates at by-elections
- favouring a limited suffrage for women
- advocating an increase in violence.

Emmeline Pethick-Lawrence said of her: 'She had great courage. She had a cool, logical mind, and a quick and ready wit. She was young and attractive, graceful on the platform, with a singularly clear and musical voice.'

Key term

DBE
Dame Commander of the Order of the British Empire. Part of a British system whereby individuals are honoured for their bravery, achievement or service.

daughter of Emmeline Pankhurst, was certainly run on democratic lines. Here, officers and delegates stood for election and were voted in. (Sylvia was expelled in 1914 for not abiding by WSPU principles.)

The points outlined above may not overthrow the hostile criticism made of the WSPU, but they certainly modify it by explaining the context in which the suffragettes worked.

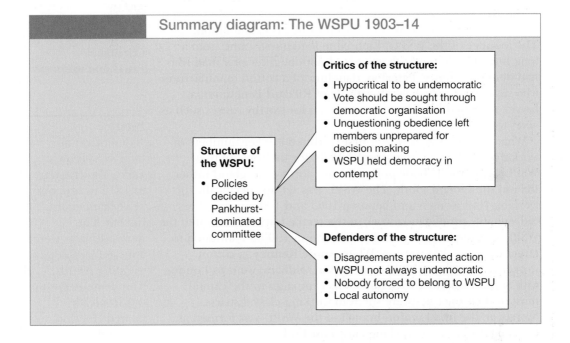

Summary diagram: The WSPU 1903–14

Structure of the WSPU:

- Policies decided by Pankhurst-dominated committee

Critics of the structure:

- Hypocritical to be undemocratic
- Vote should be sought through democratic organisation
- Unquestioning obedience left members unprepared for decision making
- WSPU held democracy in contempt

Defenders of the structure:

- Disagreements prevented action
- WSPU not always undemocratic
- Nobody forced to belong to WSPU
- Local autonomy

5 | Key Debate: Suffragette Membership

Key question
Do historians agree that the WSPU was an élitist, anti-male organisation?

One of the major criticisms levelled against the WSPU relates to its membership, which is compared unfavourably with that of the NUWSS. The first suffrage historians argued that the WSPU was an élitist organisation committed to an élitist franchise. Certainly, the WSPU was associated with middle-class and aristocratic spinsters who wanted a limited franchise based on property qualifications rather than universal suffrage. It was also believed that the WSPU was anti-men. However, these criticisms need to be reassessed.

The WSPU was an élitist organisation: arguments in favour

Key term

Viceroys
Rulers of India who were appointed by the British government. Between 1858 and 1947 India was under the control of Britain.

A number of historians point out that from 1906, when Christabel Pankhurst arrived in London, working-class women receded into the background of the WSPU to be replaced by women of an entirely different social class. The most famous example was the aristocratic and politically Conservative Constance Lytton, whose father had been one of the **Viceroys** of India and whose mother had been lady-in-waiting to Queen Victoria. These historians condemn the WSPU for recruiting upper-class women. Andrew Rosen, writing in the 1970s, regrets the decline of working-class membership, particularly when the WSPU 'ceased to envisage votes for women as a measure desirable primarily because it would benefit working-class women'. Jill Liddington and Jill Norris, too, criticise the WSPU because it had little sustained contact with working-class women.

The WSPU was an élitist organisation: arguments against

The argument that the WSPU was élitist needs examination. The founder of the WSPU, Emmeline Pankhurst, came from a long line of male political activists: granddaughter of a man who had demonstrated at **Peterloo**, daughter of a cotton manufacturer who supported anti-slavery, and wife of Richard Pankhurst, a lawyer who used his talents to campaign for worthy causes such as votes for women.

What is more, the WSPU at first recruited greater numbers of working-class women than the NUWSS, for the roots of the WSPU lay in the Labour politics of the north of England rather than in the Liberal south. The WSPU was set up specifically for working-class women and between 1903 and 1906 its members did valuable propaganda work in the textile towns. Even when the WSPU's headquarters moved to London in 1906 it continued to target working-class women. When **Annie Kenney**, a cotton worker recruited at a WSPU meeting in Oldham, went to London with Sylvia Pankhurst to organise the campaign in the capital, most of their energies were spent in working-class districts. Moreover, the first London branch of the WSPU was formed at Canning Town in the working-class East End.

In addition, later suffrage historians insist that the WSPU's strength lay with its local, regional and Scottish branches as much as its headquarters, and these branches recruited working-class women.

- Iris Dove's *Yours in the Cause*, published in 1988, argues that until 1908 the WSPU was active in Woolwich, Lewisham and Greenwich, working with the local Labour Party to recruit working-class women.
- In Scotland the links with working-class women and socialism remained strong, as argued by Leah Leneman in '*A Guid Cause': The Women's Suffrage Movement in Scotland*, which was published in 1991.
- Barbara Winslow's biography *Sylvia Pankhurst*, published in 1996, demonstrates that the WSPU branch in London's East End remained a working-class organisation. It saw itself as part of the **labour movement** and believed that women could only gain real equality under **socialism**.

Key figure

Annie Kenney
1879–1953; worked in a cotton mill until she became a paid organiser in the WSPU. She served four prison sentences. Kenney was put in charge of the London-based WSPU when Christabel Pankhurst was in exile.

Key terms

Peterloo
A demonstration held at St Peter's Field, Manchester, in 1812 in support of parliamentary reform. The demonstrators were attacked by soldiers wielding swords. The demonstration was ironically named Peterloo after a British victory over the French at Waterloo.

Labour movement
A term used to describe those who worked for improvements for the working class.

Socialism
A theory that advocates that the state should own and control businesses, factories and industry in order to promote equality.

Suffrage and working-class women: *The Suffragette*, 17 January 1913.

- In 1913, as Krista Cowman points out in '*Mrs Brown is a Man and a Brother': Women in Merseyside's Political Organisations 1890–1920*, published in 2004, the WSPU remained true to its socialist past. It recruited working-class women and invited a local Independent Labour Party leader to open its new offices in Liverpool.

Furthermore, whatever its class composition, the WSPU consistently supported issues relating to working-class women. For instance, when working-class women such as pit-brow workers, chain-makers and barmaids had their livelihoods threatened, they all received support from the WSPU. Of course, it could also be argued that the recruitment of middle- and upper-class women to the WSPU may not have been a weakness at all because this broadening of its class composition made it less exclusive. Moreover, in bringing women from different classes together, the WSPU helped to weaken the class divisions that characterised Edwardian Britain.

If you look at the cartoon from *The Suffragette* on page 55 you can see that there is a relationship between class, religion and the WSPU:

- First, the cartoon reveals that the WSPU believed in the importance of the vote for working-class women, as the central character is obviously working class, as shown by her dress and shawl.
- Secondly, it hints that the WSPU's attitude towards working-class women was informed by religious ideas. The cartoon shows a working mother with her arms outstretched in a crucifix position, a symbol of both sacrifice and shelter. In the cartoon she is regarded as both victim and saviour. Women, particularly working-class women, were seen to share with Christ in his suffering. The woman with her outstretched arms is identified, as was Christ, with the oppressed. (Many believed that mothers were like Christ. It was a time of high maternal mortality and women were seen to suffer death to give birth to a new life.)
- Thirdly, it was believed that life would improve for working-class women if they had the vote. Across her shoulders and forming a halo on her head is the slogan 'votes for working women'. If working-class women gained the vote, the WSPU cartoon suggests, women could shelter their (now) healthy, happy children and watch them pick flowers and make daisy chains. Without the vote, the cartoon implies, working-class women would be crucified.

It is perhaps important to remember that most male political organisations – be they socialist or conservative – have been led by the middle class, but historians are not so concerned about the class composition of even revolutionary groups. In contrast, historians seem obsessed about the class background of women's groups and one must ask – rather provocatively – why this is so. Of course, governments could, and sometimes did, justify their reluctance to give votes to women by pointing to the narrow composition of the suffrage movement.

Key term

The Suffragette
A WSPU newspaper published between 1912 and 1915. Each issue of the paper sold about 17,000, but this fell to about 10,000 because of police persecution.

Key question
Did the WSPU dislike men in general?

Key terms

Votes for Women
The official paper of the WSPU between 1907 and 1912. After 1912 it was edited by the Pethick-Lawrences. It had a circulation figure of over 30,000 in 1910, but after 1912, when the paper ceased to be linked to the WSPU, its editors found it difficult to keep the paper solvent.

Women's liberation movement
A movement, which began in the 1960s, that wanted equal pay for equal work, free abortion on demand, educational opportunities and equal rights for lesbians.

Men and the WSPU

Only women could be members of the WSPU, and so concern is expressed by historians that the suffragettes were anti-male. It is certainly true that the WSPU would not allow men to join the organisation and continually affirmed women's independence from the opposite sex. Yet the WSPU initially welcomed male support. In particular, it appreciated the advice of Frederick Pethick-Lawrence, who helped to edit the first suffragette newspaper *Votes for Women* and whose business acumen helped to lift the economic fortunes of the WSPU from a small provincial society to a great business enterprise.

Nonetheless, by 1913 the WSPU was unwilling to co-operate with men or with other organisations, like the NUWSS, which had male associates. By 1914 Christabel Pankhurst undoubtedly treated all men as enemies. She complained that socialist men – despite their commitment to equality – were little better than conservatives and liberals in their failure to support votes for women. Even her godfather Frederick Pethick-Lawrence (who had devoted his life to the cause) was considered to be an embarrassment purely because he was a man. Some feminist historians are not so critical of this shift for they view the WSPU as the first autonomous women's organisation and therefore the precursor of the **women's liberation movement** of the late 1960s. Certainly the WSPU saw the unity of women as more important than the division of class and suggested that the subordination of women to men was at least as significant as class oppression.

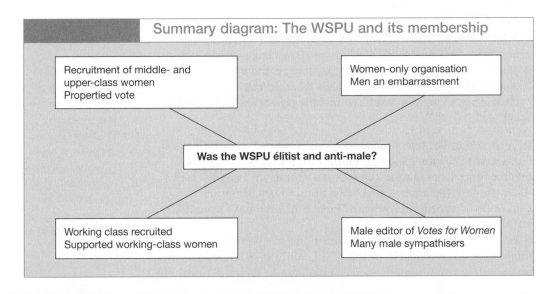

Summary diagram: The WSPU and its membership

Recruitment of middle- and upper-class women
Propertied vote

Women-only organisation
Men an embarrassment

Was the WSPU élitist and anti-male?

Working class recruited
Supported working-class women

Male editor of *Votes for Women*
Many male sympathisers

6 | Disunity in the Suffragette Movement

It is sometimes argued that splits in the WSPU arose primarily because the Pankhursts were ruthless in getting rid of those who criticised their personal control. Between 1903 and 1914 there were seven splits in the WSPU, the three most important occurring in 1907, 1912 and 1914. The first involved **Teresa Billington-Greig**, **Charlotte Despard** and others; the second the Pethick-Lawrences; and the third Sylvia Pankhurst. Neither colleagues, friends nor family could halt the march of the militant Pankhurst generals and their army.

The Women's Freedom League 1907

During 1907 differences came to a head between Despard, Billington-Greig and Emmeline Pankhurst. The first two complained that the WSPU was turning its back on the working class and cultivating upper-class and wealthy women. More importantly, Billington-Greig wanted greater organisational democracy and more independence for the branches. In 1906 she drafted a democratic constitution for the WSPU proposing annual conferences with elected leaders and members who could vote. In effect, the proposed constitution, which had been accepted by much of the membership, placed power in the hands of the branch delegates at the expense of the leadership. Unfortunately for Billington-Greig, Emmeline and Christabel Pankhurst disagreed with it and in a well-orchestrated takeover of power denounced the leaders as conspirators, tore up the proposed constitution and formed a new committee composed of those sympathetic to the Pankhurst doctrine.

The following extract written by Billington-Greig soon after the split certainly expresses a deep hostility towards the Pankhursts. But it also confirms some historians' views that the Pankhurst leadership dealt with criticism by ignoring it.

> When the Conference day came it was attended by delegates and individual members indiscriminately who assembled ready for discussion on constructive lines. But instead of discussion, there was an announcement of dictatorship put forward with all the eloquence, skill and feeling of which Mrs Pankhurst was capable. The draft Constitution was dramatically torn up and thrown to the ground. The assembled members were informed that they were in the ranks in an army of which she was the permanent Commander-in-Chief.

In response to the rejection of the constitution, Teresa Billington-Greig and Charlotte Despard, along with a fifth of the WSPU membership, left to found the Women's Freedom League (WFL). 'If we are fighting against the subjection of woman to man, we cannot honestly submit to the subjection of woman to woman', said Billington-Greig.

However, the WFL failed to establish any distinctive image as in many ways it was a hybrid of the WSPU and the NUWSS. On the one hand, it was a militant society, engaging in illegal actions, but

Key question
What were the major areas of disagreement in the WSPU?

Key figures

Teresa Billington-Greig
1877–1964; joined the WSPU in 1903. She gave up a teaching career to become a WSPU paid organiser in 1905. She resigned from the WSPU in 1907 and helped to found the Women's Freedom League (WFL). She left the WFL in 1910 because of policy disagreements. She wrote a critical history *The Militant Suffrage Movement*, which was published in 1911.

Charlotte Despard
1844–1939; daughter of an army captain and a wealthy heiress. In 1870 she married a rich Liberal and when he died in 1890 she devoted her life to politics. Poor Law Guardian; vegetarian. Joined the WSPU in 1906 but left to set up the Women's Freedom League.

Women's Freedom League founded: 1907

Key date

on the other hand, it was democratic, and thus it fell between the law-breaking suffragettes and the law-abiding suffragists. Furthermore, although the WFL was supposedly non-party, it remained loyal to its Labour origins, worked closely with local Labour groups and campaigned for Labour candidates at elections. Interestingly, the WFL too was often beset by internal divisions, so that even the rebellious Billington-Greig came to envy the alleged autocratic style of the WSPU.

The Pethick-Lawrences 1912

Friendship ties were swiftly broken whenever the Pankhursts were criticised. Emmeline and Frederick Pethick-Lawrence, who were Christabel's close friends, were expelled from the WSPU in October 1912. The Pethick-Lawrences had not only questioned the escalation of violence (see pages 85–90) but Fred, as the only man ever to take a large part in the running of the WSPU, was increasingly seen as a misfit in an all-female organisation. When Christabel Pankhurst announced that she 'disapproved of men's intimate concern' in the movement, it augured badly for Fred's future role within the WSPU. In a remarkable token of generosity, the Pethick-Lawrences left the WSPU without acrimony, continued to publish *Votes for Women* and founded the **Votes for Women Fellowship**. They later helped to found the **United Suffragists** in early 1914 and in so doing re-established links with the radical section of the Labour movement.

Sylvia Pankhurst 1914

Family bonds, too, collapsed in the event of disagreement. In January 1914 Sylvia Pankhurst was summoned to Paris by her sister Christabel – who was in voluntary exile there (see page 52) – to be informed that she must either 'toe the line' or sever all links with the WSPU. Christabel informed her that the WSPU must have only one policy, one programme and one command: those who wished to give an independent lead, or carry out programmes which differed from those laid down by the WSPU, must create an independent organisation of their own.

Undoubtedly, Christabel Pankhurst disliked her sister's emphasis on class politics. Sylvia had remained loyal to the militancy of the WSPU, but was determined to run the organisation on socialist lines. In concentrating her energies in London's East End, in forming the East London Federation of Suffragettes (ELFS), in conducting the campaign for votes for women along class lines and in forming a 'People's Army' to fight against class oppression, Sylvia Pankhurst was thought to discredit the WSPU.

The immediate cause of the split between Sylvia and the WSPU was Sylvia's public support of an Irish dock strike and its trade union leader – an obvious affront to the WSPU whose policy was non-political. And because both sides refused to compromise, the ELFS ceased to be a branch of the WSPU and became a separate organisation. This split may have permitted Sylvia Pankhurst the

Profile: Sylvia Pankhurst 1882–1960

1882 – Born in Manchester
1894 – Joined Independent Labour Party
1898 – Won a scholarship to Manchester Art School
1902 – Won a travelling scholarship
1903 – Joined WSPU
1906 – Imprisoned
1907 – Imprisoned
1911 – *The Suffragette* published
1913 – East London Federation of Suffragettes founded; imprisoned several times
1914 – Resigned from the WSPU; published *Women's Dreadnought*; met Asquith
1916 – ELFS renamed the Workers' Suffrage Federation
1917 – Newspaper renamed *Workers' Dreadnought*
1918 – Workers' Suffrage Federation renamed Workers' Socialist Federation
1927 – Gave birth to a son
1931 – The *Suffragette Movement* published
1932 – The *Home Front* published
1935 – The *Life of Emmeline Pankhurst* published
1960 – Died in Ethiopia

Sylvia, the least favoured daughter, was a serious and dedicated suffrage campaigner who lacked the glamorous appeal of her elder sister and mother. In her view, the WSPU needed to recruit working-class women and build up a mass movement rather than encourage élite women to join the suffrage ranks. Not surprisingly, she worked in the London's East End where she established the East London Federation of Suffragettes. The membership card of the WSPU, which depicted a working-class woman, was designed by Sylvia, as were suffragette banners and posters.

Sylvia suffered more than Christabel from the WSPU's advocacy of militancy, being constantly arrested, charged and imprisoned, going on hunger and thirst strikes and being force fed. For example, between February 1913 and August 1914 she was arrested eight times. Even so, Sylvia was forced to resign from the WSPU by her mother and sister who disliked her emphasis on working-class issues. Yet it was her commitment to working-class women that persuaded Asquith to receive a deputation of women from the East End in June 1914.

In 1914 Sylvia opposed the war and remained committed to campaigning for the vote (see pages 138–9). In the 1930s Sylvia joined several women's peace groups and fought against **fascism**. She campaigned against the Italian fascists when they invaded Ethiopia and soon Ethiopian politics dominated her life. In 1956 she moved to Ethiopia.

Key term

Fascism
An extreme right-wing nationalist movement that existed in Italy between 1922 and 1943. Its leader was Benito Mussolini.

freedom to pursue her own politics but, cut off from the funds of the WSPU, the ELFS did not develop into a significant suffrage organisation. Nonetheless, Sylvia founded her own paper, the ***Woman's Dreadnought***, and continued to concentrate on working-class women's suffrage.

Growth of the WSPU

The various splits and disagreements of the nineteenth century had, according to Emmeline Pankhurst, led to a weakened suffrage movement. She was determined to make sure that the WSPU was a strong fighting force. This appeared to be the case, but it is difficult to provide facts and figures because, unlike the NUWSS, the WSPU did not publish information about its membership, making it impossible to calculate accurate membership numbers. But there is no doubt that its membership grew rapidly. The attendances at the weekly meeting in London rose to about 1000 each week and by 1910 its income was £33,027. This enabled the WSPU to employ 98 women office workers in London and 26 women in charge of regional districts. The circulation of *Votes for Women* also increased to just under 40,000. However, in 1913 the wealth of the WSPU declined and it became clear that the success of its regional organisation was diminishing: 34 of its 88 branches were situated in London.

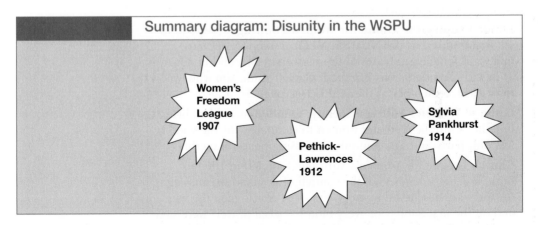

Summary diagram: Disunity in the WSPU

Women's Freedom League 1907

Pethick-Lawrences 1912

Sylvia Pankhurst 1914

Key question
How wide was the suffrage movement beyond the NUWSS and WSPU?

7 | Other Suffrage Societies

The suffrage movement was wider than the NUWSS and the WSPU who have dominated the historiography of the suffrage movement. It is important to remember that there were many other societies besides these two that campaigned for women's suffrage:

- Professional women founded their own suffrage societies: the Artists' Suffrage Franchise League, the Actresses' Franchise League, the Women Writers' Suffrage League and the London Graduates' Union for Women's Suffrage were among them.
- Similarly, different religious denominations set up suffrage groups: the Catholic Women's Suffrage Society, the Church League for Women's Suffrage, the Friends' League for

Women's Suffrage and the Jewish League for Woman Suffrage represented women from a variety of religious backgrounds.

- Women even set up suffrage organisations that reflected their political affiliations, such as the Conservative and Unionist Women's Franchise Association.

OTHER SUFFRAGE SOCIETIES

Artists' Suffrage League: founded in 1907 by women artists to help with the first suffrage demonstration held that year (see page 71). The Artists' Suffrage League designed banners, leaflets, cartoons, postcards and posters for the NUWSS, but it remained a separate organisation.

Actresses' Franchise League: founded in 1903 at the Criterion restaurant in London. It was open to anyone involved in the theatre and worked for votes for women by staging plays. The League helped both the WSPU and the NUWSS and neither supported nor condemned militancy. Two of its leading members belonged to the WSPU.

Women Writers' Suffrage League: founded in 1908 to obtain the vote for women on the same terms as men and to use methods 'proper to writers – the use of the pen'. It was founded by WSPU members.

London Graduates' Union for Women's Suffrage: founded in 1909 and linked to the NUWSS. Membership was open to male and female graduates of the University of London. One of its vice-presidents was Elizabeth Garrett Anderson who was, until 1911, a member of the WSPU (see page 5).

Catholic Women's Suffrage Society: founded in 1911 to bring together Catholic men and women to campaign for the vote. It was non-party and was committed to using peaceful methods.

Church League for Women's Suffrage: founded in 1909 to bring together members of the Church of England to campaign for the vote. It believed in the power of prayer to gain the vote and on the first Sunday of every month special prayers were said in support of women's suffrage. It used peaceful protest but would not declare itself opposed to militancy.

Friends' League for Women's Suffrage: founded around 1911 by members of the Society of Friends, who were known as Quakers.

Jewish League for Woman Suffrage: founded in 1912 to unite Jewish suffragists of all shades of opinion. It believed in peaceful methods, but synagogue services were occasionally interrupted by its members (see page 121).

Conservative and Unionist Women's Franchise Association: founded in 1908 to work for votes for women on the same terms as men. It opposed full universal suffrage. It refused to work for MPs opposed to votes for women.

From this list it seems as if most women were able to join a suffrage group that represented their profession, religion or political affiliation. The membership of these groups may have overlapped with the two national bodies, with some members joining the WSPU and some joining the NUWSS.

Suffrage groups in Ireland, Scotland and Wales

Not every country in the UK wanted to be led by either of the main suffrage organisations. The NUWSS and the WSPU had active branches all over Scotland and Wales, but they were not so successful in Ireland. Indeed, there were several Irish independent organisations: one of the most influential was the Irish Women's Franchise League (IWFL), which modelled itself on the WSPU. The IWFL was formed because Irish women had no desire to be led by Englishwomen, whether from the NUWSS or the WSPU.

Key dates

Irish Women's Franchise League founded: 1908

Women's National Anti-Suffrage League founded: 1908

Key question
Who opposed votes for women?

8 | The Opposition to Votes for Women

Some women disagreed with votes for women and campaigned against it. In 1889, Mrs Humphrey Ward persuaded 104 prominent women to sign an appeal against female suffrage. Within 2 months these original signatures were supported by another 1796 women. Indeed, female antipathy to the vote led to the formation of the Women's National Anti-Suffrage League in 1908, at a time when there was increased support for women's suffrage. In December 1908 the group established its own publication, the *Anti-Suffrage Review*. The group gathered over 337,000 signatures on an anti-suffrage petition and founded various regional branches of the organisation. By July 1910 there were 104 branches of the Anti-Suffrage League with approximately 9000 members. It then amalgamated with the Men's League for Opposing Women's Suffrage.

It is safe to say that the majority of women were probably more apathetic than antagonistic towards votes for women. Membership of the suffrage movement may have been large, but the majority of women did not belong to any suffrage group. Nor did they belong to an anti-suffrage organisation. Nonetheless, despite schisms and irreconcilable differences, the women's suffrage movement became a powerful political force within Victorian and Edwardian Britain. By 1914, largely because of its intensive campaigning, it had forced women's suffrage on to the agenda of all the political parties and had made votes for women one of the foremost issues facing the governing Liberal Party.

9 | The Key Debate

One issue that has been debated by historians of the women's suffrage movement is:

> Can women's suffrage be divided into two separate groups?

The way in which the NUWSS and the WSPU were organised is at the centre of this debate. Suffrage historians used to insist that the suffrage movement could be separated into the suffragists and the suffragettes. However, later historians argue that such an analysis is misleading.

Differences between the suffragists and suffragettes

The first suffrage historians argued that the two major suffrage organisations that dominated the twentieth century were obviously distinct. The first to be founded, the NUWSS, was led by Millicent Fawcett, whereas the other, the WSPU, was led by the Pankhursts. Each group had its own leadership, its own membership, its own aims and its own methods.

Similarities between the membership of the NUWSS and the WSPU

Later historians agree that there were distinct differences between the two groups at leadership level, but this was not the case among the general membership. As Sandra Holton, writing in the 1980s, has shown, many suffrage supporters joined both a militant and a constitutionalist society, paid two membership fees, attended two sets of meetings and campaigned for both groups. Such women may not have seen the suffrage movement as made up of antagonistic groups vying for members, but as one movement with a common aim.

Some key books in the debate:
Sandra Stanley Holton, *Suffrage Days: Stories from the Women's Suffrage movement* (Routledge, 1998).
Jill Liddington and Jill Norris, *One Hand Tied Behind Us* (Virago, 1978).

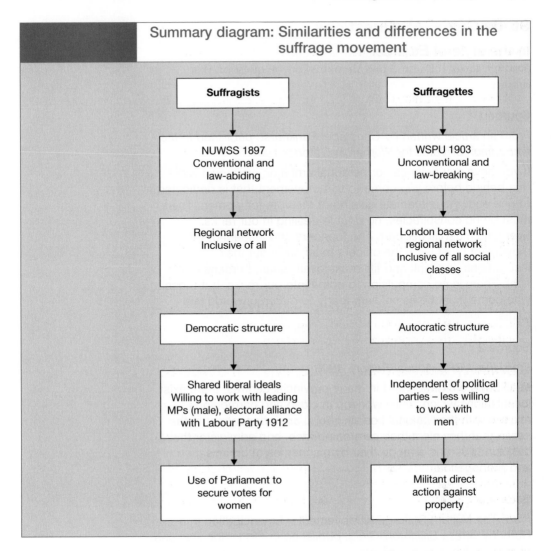

Summary diagram: Similarities and differences in the suffrage movement

Suffragists

NUWSS 1897
Conventional and
law-abiding

Regional network
Inclusive of all

Democratic structure

Shared liberal ideals
Willing to work with leading
MPs (male), electoral alliance
with Labour Party 1912

Use of Parliament to
secure votes for
women

Suffragettes

WSPU 1903
Unconventional and
law-breaking

London based with
regional network
Inclusive of all social
classes

Autocratic structure

Independent of political
parties – less willing
to work with
men

Militant direct
action against
property

Study Guide: AS Questions

In the style of Edexcel

Study Sources 1, 2 and 3 and then answer the question that follows.

Source 1

From an article written by Christabel Pankhurst, published in the first edition of Votes for Women *in October 1907.*

If you have any pettiness or personal ambition, you must leave that behind before you come to this movement that is dedicated to one end: the immediate gaining of the vote for women. There must be no conspiracies, no double dealing in our ranks. Everyone must fill her part. The founders and leaders of the movement must lead, the officers must carry out their instructions, the rank and file must loyally share burdens of the fight. There is no compulsion to come into our ranks, but those who come must be as soldiers ready to march onwards into battle.

Source 2

From the WSPU Annual Report, 1908

In all parts of London and in many provincial centres, there exist local Unions which, while working in close and harmonious relation with the National headquarters, are independent in the sense that they elect their own committee, and administer their own funds … and arrange their own schemes of organisation and propaganda.

Source 3

From The Militant Suffragette Movement – Emancipation in a Hurry *by Teresa Billington-Greig, published in 1911. She was one of the WSPU's first organisers.*

I believed in it, worked in it, suffered in it and rejoiced in it, and I have been disillusioned. I do not believe any more in votes for women as a cure for all evils. I do not believe that every principle should be sacrificed to the immediate goal of female suffrage. I condemn the militant suffrage movement and I want to expose the tone and tactics of the WSPU. The crime of the militant suffrage movement in my eyes is hypocrisy. The movement displays rebellion in its public actions while it belittles and abuses rebellion when it occurs within its own ranks.

Study Sources 1, 2 and 3

How far do these sources suggest that the WSPU was run undemocratically?   (20 marks)

Exam tips

Examiners suggest that in order to gain top marks candidates will need to focus on the 'how far' part of the question and create an argument from the evidence of the sources and/or their nature and/or their origin. A detailed comparison of similarities and differences should be given.

It is important that you recognise the similarities between two of these sources, e.g. Sources 1 and 3 both recognise that the WSPU was run like an army – note the language used: leaders, battle, rebellion. Don't forget to focus on the question – i.e. the undemocratic nature of the WSPU – and stress that both writers emphasise the need for conformity within the organisation. Billington-Greig accuses the suffrage movement of hypocrisy because it did not practise what it preached: i.e. support for rebellion (also of course democracy). The WSPU belief that members should be committed to one aim – to gain the vote for women – and that every principle, including that of democracy, should be sacrificed to that aim was anathema to Billington-Greig. Of course, the provenance of a source is important – after all, Teresa Billington-Greig had resigned from the WSPU in 1907 and Christabel's speech was a response to that rebellion.

In contrast, Source 2 suggests that local organisations were independent and democratic. However, one must bear in mind that the source is dated 1908 and it is from an Annual Report, a source that tends to interpret the year's events positively. A conclusion which focuses on the 'how far' part of the question would be useful: the evidence is contradictory.

4 The Suffrage Campaigns 1860–1914

POINTS TO CONSIDER

This chapter starts by considering whether or not a distinction can be made between the methods of the suffragists and the methods of the suffragettes. It goes on to look at the different methods of campaigning for the vote that were used between 1860 and 1914 and how effective these methods were. It does this through the following headings:

- Peaceful methods of campaigning
- Parliament and women's suffrage
- Increasing militancy

Key dates

1905		Christabel Pankhurst and Annie Kenney arrested
1907	February	'Mud March'
	February	First Caxton Hall meeting
1908	January	WSPU members chained themselves to railings of 10 Downing Street
	February	Trojan horse raid
	June	Window-smashing began
	October	'Rush' on the House of Commons
	October	WFL members chained themselves to grille in House of Commons
1909		First hunger strike
		Tax Resistance League founded
1910	July	Prison to Citizenship procession
1911		Constance Lytton imprisoned as a working-class woman
	April	Boycott of census
	June	Coronation procession
	December	First post-box destroyed
1912		NUWSS–Labour Party alliance established
		WSPU opposed Labour Party candidates
1913	February	Lloyd George's country home set on fire

	June	Emily Wilding Davison died from injuries at the Derby
	August	NUWSS pilgrimage
1914	March	Velázquez's painting attacked
	June	Group of women from London's East End met Asquith
		Militancy ceased when First World War declared

1 | Introduction

Key figure

David Lloyd George
1863–1945; a leading Liberal politician: President of Board of Trade 1906; Chancellor of the Exchequer 1908. In 1915 he was Minister of Munitions, making sure that the armed forces had enough weapons to fight the war. He became Prime Minister in 1916.

In the early months of 1913 suffragettes placed gunpowder containers laced with nails in **David Lloyd George's** house at Walton Heath, Surrey. They also set fire to several other country houses, burned down a grandstand at a popular racecourse and destroyed part of a railway station by putting a home-made bomb in it. Telephone and telegraph wires were cut and letters in post-boxes were destroyed by acid or ink being placed in them. Hundreds of orchids in Kew Gardens were destroyed, several golf courses were damaged and windows were broken. Windsor Castle was closed to the public.

Meanwhile suffragists continued to campaign peacefully, helping to organise by-elections for their supporters, publishing their newspaper, preparing for demonstrations and deputations and collecting petitions. At first the Women's Social and Political Union (WSPU) also favoured conventional methods, only resorting to violence when peaceful campaigning seemed to fail.

Key question
Were legal methods of campaigning effective?

2 | Peaceful Methods of Campaigning

Between 1860 and 1914 various methods were used to publicise the issue of votes for women. For a lot of this time both the suffragists and suffragettes used peaceful and legitimate measures copied from other reform groups. They organised public meetings, demonstrated, wrote propaganda literature, raised money, lobbied MPs and petitioned Parliament, all of which were traditional middle-class methods of persuasive campaigning. Later on, when the WSPU adopted law-breaking methods, they continued to combine more traditional methods with the new.

Meetings

Meetings were organised by all the suffrage organisations to consolidate support, recruit new members, collect money and sell papers. The first meetings took place in London (1866) and in Manchester (1874). At first, meetings took place in people's homes and only invited guests were welcome. Public meetings, initially advertised for women only, were later organised. Here are some examples:

- Lydia Becker (see pages 37–8) and National Society for Women's Suffrage (NSWS) members spoke at mothers' meetings, Church groups and political organisations.

- Millicent Fawcett and the National Union of Women's Suffrage Societies (NUWSS) raised the question of women's suffrage at trade union conferences and in the major cotton towns.
- The North of England Society and the Lancashire and Cheshire Textile and Other Workers' Committee spoke to workers outside the cotton factory gates.
- The WSPU and others spoke in Hyde Park and at Trafalgar Square in London and other squares throughout the country.

Supporters soon became used to suffragists and suffragettes speaking wherever women were to be found in large numbers: local market squares, bus and tram stations, factories, shops and even breweries. However, as the photograph of the NUWSS below shows, women did not attend these outdoor events in large numbers.

Whatever the venue, suffragists spent a lot of time talking to others about the need for votes for women. During the last few months of 1909 Millicent Fawcett, for example, was engaged to speak in Cardiff, Manchester, London, Shrewsbury, Sussex, Kent, Glasgow and Edinburgh. Between 1866 and 1903 the NUWSS had organised at least 1400 public meetings.

Similarly, WSPU members were kept busy speaking in support of votes for women. In 1909, the WSPU held large meetings in the Royal Albert Hall and the Queen's Hall, London; the Colston Hall, Bristol; the Sun Hall, Liverpool; the Albert Hall, Nottingham; the Town Hall, Birmingham; the Synod Hall,

The NUWSS at Hyde Park in London in 1913. How useful would this photograph be to a historian researching the women's suffrage campaigns between 1903 and 1914?

Key dates

First Caxton Hall meeting: 13 February 1907

'Mud March': February 1907

Prison to Citizenship procession: July 1910

Coronation procession: June 1911

Edinburgh; St Andrew's Hall, Glasgow; and the Rotunda, Dublin. The WSPU also held regular meetings at Caxton Hall in London, just across the square from the House of Commons, and called these meetings the Women's Parliament as a protest against their exclusion from the franchise.

Response to female speakers

In the nineteenth century, many believed that it was just too daring, unladylike and improper for women to speak in public. It was expected that women should stay at home and look after the family rather than be active in politics (see page 8). In 1869, Victorian society was scandalised when Millicent Fawcett and another suffragist spoke to a mixed audience in London. One MP was so shocked by this unseemly behaviour that he mentioned the incident in Parliament. In his speech he referred to two ladies who had recently disgraced themselves by speaking to a mixed public audience, but refused to mention their names in case it caused further embarrassment. However, by the end of the century public speaking had generally become unexceptional unless it took place in unusual circumstances. For instance, in 1908, when Fawcett became the first woman to debate at the **Oxford Union**, she once again received a great deal of publicity.

Demonstrations and pilgrimages

Demonstrations and **pilgrimages** were traditional ways to show discontent, attract government attention and gain publicity for reform. In 1880 Lydia Becker helped to organise women-only marches throughout Britain that attracted large crowds and a good deal of publicity. Between 1907 and 1913 all the suffrage societies organised demonstrations attended by large numbers of supporters, as the following list shows:

Key terms

Oxford Union
Formed in 1823 as a debating society at the University of Oxford. It enjoys a reputation for the quality of its debate and has proved to be a training ground for many British politicians. It has always invited prestigious people to speak on behalf of a controversial issue.

Demonstrations
Public marches for a political purpose.

Pilgrimages
Journeys taken for religious, political or sentimental reasons.

- In February 1907 the first of the big suffrage twentieth-century marches, organised by the NUWSS, became known as the 'Mud March' because of the heavy rain which poured down on the demonstrators.
- Another demonstration in June 1908 organised by the NUWSS drew between 10,000 and 15,000 women.
- A week later, Emmeline Pankhurst, determined not to be outdone, led the first of the WSPU's large-scale processions where seven different groups from around the country met in Hyde Park in London.
- In 1910 the WSPU and the Women's Freedom League (WFL) organised another, which was even bigger and better. Here, Mrs Pankhurst headed a column of over 600 ex-prisoners, each carrying a prison arrow as a symbol of their former imprisonment. It was known as the Prison to Citizenship procession.
- In 1911 a Coronation procession, held in honour of the new king, George V drew approximately 40,000 demonstrators from every single one of the various suffrage societies, both peaceful and militant.

Indian women on the Coronation procession, London, June 1911. It was part of the Empire section. How useful would this source be to a historian studying women's suffrage 1903–14?

Suffragettes also went on longer walks. In 1912 thousands of suffragists went on a month-long pilgrimage from Edinburgh to London. Similarly, a pilgrimage in August 1913 organised by the NUWSS (from all parts of Britain to the capital city) enjoyed great success. The 'pilgrims' left in the middle of June and spent 6 weeks walking, holding meetings and raising £8000 for their cause.

It took a lot of courage to march in the streets. Even in 1910 many thought that it was disreputable for women to demonstrate, so the women who took part risked their respectability and sometimes their employment.

NUWSS pilgrimage: August 1913

Key date

WSPU influence on demonstrations

The WSPU gave demonstrations a new direction as, with impressive skill, they introduced a touch of melodrama to an old form of protest. Some members were great extroverts and livened up demonstrations by making them into dramatic performances. The black and white photographs of the period do not show how vivid these suffrage parades were. When Emmeline Pethick-Lawrence chose the colours of purple for dignity, white for purity and green for hope to represent the suffragettes, she created a potent symbol. Suffragettes proudly wore these colours in public to show their commitment to the WSPU.

In the jointly organised Coronation procession of 1911 suffragettes and suffragists dressed up in the following styles:

- plain white with sashes in the colours of the WSPU, the NUWSS or other organisations (e.g. members of the NUWSS wore red, white and green sashes; the Actresses' Union pink and green; the WFL green, white and gold)
- in the costumes of famous women (Joan of Arc and Elizabeth I were popular figures)
- in their working clothes (as pit-brow women, factory workers, doctors, teachers)
- in their national costume (Scottish women wore tartan, Welsh women their shawls and hats)
- as ex-prisoners (dressed in prison clothes).

Demonstrators carried 8-foot high banners and enormous posters with the portraits of the leadership on them. Various bands, including a suffragette drum-and-fife band dressed in the WSPU colours of purple, white and green, accompanied these bright and dazzling processions. Many women sang the latest suffrage song, 'The March of the Women', composed by **Ethel Smyth**. The following passionate, military and evangelical words are taken from this hymn-like song, from which, with its catchy tune and memorable lyrics, it is clear that the WSPU regards itself as an army, marching to freedom with the help of God.

> Shout, shout – up with your song,
> March, march, swing you along,
> Wide blows our banner, and hope is waking.
> Song with its story, dreams with their glory,
> Lo!, they call, and glad is their word!
> Hark, hark, hear how it swells,
> Thunder of freedom, the voice of the Lord!

Key figures

Ethel Smyth
1858–1944; a composer who wrote several operas, a mass and various pieces for the orchestra. She met Emmeline Pankhurst in 1910 and was imprisoned with her 2 years later.

Elizabeth Robins
1862–1952; a famous actress, distinguished dramatist, an active member of the WSPU and founder of the Actresses' Franchise League.

Key question
Why was propaganda used?

Propaganda techniques
Some of the methods used in the early twentieth century, particularly by the WSPU, suggest a playfulness and sense of humour that was far removed from the usual gloomy and stern image of the suffragette. The WSPU was innovative in its propaganda techniques, rarely missing an opportunity to promote votes for women.

Performances
The Actresses' Franchise League wrote and performed plays to strengthen the morale of sympathisers, to persuade others to join and, of course, to make money for the cause. In these dramas, the female was generally portrayed as a heroine pitted against an unyielding and intransigent male. Plays such as *How the Vote Was Won* written by **Elizabeth Robins** were performed to sympathetic audiences throughout Britain. At the Women's Exhibition and Sale of Work held in London in 1909 a photographic history of the suffrage movement, a reproduction of a prison cell and plays

performed by the Actresses' Franchise League entertained – and educated – the vast numbers who attended. In the 2 weeks in which the exhibition was open it collected £6000 and recruited over 200 women.

A film about the struggle for women's suffrage, called 'True Womanhood', was regularly shown to sympathetic audiences. Poems and limericks were used to emphasise the political point. On 10 February 1911 a poem entitled 'Woman This, and Woman That', written by **Laurence Housman**, was recited outside Woolwich Town Hall to an audience of hundreds:

> We went before a magistrate who would not hear us speak;
> To a drunken brute who beat his wife he only gave a week:
> But we were sent to Holloway a calendar month or more,
> Because we dared, against his will, to knock at Asquith's door.
> When women go to work for them the Government engage
> To give them lots of contract jobs at a low starvation wage;
> But when it's men that they employ they always add a note –
> 'Fair wages must be paid' – because the men have got the vote.
> You talk of sanitation, and temperance, and schools,
> And you send your male inspectors to impose your man-made rules;
> 'The woman's sphere's the home' you say? then prove it to our face;
> Give us the vote that we may make the home a happier place!

Laurence Housman 1865–1959; author of over 100 works that included poetry, novels, plays, non-fiction and stories for children. He was a firm supporter of votes for women and brother of the famous poet A.E. Housman.

Key figure

Newspapers and novels

The regular production of suffrage newspapers, such as *The Women's Suffrage Journal* from 1870, *Votes for Women* from 1907, the *Common Cause* from 1909 and *The Suffragette* from 1913, proved to be a valuable means of both publicising the women's suffrage cause and keeping the various groups and associations in touch with one another.

Novels, often seen to be a female pastime, were written and read. Elizabeth Robins wrote a popular novel, *The Convert*, a book that deals with how men sexually exploit women, a favourite topic of suffrage sympathisers. Vida, the heroine of the story, became a suffragette after she had been seduced by a Conservative MP and forced to have an abortion. (The heroine was at first called Christabel after Christabel Pankhurst, but when Emmeline Pankhurst objected the name was changed to Vida.) Gertrude Colmore's 1911 novel, *Suffragette Sally*, deals with another popular suffrage question: that of class. In this story the lives of three very different women – working class, middle class and upper class – are explored, with Lady Constance Lytton's (see page 90) experiences in prison fictionalised as the upper-class heroine. Of course, it is impossible to gauge the readership of these books, but the fact that they were published and the authors paid a fee suggests that they were bought, if not read, by large numbers of people.

Suffragette ephemera

The WSPU used every kind of propaganda to publicise the cause of votes for women. They even designed, advertised and marketed a wide variety of **ephemera**. Tea caddies, soap, cakes,

Ephemera
Everyday, seemingly unimportant items.

Key term

dolls, cards, crackers, badges and even the ubiquitous stock cube were designed for sale in purple, white and green. A suffragette could fully clothe herself in suffragette colours, buy a white summer blouse, a green bag, a purple belt and a scarf in full matching colours – and become a fashionable walking advertisement for the WSPU. The WSPU sewed for votes: one member of the WSPU made a quilt with the names of suffragette hunger strikers embroidered on it and sold it for over £1700 at a bazaar held by the suffragettes in Glasgow.

Other techniques

Groups of women went out regularly on bicycles decorated with the suffragette colours to advertise demonstrations. They used innovative methods to get across their point of view. For example:

- At the 1908 Football Cup Final, held at Crystal Palace in London, the WSPU distributed envelopes with the teams' colours on them inviting the wives of the male spectators to meetings. On the day of the match they flew a kite with 'Votes for Women' written on it above the pitch and distributed suffragette leaflets at nearby railway stations.
- At one of the annual boat races between Oxford and Cambridge universities, the WSPU hired a launch and filled it with 'Votes for Women' banners.
- The WSPU sailed a boat to outside the House of Commons and harangued MPs taking tea on the terrace.
- One member of the Women's Freedom League borrowed a balloon to fly across London to drop leaflets supporting votes for women.

Key question
Why did women use the courts to try to get votes for women?

Challenging in the courts

In the 1860s suffragists attempted to use the legal system to gain the vote. In 1867 a widowed shop-keeper named Mrs Lily Maxwell had been mistakenly put on the electoral register and went to cast her vote publicly on the hustings accompanied by a large number of suffrage supporters. Her vote was accepted and inspired over 5000 other female householders, encouraged by Lydia Becker, to do the same (see page 37). Eventually, in 1868, in a case known as *Chorlton* v. *Lings*, the High Court examined the validity of the women's claims. Sir John Coleridge and Richard Pankhurst represented the women, both arguing that women had once enjoyed the right to vote but had been excluded in the 1832 Great Reform Act. In addition, it was argued that the term 'male' (used in the 1832 Act) also included women. The two lawyers drew their argument from an Act of 1850 that specifically stated that in law the word 'male' meant both men and women unless it said otherwise. A similar case, *Brown* v. *Ingram*, took place in Scotland, but both the English and the Scottish petitioners lost when the courts refused to accept the validity of their claim.

Key dates
Campaign to get women's names on the electoral register: 1867

Chorlton v. *Lings* case: 1868

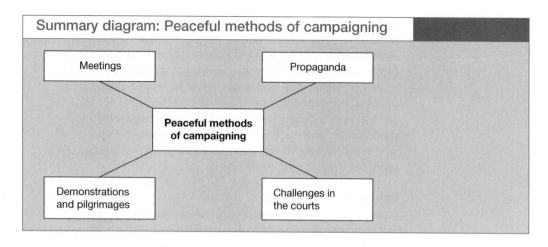

Summary diagram: Peaceful methods of campaigning

- Meetings
- Propaganda
- **Peaceful methods of campaigning**
- Demonstrations and pilgrimages
- Challenges in the courts

3 | Parliament and Women's Suffrage

Persuading Parliament

Only Parliament could give women the vote, so suffragists tried desperately to convince MPs of the logic of women's suffrage. At first, conventional middle-class methods of pressure were used: MPs were petitioned, lobbied and, if they were in favour of votes for women, supported in election campaigns. It was the politics of persuasion rather than the politics of confrontation. The NUWSS, until they became disillusioned with the Liberal Party (see page 78), remained committed to *convincing* individual MPs to put forward a private member's bill. This changed from 1906 as the WSPU sought to *force* the **Liberal government** into conceding votes for women. The leadership of the WSPU also realised that private member's bills were doomed: by this time almost all laws that were passed were proposed by the government and not by individual MPs.

Petitioning Parliament

Petitioning the House of Commons was a popular and successful method used by a number of male reform groups. Suffragists favoured the petition, first because it indicated to the government that large numbers were in favour of votes for women and secondly because it helped to arouse public interest in the campaign.

Women, of course, were without the vote and their petitions were not received with much sympathy. In 1866 Emily Davies and Elizabeth Garrett delivered a petition containing 1499 signatures to John Stuart Mill, who presented it to Parliament. Between 1870 and 1880 a yearly average of 200,000 people signed their names to various women's suffrage bills. In 1894, a petition signed by a quarter of a million women was exhibited in Westminster Hall. Large petitions, of course, gained publicity, especially when Davies sent copies of one petition to 500 newspapers. Petitioning continued in the twentieth century: in 1910 NUWSS members stood outside polling stations at election time and persuaded 300,000 male voters to sign a women's suffrage petition.

Key question
How and why did suffragists try to persuade Parliament?

Liberal government
The Liberals swept into power in 1906, fought two elections in 1910 and remained in power until 1922.

Key term

Key figures

Henry Campbell-Bannerman
1836–1908; elected Liberal MP in 1868. He became Secretary of Ireland in 1884 and Leader of the House of Commons in 1898. He opposed the Boer War and supported social reform.

Herbert Asquith
1852–1928; became Home Secretary in 1892, Chancellor of the Exchequer in 1906 and Prime Minister in 1908.

Key date

Group of women from London's East End met Asquith: June 1914

Key term

Plural Voting Bills
Men had the right to vote in their own constituency, as university graduates and as business owners. The Plural Voting Bills aimed to stop men from voting more than once.

Deputations to Parliament and to prime ministers

Both the suffragists and the suffragettes visited MPs and ministers to persuade them to put forward a women's franchise bill. In May 1906, the newly elected Prime Minister, **Henry Campbell-Bannerman**, received a deputation of MPs, suffragists, suffragettes and other women's leaders who sought to convince him of the need for votes for women. On this occasion, suffrage groups and representatives from various trade unions came from all over Britain in support of the deputation. In October of that same year, Emmeline Pankhurst led another deputation to Parliament, but when they were inside, her daughter Adela and several other women tried to make speeches in the lobby of the House of Commons and so were arrested.

When **Herbert Asquith** became Prime Minister in 1908 both suffragists and suffragettes tried to meet him to discuss the question of votes for women. For example:

- Millicent Fawcett led a deputation to Asquith in 1910, but although Asquith accepted the deputation, he promised little.
- Towards the end of 1911 Asquith received a deputation from all the suffrage societies and made a promise that women could be included in an amendment to a male suffrage bill being drafted by the government. (Yet, about the same time, he told a group of anti-suffragists that women's suffrage would be 'very disastrous'.)
- In 1913, after the women's pilgrimage, Fawcett led another deputation, but once more the Prime Minister seemed reluctant to grant votes for women.
- In June 1914, when Sylvia Pankhurst stated that she would hunger strike until death (see page 60), it seemed hopeful that Asquith might listen. He met and listened attentively to a group of six working mothers.

Lobbying MPs

Suffragists lobbied MPs and prime ministers to gain their support for women's suffrage. In June 1887 Lydia Becker formed the first Committee of Members of Parliament who pledged their commitment to votes for women. Seventy-one MPs joined. As a result of the work of this committee and the NUWSS, a private member's bill in support of women's suffrage was brought in almost every year. But they all failed. In addition, efforts were made to amend government franchise bills to include women's suffrage. In 1867 the Liberal MP and philosopher John Stuart Mill introduced the first ever women's suffrage amendment to the Second Reform Act, while William Woodall, a Liberal MP for Stoke-on-Trent, tried to secure the inclusion of a woman's suffrage amendment to the Third Reform Bill of 1884. The three **Plural Voting Bills** of 1906, 1913 and 1914, and the 1912 Irish Home Rule Bill each had an amendment attached in support of votes for women. All of the amendments failed too. Eventually, groups of MPs from across the political spectrum formed a Conciliation Committee and three times put forward a Conciliation Bill to enfranchise women. Again each of these Bills failed, despite the fact that the WSPU called a truce while each Bill was debated (see pages 101–2).

Canvassing for MPs

In the late nineteenth and early twentieth centuries suffragists worked hard for Liberal MPs who supported votes for women. The NUWSS canvassed for votes for sympathetic Liberal MPs at general elections and by-elections. For example:

- In 1906, Wigan textile workers canvassed for MPs who supported women's suffrage.
- In 1907, the NUWSS canvassed in Hexham, Jarrow, Kirkdale and Wimbledon. In Wimbledon the NUWSS ran the entire election campaign of the women's suffrage candidate.
- In the 1910 general election, the Birmingham branch of the NUWSS wrote to 52 parliamentary candidates to see whether they were in favour of votes for women, undertook door-to-door canvassing and stood outside election booths to persuade voters to vote for those who did support votes for women.

Until the Liberal landslide victory of 1905, the NUWSS concentrated much of its energies on opposing Conservative candidates. However, the Liberal victory left the NUWSS with a political dilemma. Although the Liberals brought women's suffrage no further forward, suffragists had no wish to embarrass a government which so many of them supported and to which many of their male relatives belonged. Yet by 1910 the patience of the NUWSS had worn thin and it became official NUWSS policy to give support to suffrage candidates against opponents from all of the major political parties, including the Liberals.

From 1912 onwards the NUWSS, disillusioned by what it perceived as the continuing duplicity of the Liberal Party, redirected its loyalty to the Labour Party. It subsidised Labour MPs in Parliament who were sympathetic to women's suffrage and set up an election fighting fund to defeat the Liberals. These tactics were, by and large, successful. In the last by-election campaign supported by the election fighting fund (fought in Midlothian, Scotland, in 1912), the NUWSS claimed that the Liberals had been defeated because their Labour candidate had taken away valuable Liberal votes.

The WSPU, which claimed to be non-partisan and to support no political party, did not usually help even sympathetic MPs to be elected. Even so, Emmeline Pankhurst often helped **Keir Hardie** in his electoral campaigns when they remained friends and WSPU members helped sympathetic Liberals in the general election of December 1910.

However, by 1912 the WSPU opposed both the Labour Party and the Liberals at elections.

Provoking Parliament and authority

The beginnings of militancy

The WSPU came to prefer confrontation to the politics of persuasion, believing that they could force the government to grant women the vote. The first incident occurred during the 1905 election campaign when Christabel Pankhurst and

Key date

NUWSS–Labour Party alliance established: 1912

Key figure

Keir Hardie 1856–1915; the first Labour MP. He was elected the Chair and Leader of the Independent Labour Party that he helped to found in 1893.

Key question
Why did the WSPU try to provoke politicians?

Key figures

Sir Edward Grey
1862–1933;
Secretary of State
for Foreign Affairs
in the Liberal
government
1906–16.

Winston Churchill
1874–1965; a
Conservative MP in
1900 and a Liberal
MP in 1904. He
held numerous
posts in the Liberal
government:
President of the
Board of Trade
1908; Home
Secretary 1910;
First Lord of the
Admiralty 1911. He
was Conservative
Prime Minister
twice (1940–5 and
1951–5).

Annie Kenney interrupted **Sir Edward Grey** and **Winston Churchill** at a meeting in Manchester's Free Trade Hall. The two women were evicted from the hall. When Christabel and Annie Kenney spoke to the crowd that had gathered outside the Hall, they were arrested, fined and charged with disorderly behaviour and obstruction. They refused to pay the fine – or even accept the payment of the fine by Churchill – and so were imprisoned.

This event created what Christabel Pankhurst wanted: much needed publicity for women's suffrage. Imprisonment was news. Despite criticism from the press about the unladylike behaviour of Kenney and Christabel Pankhurst, the WSPU began to attract sizeable audiences, enjoyed an increase in membership and, perhaps more importantly, gained greater news coverage for the cause.

Interrupting MPs

The 1905 heckling of Churchill and Grey was re-enacted on numerous occasions. Women interrupted government leaders, were arrested, refused to pay fines and were imprisoned and then received what was in essence free publicity and, as a consequence, the organisation increased its membership. It was a heady formula for success. All the leaders of the Liberal Party – Churchill, Campbell-Bannerman, Asquith, Lloyd George and Grey – suffered from WSPU disturbances at their meetings, whether they supported women's suffrage or not.

For example, Churchill regularly had his speeches interrupted because, as a senior member of the Liberal government, he was also held responsible for its refusal to grant women the vote. The WSPU claimed their greatest success when Churchill lost his seat at a Manchester by-election and was forced to flee to Dundee in 1908 to fight another. And when Churchill, by now MP for Dundee, was due to speak at the Kinnaird Hall in Dundee, suffragettes concealed themselves in a building nearby so that they could throw stones at the windows in the roof's skylight.

Even when MPs spoke at suffrage meetings they were not safe. In 1908, WSPU members wearing prison uniforms continually interrupted Lloyd George's speech at a women's suffrage meeting sponsored by the Women's Freedom League.

Whenever the government took the step of banning women from political meetings or else used a heavy police presence to protect themselves, suffragettes responded by using surprise and disguise to heckle them. Suffragettes concealed themselves between organ pipes or lurked under platforms. Some were lowered into political meetings at the end of ropes. Ray Strachey, a suffragist, noted that 'they peered through roof windows, and leapt out of innocent-looking furniture vans; they materialised on station platforms, they harangued the terrace of the House from the river, and wherever they were least expected there they were'. In October 1908, Christabel Pankhurst organised the 'Trojan horse' raid on the House of Commons when approximately 26 women jumped out of a seemingly innocent van parked outside the House of Commons and tried to force an entrance.

Key dates

Christabel Pankhurst
and Annie Kenney
arrested: 1905

Trojan horse raid:
February 1908

At first it was just the Liberal Party that suffered from interruptions, but in October 1912 the WSPU decided to oppose Labour Party MPs too. This was a calculated reaction to Labour's decision to pledge support to a Liberal government which force-fed women (see pages 115–17). At the same time, the WSPU cultivated the support of the Conservatives. For example, Christabel Pankhurst wrote regularly to the former Conservative Prime Minister Arthur Balfour (brother-in-law to Lady Betty Balfour, a leading suffragist) to gain his support for votes for women. Christabel insisted that the Tories were more likely to grant votes for women as, after all, they had enfranchised a large section of the working class in 1867.

Why did suffragettes interrupt politicians?

Jane Marcus, a feminist historian, argues that interrupting the speeches of male politicians marked a watershed in suffrage history. By stopping MPs speaking, suffragettes not only challenged male authority, but claimed a political voice for women who were supposed to remain silent. Of course, this is historical speculation: the WSPU perhaps had more matter-of-fact reasons for interrupting the government. Indeed, they were probably more influenced by **Charles Parnell**'s behaviour in the Irish Home Rule campaign of the 1880s than in interrupting men to make a feminist point. Parnell heckled all Liberal candidates at elections whether or not they supported Home Rule because the Liberal government was held responsible for the situation in Ireland. Emmeline Pankhurst was all too aware that her late husband, Richard Pankhurst, who had stood for Parliament as a Liberal candidate and was a keen supporter of Home Rule, had been defeated in 1885 because of Irish opposition. If the WSPU could similarly embarrass the Liberal government then the vote could not be far off – or so it was thought. Unfortunately, the WSPU leadership had misread their history. When Parnell opposed the Liberal Party he had a group of disciplined MPs and a huge male electorate in Ireland behind him. The WSPU had no such advantage.

Entering the House of Commons

Suffragettes lobbied MPs in Parliament, but when they succeeded in gaining entry into the House of Commons they often misbehaved. On October 1906, for example, 30 well-dressed suffragettes entered the lobby of the House of Commons and were met by a large number of inquisitive MPs who were not all sympathetic to votes for women. When MPs refused to support the suffragettes, **Mary Gawthorpe** stood on a sofa and made a speech advocating votes for women. Chaos followed. She was arrested by the police, but another woman jumped up on the sofa and spoke, and when she too was arrested yet more women took her place. All this happened amidst a lot of shouting, scuffling and general disturbance.

Key date

WSPU opposed Labour Party candidates: 1912

Key figures

Charles Parnell 1846–91; in 1879 Parnell founded the Irish Land League, which aimed to provide tenant farmers with a fair rent, a fixed lease and an opportunity to buy the land on which they farmed. Between 1880 and 1889 he was the acknowledged leader of the Home Rule Party. In 1889 he lost his leadership role when he was accused of adultery in a divorce case. He died soon afterwards.

Mary Gawthorpe 1881–1973; daughter of a leather-worker. She trained as a teacher, but in 1906 she left her job to become a paid organiser for the Leeds WSPU. She was imprisoned several times.

Key date
'Rush' on the House of Commons: October 1908

Christabel Pankhurst, knowing that suffragettes were often refused entry to the House of Commons, wrote a leaflet saying that the suffragettes would 'rush' the House of Commons on 13 October 1908. By this, she meant to rush into the Commons, go through the doors into the debating chamber and confront the Prime Minister. On the day several groups of suffragettes tried to enter the House only to be repelled by the police officers sent by the government to stop them. This tactic was used time and time again by the suffragettes.

Key question
Why did the suffragettes harass the Church?

Suffragettes and the Church

The WSPU objected to the male authority of the Church. They attacked the Church because it was seen, paradoxically, both as the servant of government and as a symbol of resistance against authority (see pages 119–21 for the Church response to the suffrage movement). Either way, the suffragettes confronted the Church with remarkable fervour and dedication.

- The Church was criticised because it did not practise what it preached – the Christian doctrine of equality.
- By not actively supporting votes for women, the Church was agreeing with an unjust system which denied democracy to half of Britain.
- Moreover, because Jesus Christ was regarded as a rebel who spoke out against injustice, the Church needed to be reminded of its historical role in championing the oppressed.
- In a leaflet written around 1912 Christabel Pankhurst condemned the Church for its 'shameful and obsequiously compliant attitude' in not speaking out against the perceived torture of imprisoned suffragette martyrs.

There were widespread protests in various churches and cathedrals where suffragettes interrupted services to offer prayers in support of votes for women. For example, in 1913 at St Mary's Baptist Chapel in Norwich, a woman rose during the service to say 'Oh Lord Jesus, who dost at all times show tender compassion to women, hear now our petitions for our sisters who are being tortured in prison … by men calling themselves Christians.' Annie Kenney even arrived with her luggage at Lambeth Palace

Key term
Sanctuary
The most sacred part of the Christian Church where a fugitive from the law could take refuge against arrest.

to seek **sanctuary** at the official residence of the Archbishop of Canterbury until the vote had been won, but after providing her with lunch and tea the Archbishop called the police who promptly arrested her.

Despite the efforts of the suffragists and the somewhat alienating tactics of the suffragettes, votes for women seemed no further forward. As a consequence, the suffragettes turned to other forms of political action to get their voice heard. And it is this type of action that has aroused the most controversy.

Summary diagram: Parliament and women's suffrage

Suffragists

Suffragettes

Persuading Parliament:
• Petitioning
• Deputations
• Lobbying
• Canvassing for MPs

Provoking Parliament and authority:
• Interrupting MPs
• Entering the House of Commons
• Harassing the Church

4 | Increasing Militancy

Key question
Why did the WSPU turn to violence?

From 1908 the WSPU intensified the political pressure and promoted new and confrontational methods to force MPs to give women the vote. The reason for this turn to violence is open to debate. Nonetheless it is important to remember that the WSPU often called a truce and stopped militancy. Unsympathetic observers have either viewed militancy humorously or else thought that suffragettes were mad or abnormal. Militancy, for some anti-suffragists, was seen as a reflection of the widespread instability of women, and of their fanatical and hysterical tendencies. To them, it was proof that women should not be allowed to vote.

How the suffragettes justified militancy
Suffragettes argued that violence emerged and escalated for a number of core reasons which served to justify it:

• Militancy was adopted because politicians had taken little notice of the years of peaceful campaigning.
• Militancy was a reaction to the 1906 Liberal government which, by excluding women from public meetings and refusing to meet suffrage deputations, had denied suffragettes the main forms of agitation open to the disenfranchised. Suffragettes, forbidden access to peaceful protest, believed that they were left with only one alternative: violence.
• Militancy was seen as a retaliatory measure against a government that encouraged police brutality, arrested, imprisoned and force-fed those who participated in direct action (see pages 115–17). If the government chose to treat women roughly then it too would be intimidated.
• Suffragettes believed themselves to be continuing a long-respected tradition of protest, as previous extensions to the franchise, for instance in 1832 and 1867, had been preceded by great disturbances. The WSPU drew on historical examples of the unlawful exercise of physical force to justify its tactics

and identified the suffragettes with past revolutionary and resistance heroes. In 1907, one male supporter of votes for women remarked ironically:

> Of course, when men wanted the franchise, they did not behave in the unruly manner of our feminine friends. They were perfectly constitutional in their agitation. In Bristol, I find they only burnt the Mansion House, the Custom House, the Bishop's Palace, the Excise Office, three prisons, four tollhouses, and forty-two private dwellings and warehouses, all in a perfectly constitutional and respectable manner … Four men were respectably hanged at Bristol and three in Nottingham … In this and other ways the males set a splendid example of constitutional methods in agitating for the franchise.

Ulster Unionists
A political organisation whose members wanted the northern province of Ulster in Ireland to remain British. When the Liberals introduced another Home Rule Bill in 1912 the Ulster Unionists threatened to rebel.

Civil disobedience
Disobeying the civil law, e.g. laws concerning taxes.

Key terms

- Suffragettes believed that the government would not grant women the vote until they were forced to do so. Comparisons were drawn between the suffragettes and other pressure groups who advocated violent methods. Christabel Pankhurst, for instance, noted that miners had succeeded in gaining improved pay and conditions in 1911 because they made themselves a nuisance. Similarly, the tactics of the **Ulster Unionists** were successful in stopping the move towards Irish Home Rule. The suffragettes believed that the achievements of these groups demonstrated that the vote would only be obtained through violent action.

Tax evasion and census resistance

The popular image of the militant is of an expensively well-dressed woman producing a hammer from an innocent-looking handbag and smashing windows in the main shopping streets of London. In fact, the first illegal methods used were little more than mild forms of **civil disobedience**. Initially, women tried to undermine the business of the government by refusing to support a state that denied them recognition. Two of the most common ways to achieve this were tax and census evasion.

Tax evasion

The refusal of women to pay their taxes had a long history in the annals of the suffrage movement, since from at least 1870 women were quick to claim that taxation and representation were inseparably united (see page 17). The Women's Freedom League, under the direction of Charlotte Despard (see page 58), adopted a similar policy when it was founded in 1907 and described tax evasion as 'constitutional militancy'.

A number of wealthy suffragists lost property and faced heavy fines for non-payment of taxes, but continued to believe that the sacrifice was worthwhile.

Key question
Why did women refuse to pay their taxes?

Dora Montefiore
1851–1934; member of the Women's Liberal Association, the Central Committee for Women's Suffrage and the WSPU.

Key figure

- In 1870 two Quaker suffragists had their property seized by bailiffs when they refused to pay taxes.
- More than 35 years later **Dora Montefiore** barricaded herself in her Hammersmith house in defiance of the bailiffs sent to seize her home for non-payment of tax.

- In 1911, the West Midlands suffragist, Emma Sproson was sentenced to 7 days' imprisonment for refusing to pay for a dog licence. Her dog was shot.
- In 1913 **Duleep Singh** had a pearl necklace and a gold bangle studded with pearls and diamonds confiscated because she would not pay for a dog licence or a licence for her servant.
- Evelyn Sharp, a leading journalist, was declared bankrupt as a result of her refusal to pay taxes.

In 1909 a Tax Resistance League was set up by the Women's Freedom League to help women to resist paying taxes. When bailiffs seized the property of tax resisters in lieu of taxes and put it up for auction, the Tax Resistance League made sure that sympathisers bought the restrained goods and returned them to their owners. The League was not affiliated to any suffrage society and held meetings in both NUWSS and WSPU premises.

Census evasion

All the suffrage groups linked the census with citizenship and citizenship with suffrage so that 'no-vote, no-census' became one of their rallying cries. The Women's Freedom League organised a boycott of the 1911 census, and this was endorsed by the WSPU and the NUWSS. On 2 April 1911, the day of the census, large numbers of women made elaborate arrangements to be away from home for the night in order to avoid the **census enumerator**. For example:

- Women with large houses offered overnight accommodation to those who were away from home.
- In Edinburgh, a large café was hired by the WSPU so that women who wanted to evade the census had somewhere safe to stay.
- Others stayed in the Women's Freedom League headquarters in Glasgow or the WSPU offices elsewhere.
- Some went to the all-night entertainments put on by the various suffrage societies.
- Emmeline Pankhurst attended a concert organised by the WSPU and walked around Trafalgar Square in London until midnight, when she joined other suffrage census resisters at the Aldwych Skating Rink.

Key figure

Duleep Singh
1876–1948; Indian princess who was the daughter of a Maharaja. She was a member of the WSPU.

Key dates

Tax Resistance League founded: 1909

Boycott of census: April 1911

Key question
Why did women refuse to answer the census?

Key term

Census enumerator
Someone who collects census information from householders.

Key question
Why did the WSPU
begin to smash
windows?

Key date

Window-smashing

One of the WSPU's first violent tactics was breaking windows: an act borne of desperation rather than a coherent political strategy. The first window-smashing began as a response to the treatment that women received outside the House of Commons in 1908. Prime Minister Asquith had refused to receive a deputation of suffragettes who were subsequently assaulted by the crowd gathered outside. Exasperated, Edith New and Mary Leigh smashed two windows at the Prime Minister's official residence, 10 Downing Street.

The next bout of window-smashing occurred in 1909 when Emmeline Pankhurst and a group of elderly suffragists were evicted from the House of Commons and arrested when trying to deliver a petition. This event prompted women to break windows at the Treasury and the Home Office in protest against such treatment. Once again, window-breaking was not authorised by the WSPU leadership, but was an angry and impassioned response to government intransigence and police violence. Yet window-breaking soon gained approval from the leadership of the WSPU, and then it became official policy. When Mrs Pankhurst remarked that 'the argument of the broken window pane is the most valuable argument in modern politics', she endorsed this new tactic. Soon afterwards, the smashing of windows became part of a well-orchestrated campaign.

Even so, window-smashing was generally used as a response to events. For instance, when Asquith rejected a Second Conciliation Bill (see page 101) for women's suffrage in November 1911, the WSPU membership reacted immediately by shattering windows at the Home Office, the War Office, the Foreign Office, the Board of Education, the Board of Trade, the Treasury, Somerset House, the National Liberal Club, Guards Club, the *Daily Mail* and the *Daily News*.

On another occasion, when a Liberal cabinet minister commented that the women's suffrage movement had not generated the kind of popular uprising associated with previous pressure groups, the suffragettes responded with a day of unprecedented destruction. On 1 March 1912, *The Times* reported that groups of fashionably dressed women smashed windows in several parts of London: the Strand, Cockspur Street, Haymarket, Piccadilly, Coventry Street, Regent Street, part of Oxford Street and Bond Street. Apparently, the attack was made simultaneously in the different streets, and in spite of the amount of damage done the whole disturbance occurred over a short period.

Setting fire to property

Setting fire to property, like window-breaking, was initiated by individuals and only later became official WSPU policy. **Emily Wilding Davison**'s destruction of a post-box in December 1911 shifted militancy on to a new level – a level given the seal of approval by Emmeline Pankhurst, who in an inflammatory speech at the Albert Hall in October 1912 encouraged her members to do whatever they could to force the government to give votes to women.

Although there were a few sporadic arson attacks before 1913, the partial destruction of Lloyd George's country house in Surrey that year marked a watershed in suffragette violence. 'We have tried blowing him up to wake his conscience', said Emmeline Pankhurst.

Many of the arson attacks were, like window-smashing, a response to particular political events. At least four of the major acts of arson committed in March 1914 were precipitated by the arrests of Emmeline Pankhurst. The arson campaign was widespread throughout Britain, as you can see from 'A Year's Record' on page 87, but not one person was injured because the suffragettes only attacked empty buildings.

'A Year's Record' on page 87

Key question
Why did suffragettes set fire to property?

Key dates

First post-box destroyed: December 1911

Lloyd George's country home set on fire: February 1913

Key figure

Emily Wilding Davison
1872–1913; left her teaching job in 1906 to fight for votes for women. She was imprisoned several times. She died from injuries sustained at the Derby where she ran in front of a horse to gain publicity for votes for women.

The house of Arthur du Cross at Hastings, burnt down by suffragettes in 1913.

258   THE SUFFRAGETTE   December 26, 1913.

A YEAR'S RECORD.

The following are the more serious attacks on property which have been attributed to Suffragettes during the year 1913.

January 13.—Estimate that women have broken glass worth from £4,000 to £3,000.

January 28.—Women sentenced for damaging Windsor Castle. Fifty women arrested for window-smashing in West End of London.

January 30.—Windows of Lambeth Palace broken.

February 3.—Case smashed in jewel-room at Tower of London.

February 8.—Hundreds of orchids destroyed at Kew Gardens.

February 12.—Kiosk burnt in Regent's Park : damage £400.

February 16.—Wholesale raid on golf links, many greens being damaged.

February 17.—Great Central Railway carriage fired at Harrow.

February 19.—House building for Mr. Lloyd George blown up at Walton Heath.

March 10.—Saunderton and Croxley Green stations destroyed by fire.

March 11.—Revolver shots and vitriol thrown at Nottingham Suffragette meeting.

March 16.—£2,000 house burnt at Cheam.

March 20.—Lady White's house, Staines, burnt down; £3,000 damage.

March 24.—House set on fire at Beckenham.

March 27.—House fired at Hampstead : petrol explosion.

April 2.—Church fired at Hampstead Garden Suburb.

April 3.—Four houses fired at Hampstead Garden Suburb.

April 4.—Mansion near Chorley Wood destroyed by fire; bomb explosion at Oxted Station; empty train wrecked by bomb explosion at Devonport; famous pictures damaged at Manchester.

April 5.—Ayr racecourse stand burnt : £3,000 damage; attempt to destroy Kelso racecourse grand stand.

April 6.—House fired at Potter's Bar; mansion destroyed at Norwich.

April 8.—Plot to destroy Crystal Palace stands before the Football Cup tie.

April 8.—Explosion in grounds of Dudley Castle; bomb found in heavily-laden Kingston train at Queen's Road, Battersea.

April 11.—Tunbridge Wells cricket pavilion destroyed.

April 12.—Council schools, Gateshead, set on fire.

April 15.—Mansion fired at St. Leonard's : damage £9,000—Home Office order prohibits Suffragette meetings.

April 19.—Attempt to wreck Smeaton's famous Eddystone Lighthouse on Plymouth' Hoe.

April 20.—Attempt to blow up offices of "York Herald," York, with a bomb.

April 23.—Attempt to burn Minster Church, Isle of Thanet.

April 24.—Bomb explodes at County Council offices, Newcastle.

April 26.—Railway carriage destroyed by fire at Teddington.

April 30.—Boathouse burned at Hampton Court : £3,500 damage; Suffragettes' headquarters seized by police, five leaders arrested.

May 1.—Buildings burned at Hendon.

May 3.—Amazing Suffragette plots disclosed at Bow Street.

May 6.—Woman Suffrage Bill defeated in Commons; St. Catherine's Church, Hatcham, burned down.

May 7.—Bomb found in St. Paul's Cathedral : two bungalows damaged near Bexhill; bowling-green chalet, Bishop's Park, Fulham, destroyed.

May 9.—Oaklea, near Barrow, fired.

May 10.—Farringdon Hall, Dundee, destroyed : damage £10,000; private house, Beckenham, fired.

May 12.—Boathouse on the Trent destroyed : damage nearly £2,000.

May 13.—Private house, Hendon, badly destroyed.

May 14.—Private house Folkestone, fired : damage from £700 to £1,000; Penn Church damaged.

May 15.—St. Anne's Church, Eastbourne, damaged.

May 18.—Parish Rooms, St. Anne's, Eastbourne, damaged by fire; private house, Cambridge, destroyed by fire : damage between £700 to £1,000; buildings belonging to University, Cambridge, damaged.

May 21.—Bomb explosion, Blackford Observatory, Edinburgh : serious damage.

May 22.—Trinity Wesleyan Church, Stamford, burned; stables, Stamford Hotel, damaged.

May 23.—South Bromley Station damaged by fire.

May 28.—Good's Yard, G.C. Railway Station, Nottingham, timber stacks destroyed.

May 31.—Shields Road Station, Glasgow, damaged.

June 3.—Rough's boathouse, Oxford, destroyed : damage £3,000; Westwood Manor, Trowbridge, destroyed by fire : damage £15,000.

June 7.—North Middlesex Cricket Club pavilion destroyed by fire : business premises at Bradford destroyed : damage £80,000.

June 8.—Boathouse, Hollow Pond, Whipp's Cross, destroyed.

June 11.—Private house, East Lothian, destroyed : damage £7,000.

June 12.—Assembly Rooms and Pier Hotel, Withernsea, destroyed.

June 13.—Eden Park Station damaged; three further outbreaks in Bradford.

June 18.—Rowley Regis Church, near Dudley, destroyed : damage £6,000.

June 19.—Private house, Olton, destroyed.

June 21.—Gatty Marine Laboratory, St. Andrew's University, partially destroyed.

June 25.—Hazlewell Railway Station damaged.

June 30.—Ballikinian Castle, Stirlingshire, destroyed : damage £70,000; Lencross Railway Station destroyed : damage £2,000.

July 4.—Private house, South Coldfield, destroyed : damage £4,000.

July 8.—Sir W. Lever's bungalow destroyed.

July 21.—Private house, Perry Bar, damaged.

August 4.—Private house, Woldingham, damaged.

August 5.—Holiday House, Lyton, destroyed : damage £10,000; motor car burned.

August 8.—School, Sutton-in-Ashfield, damaged; private house, Finchley : damage £500; hayricks fired, Abergavenny : damage £50.

August 13.—Laxey Glen Pavilion, Isle of Man, destroyed : damage £5,000.

August 14.—Carnarvon School-House damaged.

August 15.—Haystacks burned near Liverpool : damage £350; Willesden Park pavilion destroyed : damage £250.

August 16.—Private house, Bangor, damaged.

August 19.—Bedford Timber Yard : damage £200.

August 22.—Private house, Edinburgh : damage £300; Fettes College, Edinburgh, damaged.

August 23.—Haystacks burned Littlemore, Burnham Beeches, and Maltby : damage about £300; motor cars burned at Hunsworth, Birmingham.

September 1.—Bomb found in Cheltenham Town Hall; house fired at Newcastle; school fired at Oldbury; International Correspondence Schools fired at Finchley.

September 5.—Fire at Dulwich College : damage £300.

September 11.—Stanstead House, Seaton, fired : damage £500.

September 13.—Kenton Station gutted : damage £1,000.

September 16.—Wheat rick destroyed at Berkhampstead; Penshurst Place burnt.

September 19.—House fired at Finchley; house fired at Liverpool.

September 23.—Seafield House, Derby, completely gutted : damage £80,000.

September 22.—Withernsea Town Hall gutted; The Cedars, Waltham Cross, destroyed by fire; fire at Warren Hill, Loughton.

September 27.—Fire at timber yards, Yarmouth : damage £40,000.

September 28.—Fire at Frensham Hall, Farnham; Football Ground stand at Plumstead destroyed by fire : damage £1,000; hayricks fired near Oldbury : damage £200.

October 2.—Hayricks and farm fired at Willesden.

October 4.—The Elms, Hampton-on-Thames burnt out : damage £3,000.

October 7.—Two houses fired at Bedford.

October 10.—Yarmouth Pier fired.

October 12.—Wrighley Head Mill, Failsworth, fired.

October 19.—Red House, Loughborough, fired.

October 23.—Bristol Line Athletic Ground destroyed by fire : damage £2,200.

October 22.—Two stations in Birmingham fired.

October 26.—Brooklands, Farnham Royal, destroyed by fire.

October 28.—Shirley Manor, Wyke, completely destroyed by fire : damage £5,000; Mill House, Bramshill, destroyed by fire; Station fired at Oldbury.

November 2.—Streatham Station fired.

November 8.—Stockton Grand Stand fired.

November 11.—Bomb explosion in Cactus House, Alexandra Park, Manchester : damage to glass alone £200; Begbrook, Bristol, fired : damage £3,000; Bowling Green Club pavilion at Catford burned to ground : damage £1,500.

November 15.—Bomb found in Palm House, Sefton Park, Liverpool.

November 16.—The Priory, Sandown Park, Liverpool, fired : three floors and roof destroyed.

November 17.—Newton Road Station, Birmingham, fired.

November 20.—Mill at Ashton-under-Lyne fired : damage £200; fire at timber yard, Oxford : damage £3,000.

November 22.—Football Stand, Blackburn, fired.

November 23.—Bristol boathouse burned : damage £300.

November 24.—Castle Bromwich Station fired.

November 27.—Caerleon Training College, Newport, fired : damage £40,000.

November 24.—Hurristfield, hayricks burned : damage £2,000.

December 5.—Kelly House, Wemyss Bay, fired : damage £60,000.

December 6.—Rusholme Exhibition, Manchester, fired : damage £12,000; Liverpool Exhibition fired.

December 13.—Scottish mansion (Ardgare) fired : damage £10,000.

December 15.—Devonport timber yards fired, more than £2,000 damage; Bristol mansion burnt.

December 16.—Liverpool church fired.

December 18.—Explosion at Holloway Prison.

MRS. PANKHURST'S LICENCE.

Readers are asked to note that Mrs. Pankhurst's last licence is on sale for the highest bidder.

The Suffragette, 1913. How useful is this source to a suffrage historian examining the campaign for votes for women?

Other damaging behaviour

Suffragettes tried to destroy valuable works of art as a protest against the higher value placed on property than on people.

- The most famous case centred on **Mary Richardson**, who, in early 1914, walked into the National Gallery in London and attacked the painting 'Venus' by Velázquez with an axe. Richardson, later known as 'Slasher Mary', wanted to draw a parallel between the public's indifference to Emmeline Pankhurst's health and their respect for a valuable object. She said that 'You can get another picture, but you cannot get a life, as they are killing Mrs Pankhurst.' (Emmeline Pankhurst was very weak at this time due to constant imprisonment and hunger-striking.)
- Other suffragettes used similar tactics. In the same year, a woman spoiled a painting by Romney that hung in Birmingham Art Gallery, while another tried to mutilate the picture of the King in the Royal Scottish Academy.
- The WSPU cut telegraph wires, wrecked plants in the Royal Botanic Gardens in Kew, burnt messages with acid into golf courses saying 'No Votes, No Golf', and chained themselves to railings and to the grille of the **Ladies' Gallery** in the House of Commons. In 1908 **Flora Drummond** and others chained themselves to the railings outside 10 Downing Street.
- Suffragettes disrupted plays about female characters. On one occasion three suffragettes barricaded themselves into a box at the Royal Opera House in Covent Garden to interrupt a production of *Joan of Arc*. Their aim was to draw similarities between the treatment of Joan and the treatment of the suffragettes at the hands of a hostile government.

These particular law-breaking activities were well orchestrated and more reminiscent of a minor form of terrorism than traditional forms of political protest. In Scotland, for example, post-box attacks were organised with great precision. Activists would meet at a prearranged time and place. They would be handed bottles of acid, which had usually been obtained from sympathetic members who were chemists, and told exactly when to drop them into the boxes for the greatest effect. While doing this kind of work suffragettes tried to remain anonymous: one activist always dressed as a domestic servant, wearing a black dress and white muslin apron, to avoid suspicion. To ensure secrecy, all messages to WSPU activists were written in code. At first the code word ANNOUNCEMENT was used until the secret was discovered by the press and the more impenetrable PORTUGUESE EAST AFRICA replaced it.

Even at the height of militancy there were periods of truce where the WSPU ceased breaking the law and concentrated on peaceful propaganda. For example:

Key question
Why did suffragettes damage other property?

Key dates

WSPU members chained themselves to railings of 10 Downing Street: January 1908

WFL members chained themselves to grille in House of Commons: October 1908

Velázquez's painting attacked: March 1914

Key term

Ladies' Gallery
A separate place for women to sit in the House of Commons; protected by an iron rail, called a grille.

Key figures

Mary Richardson
1889–1961; drum major for the WSPU's Fife and Drum Marching Band. She carried out several window-smashing raids, set fire to a country house and bombed a railway station. Richardson was with Davison at the Derby.

Flora Drummond
1879–1949; Labour Party member who joined the WSPU in 1906. She was imprisoned nine times for suffragette activities and went on hunger strike but was never forcibly fed.

Key term

First and second readings
The first reading announces the main parts of a proposed Parliamentary Bill. At the second reading, it is read out in full and discussed; amendments can be added. It then proceeds to the third reading and to the House of Lords. If both Houses agree, the Bill is given to the monarch to sign.

Key question
Why did the suffragettes go on hunger strike?

Key date
First hunger strike: 1909

Key term
Hunger strike
A refusal to eat in order to increase sympathy for a cause.

- between January 1910 and November 1910, when a Conciliation Bill which would give propertied women the vote (see page 101) was going through its **first and second readings** in Parliament; the WSPU resumed militancy when the government resigned before giving the Bill time for a third reading
- during the general election of December 1910, when the WSPU stopped smashing windows and other violent activities; members of the WSPU even campaigned for Liberal candidates who supported the Second Conciliation Bill
- for most of 1911, when the Second Conciliation Bill was being debated.

Damage to themselves
Yet, perhaps the greatest damage the suffragettes did was to themselves. Suffragettes regularly put themselves in danger from physical harassment when they spoke in front of unsympathetic crowds and often suffered lasting after-effects from their regular imprisonments.

Hunger-striking
By engaging in illegal activities, the suffragettes were liable to arrest and imprisonment; once imprisoned, large numbers went on **hunger strike** to protest that their detention was unfair, that they should be awarded the status of political prisoner, and to gain publicity (see page 114). As with the first window-smashers and the first arsonists, the first hunger-striker, Marion Wallace-Dunlop, conceived of the idea independently in 1909 when imprisoned for stencilling a quotation from the Bill of Rights on a wall in the House of Commons.

Hunger strikes soon become official WSPU policy, especially when it was realised that those who refused food were released from prison when their health was seen to be in danger. Even the leadership took part. Between April and December 1913 Emmeline Pankurst was on hunger strike in prison, was released and re-arrested six times, getting visibly thinner with each imprisonment. During a 3-day imprisonment in mid-July 1914 she lost 6 kg in weight and suffered greatly from nausea. By this time she was in a weak and exhausted condition, and was suffering with heart problems, so that she had to be transported everywhere by ambulance.

The government, fearful of public criticism, never force-fed Emmeline Pankhurst, but released her from prison when her health was critical. The composer Ethel Smyth visited Pankhurst soon after one of her many releases from prison, noting that her skin was so 'yellow and so tightly drawn over her face that you wondered the bone structure did not come through; her eyes deep sunken and burning, and a deep dark flush on her cheeks'. At this point, Pankhurst was very near death.

The WSPU used the experiences of hunger-strikers to gain widespread sympathy. Stories regularly appeared in *Votes for Women* about the brutal way in which women were treated. The paper often drew attention to the class differences within prison by informing readers that when working-class women were forcibly fed they were not given any medical aid or examined to see if they were fit. Selina Martin, a working-class woman arrested in Liverpool, was kept in chains and frog-marched to her cell. In contrast, upper- and middle-class women were given preferential treatment and shown greater consideration.

Lady Constance Lytton

These discrepancies prompted Lady Constance Lytton, in 1911, to disguise herself as a working-class woman. Lytton had been imprisoned twice in 1909, first in February for participating in a deputation to the House of Commons and again in October for throwing a stone at a car in which Lloyd George was travelling. Each time she was arrested, tried and sent to prison; each time she went on hunger strike, was medically examined, found unfit to be force-fed and subsequently released. In her view, she had received preferential prison treatment because of her privileged position and was determined to put her theory to the test.

> Key date
> Constance Lytton imprisoned as a working-class woman: 1911

Quite deliberately, she cut off her hair, dressed in cheap clothes, covered herself in suffrage badges and changed her name to Jane Wharton. In this assumed identity, she dropped some stones over the garden hedge of the Governor of Walton Gaol, was arrested, convicted and sent to prison. This time she was shown no such respect. After 4 days of hunger strike, 'Jane Wharton' was informed by the medical officer that she would be force-fed. Two wardresses held her down, a steel gag was inserted into her mouth and the forcible feeding began. In her biography, *Prison and Prisoners*, Lytton writes of this experience:

> The pain of it was intense ... he [the medical officer] put down my throat a tube which seemed to me much too wide and was something like four feet in length ... I choked the moment it touched my throat ... then the food was poured in quickly, it made me sick a few seconds after it was down and the actions of the sickness made my body and legs double up, but the wardress instantly pressed back my head and the doctor leant on my knees ... I was sick over the doctor and wardresses, and it seemed a long time before they took the tube out.

She was forcibly fed seven times before her real identity emerged and she was released. This case attracted much publicity and enabled the WSPU to draw attention to the status differences which existed both in prison and in the wider society and which the female vote might help to eliminate. The consequences were far more severe for Lytton, who never fully recovered, suffered a stroke in 1912 and died in 1923.

Dying for the cause

The best known and the most tragic incident involved Emily Davison at the 1913 Derby, when she jumped out in front of the

Key date

Emily Wilding Davison died from injuries at the Derby: June 1913

king's horse and died later as a result of the injuries she sustained. She was not the only one to die in the suffrage cause: Ellen Pitfield died of incurable injuries received on Black Friday 1910 (see pages 113–14). Others, beside Lytton, were physically weakened by their treatment in prison, by hunger strikes and so on, and many died at an early age. Mary Clarke, the younger sister of Emmeline Pankhurst, died on Christmas Day 1910 from heart failure; 3 days after her release from prison.

The WSPU leadership and illegal actions

Key question

Did the WSPU leadership force its members to commit crimes?

It is often assumed that violent behaviour was orchestrated by a dictatorial WSPU leadership that marshalled an obedient membership and directed it to commit crimes. Militancy, however, often began at a local level with a few ardent activists and was only adopted as WSPU policy when it had received overwhelming support from the membership. Lytton, for example, acted independently and only told a few close friends her intentions. As Sandra Holton, the suffrage historian, has pointed out, window-smashing, arson, letter-burning and hunger-striking were all initiated by ordinary members rather than the leadership. Indeed, there is evidence to suggest that rather than encourage impetuous behaviour, the WSPU executive tried to restrain the enthusiasms of its membership. When a group of women under 30 committed to '**danger duty**' formed a **Young Hot Bloods** group, Emmeline Pankhurst discouraged illegal activities and often froze in disapproval when the young women members announced their willingness to be arrested.

The NUWSS

Key terms

Danger duty
Term used by the WSPU for illegal activities.

Young Hot Bloods
A name given to the members of a WSPU group. Being a hot blood meant being passionate, possibly overzealous, about an issue.

Meanwhile, the NUWSS continued to use the well-tried methods of pressure-group politics: they held meetings, they organised petitions, they published political tracts and newspapers, they spoke in debates, they tried to persuade MPs of the value of their cause, and they set up an election fighting fund to campaign for Labour Party candidates. Unlike the methods of the suffragettes, the suffragists were legal and legitimate and above reproach. Indeed, the NUWSS believed that the actions of the suffragettes damaged the cause of women's suffrage.

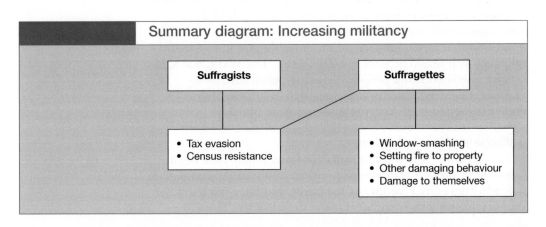

Summary diagram: Increasing militancy

5 | The Key Debate

A question which continues to interest historians is:

> Was the violence of the suffragettes self-defeating?

Historians disagree over whether militancy helped or hindered the cause. On the one hand, it is claimed that violence exasperated politicians so much that they refused to enfranchise women while suffragettes smashed windows and burned down buildings. On the other hand, it is argued that militancy helped because it brought votes for women to public attention.

It is important to remember that the violence which the WSPU used was targeted against property rather than people. It was also very disciplined: between January 1910 and 7 November 1911, apart from a week, the WSPU called a truce while the Conciliation Committee tried to bring a women's suffrage Bill into Parliament. By modern standards, suffragette violence was also restrained. Suffragettes had no wish to endanger the lives of other human beings. Although they were prepared to sacrifice their own lives in the pursuit of votes for women, the suffragettes generally confined themselves to attacks on property rather than people. Certainly, up until 1914, when the WSPU ceased its campaigning, cabinet ministers and others were rarely in any personal danger because Emmeline Pankhurst proclaimed that the WSPU did not wish to harm people, only property. However, it is tempting to speculate whether this belief in the sacredness of human life would have lasted if war had not broken out as, after all, the suffragettes had already begun to throw slates and other missiles at government ministers.

Sandra Holton criticises those who see that militancy defeated the women's cause and points to the prejudices of Asquith and the cynical wheeler-dealing of Lloyd George as factors stopping women's enfranchisement. Is she correct?

Arguments against militancy
Militancy lost government support
It is sometimes argued that militancy lost the WSPU the sympathy and support of the country at large and provided the Liberal government with the perfect excuse to deny women the vote. The government, it was argued, could not possibly give in to female militancy as it would be seen to be too weak. The WSPU was said to have alienated many people, including politicians, by its violence. Often suffragettes were regarded as fanatics, hysterics and lunatics (see page 122) because they were militant.

Suffrage and peaceful protest
Moreover, it was believed that votes for women may have been winnable by other less destructive means. Millicent Fawcett had defended the early militancy of the WSPU but later retracted her support, blaming the militants for the defeat of the Third

Conciliation Bill in March 1912. 'I am personally of the opinion', she stated, 'that the militant suffragists have destroyed for the time being much of the sympathetic support that the women's movement has hitherto enjoyed from the general public'. Over the years, they had tried to prove that they (and, by association, women in general) were calm, sensible and rational beings. Accordingly they put forward measured arguments and used democratic methods to get their message across.

It was feared that the use of violence discredited the suffrage movement and undermined suffragist efforts to be seen as mature adults who could be trusted with the vote. In Fawcett's view, and in the view of the NUWSS, militancy was doing the 'greatest possible harm to the suffrage cause'. Between 1912 and 1914, the NUWSS increasingly disassociated itself from the violence perpetrated by the WSPU, continually arguing that the increase in militancy was 'the chief obstacle' to the success of votes for women. However, the NUWSS leaders were reluctant to criticise the WSPU too openly and publicly in case this exacerbated the government's obstinacy.

NUWSS larger than WSPU
Undoubtedly, the NUWSS had a larger membership and more regional groups (by 1914 there were over 600 member societies and more than 100,000 members) than the WSPU (which allegedly had only 2000 members), which points to lack of support for militancy. Andrew Rosen, a twentieth-century historian, claims that just before the First World War all the best minds such as Emmeline Pethick-Lawrence, had deserted the WSPU because of its increase in violence.

Lack of support among women
Some historians agree with this and point to the lack of support among 'ordinary' women for the vote. Certainly, the suffragettes were unsuccessful in persuading the majority of women to join the struggle for the vote. In the early part of the twentieth century there were approximately 10.5 million women in Britain but only a small percentage joined the suffrage movement. Of course, it is impossible to find out about the changing sympathies of the majority of women. Many may have wanted the vote but did not want to join an organisation.

Arguments in support of militancy
Not surprisingly, the WSPU leaders denied the accusation that violence was counter-productive. On the contrary: to believe that militancy damaged the suffrage cause was to be ignorant of all the lessons taught by history. In their view, peaceful tactics were ineffective as they failed to bring about any change in the law.

Militancy produced results
Indeed, it is an uncomfortable political reality that violent behaviour is often rewarded. Before men got the vote, Emmeline Pankhurst maintained, 'they asked for it nicely, and when they

found that asking for it nicely did not give it to them they began to do things – they burned down public buildings, assaulted bishops and archbishops, and created a revolution'. Certainly, by 1909 when Emmeline made this remark in Torquay, the WSPU had run out of patience and now hoped to force the government into conceding votes for women by a sustained campaign of violence.

Militancy gained support

Some historians point out that, although the government may have been exasperated by WSPU violence (see pages 110–18), suffragettes received considerable support. By 1909 the WSPU had 75 office staff who were assisted by hundreds of unpaid volunteers, the readership of *Votes for Women* increased year on year, and donations kept rolling in. The amount of money donated to the WSPU was impressive: between March 1913 and February 1914 it collected over £28,000 in subscriptions and at one meeting alone people pledged £16,350 to the suffragette struggle, a staggering sum at the time. In addition, the WSPU attracted bigger audiences both at their meetings and on their processions than the NUWSS.

Moreover, the research of historian Leah Leneman contradicts the arguments put forward by Rosen that the WSPU was losing members. On the contrary, she argues, many former suffragists, fed up with the failure of the Conciliation Bills, joined the WSPU because they feared that non-militant methods were failing. For example, in 1912, a niece of **Lord Kitchener** and former suffragist was caught trying to burn down the cottage where the famous Scottish poet Robbie Burns was born.

Militancy increased interest in votes for women

In addition, despite the lack of success in recruiting the vast majority of women, there is no doubt that the numbers of women involved in the suffrage movement increased largely because of the publicity generated by the WSPU. When the WSPU burst onto the political scene in 1903, its novel and exciting methods electrified the country and awakened women to the suffrage cause. Between 1906 and 1914 thousands of women pledged their time, money and energy to the campaigns.

Historians generally acknowledge that the early militancy of the suffragettes increased interest in women's suffrage as never before. Between 1907 and 1914 over 50 new women's suffrage societies were founded. And even Millicant Fawcett credited suffragette militancy with a rise in the membership of the NUWSS. Indeed, between 1897 and 1903, when the WSPU was formed, the NUWSS had only 16 branches, but by 1909 this had increased to 207, allegedly helped by the publicity generated by the WSPU.

And whatever arguments one might have about the effectiveness of the suffragettes in gaining the vote, there is no doubt that the WSPU provided the vital spark to electrify a fading movement. Suffragists had systematically and methodically over

Lord Kitchener 1850–1916; a national military hero who fought in the Sudan (1898) and the Boer War (1899–1902). He became Commander-in-Chief of India and Military Governor of Egypt. In 1914 he was appointed Secretary of State for War.

Key figure

the years petitioned, lobbied, leafleted, demonstrated, published articles and newspapers and canvassed in support of MPs sympathetic to women's suffrage. But before the arrival of the WSPU the suffrage movement was moribund. The suffragettes' exciting, unconventional, innovative approach to politics was a refreshing change from the rather staid, conventional and old-fashioned approach used by the suffragists. Suffragettes challenged the fundamental stereotype of Edwardian women (see page 8) and, in spite of widespread criticism, they made votes for women one of the foremost political questions for women facing the Liberal government. From 1905 onwards it was impossible to ignore the suffrage movement, whether one agreed with votes for women or not.

Some key books in the debate:
Brian Harrison, *The Opposition to Women's Suffrage in Britain* (Croom Helm, 1978).
Sandra Holton, *Feminism and Democracy* (Cambridge, 1986).
Leah Leneman, *A Guid Cause* (Aberdeen University Press, 1991).
Jane Marcus, *Suffrage and the Pankhursts* (Routledge, 1987).
Martin Pugh, *The March of the Women* (Oxford, 2000).
June Purvis and Sandra Holton (editors), *Votes for Women* (Routledge, 2000).

Summary diagram: Was the violence of the suffragettes self-defeating?

YES!	NO!
Militancy:	**Militancy:**
• Lost government support	• Produced results
• Destroyed public support	• Increased financial support
• Lost active members	• Increased suffrage membership
• Lost female support	• Increased interest in suffrage

Study Guide: AS Questions

In the style of Edexcel

Study Sources 1–4 below and then answer the questions that follow.

Source 1

From a song 'The March of the Women', composed by Ethel Smyth in 1911 and dedicated to the WSPU. The suffragettes adopted it as their marching song.

Long, long – we in the past
Cowered in dread from the light of heaven,
Strong, strong – stand we at last
Fearless in faith and with sight new given.
Strength with its beauty, Life with its duty
(Hear the call, oh hear and obey!)
These, these – beckon us on!
Open your eyes to the blaze of the day.

Source 2

Suffragettes at Torquay Regatta.

Source 3

Extracts from a speech by Emmeline Pankhurst, Albert Hall, London, 1912.

Those of you who can express your militancy by facing Party mobs at Cabinet Ministers' meetings when you remind them of their falseness to principle – do so. Those of you who can express your militancy by joining us in our anti-Government by-election policy – do so. Those of you who can break windows – break them. Those of you who can still further attack the secret idol of property so as to make the Government realise that property is as greatly endangered by Women Suffrage as it was by the Chartists of old – do so. And my last word to the Government: I incite this meeting to rebellion.

Source 4
From The Pankhursts *by Martin Pugh, published in 2000.*

There was, in fact, much to be said for Christabel and Emmeline's insistence on having autocratic control of the movement. Militancy led the campaign to develop into something very like a series of terrorist attacks on the authorities, who eventually tried to close down the WSPU. Having gained unquestioning support from their members, the WSPU leaders were in a position to make swift decisions and changes of tactics in order to take advantage of any new developments. Emmeline and Christabel eventually undermined the WSPU, although this did not become clear until 1913. By then, the leaders were fighting amongst themselves and there was no one capable of filling their places.

(a) **Study Sources 1, 2 and 3**
    How far do the sources suggest that the WSPU was a militant movement? (20 marks)
(b) **Study Sources 3 and 4**
    Do you agree with the view that votes for women were won mainly because of the leadership of the Pankhurst family? Explain your answer, using these two sources and your own knowledge. (40 marks)

Source: question (b) adapted from Edexcel, June 2004

Exam tips
The cross-references are intended to take you straight to the material that will help you to answer the questions.

(a) It is important that you do not just paraphrase the sources. When answering these types of question it is important to focus on the 'how far' in the question and create an argument from the evidence of the sources and/or their nature and origin, offering a detailed comparison of their similarities and differences. You need to be able to offer contrasting cross-references and discuss the limitations of the sources in specific, non-general terms.

Superficially, it seems as if Sources 1 and 2 and the words of Emmeline Pankhurst in Source 3 are contradictory. The first two sources certainly seem to stress the peaceful, constitutional nature of the WSPU rather than its militancy. (But this depends on how militancy is defined: is it any challenging political activity or can it be confined to violent action?) For example, in Source 1 you should note that the suffragettes marched fearlessly to get the vote; that they were cheerfully defiant in their determination to get what was right; that it was a marching, rallying song rather than a tuneful little jingle. This could be construed as militant.

Source 2 seems to undermine the idea of militancy – two women, dressed elegantly in white walk by the side of a horse and trap advertising votes for women. But remember that it was a very brave gesture to advertise votes for women in public, especially at such a conventional venue like a Regatta (see page 72). Nonetheless, as the first two sources indicate, the WSPU continued with its peaceful propaganda work throughout the militant campaign – something which Emmeline Pankhurst excelled at, even though she espoused militancy in her speeches. Source 3 definitely suggests that the WSPU was characterised by its militancy. In this hard-hitting speech, Emmeline Pankhurst is uncompromisingly militant. Remember, too, to consider Pankhurst's own position – if the leader of the movement is calling for militancy, you could comment on the weight that adds to evidence suggesting that the WSPU was a militant movement.

(b) Examiners require you to use the sources and knowledge to show a clear analytical understanding of the situation and an ability to explore the interrelationship of factors. Candidates who do well in this question are those who are able to offer a range of relevant, specific detail, combine the two given sources, and link them clearly to the question. It is important to focus on the Pankhursts' *leadership* and not simply on what they did.

As Source 3 shows, Emmeline Pankhurst was a stirring speaker, encouraging her 'troops' to do what they could to force the government to grant votes to women. Pugh confirms Pankhurst's rebellious rhetoric by showing that militancy developed into terrorist attacks. This type of action certainly helped to make votes for women headline news. Nevertheless, it is unlikely that the WSPU heralded a full-blown female insurgency, sustained by Pankhurst rhetoric, which would force the government into action. Rather, the Pankhursts remained a sporadic irritant to those unsympathetic to, and indeed to supporters of, votes for women. It is argued that the Pankhurst leadership, with its emphasis on violent militancy, lost votes for women widespread support and thus hindered, rather than advanced, the cause.

As Pugh indicates, the Pankhurst leadership, with its emphasis on personal loyalty, led to a series of splits in the organisation that eventually weakened it (see pages 58–61). Nonetheless, such a fiery dynamic leadership was at times advantageous since it allowed the leaders to make 'swift decisions and changes of tactics'.

It is important to remember that the suffragette story was not the only story, for it was the painstaking methods of the NUWSS and other groups which also paid dividends. The outbreak of war, the women's suffrage responses to it and changes in government were also important factors in winning the vote.

5 Men and Votes for Women

POINTS TO CONSIDER
This chapter will examine the extent to which men supported or opposed women's suffrage. It will analyse the attitudes of the political parties to women's suffrage and assess why the Liberal government did not enfranchise women. Outside formal political circles, men tended to react differently to the notion of votes for women. This chapter will explain the diversity of male responses to this complex political issue by examining:

• The political parties
• The Liberal government 1906–14
• The alternative establishment
• Male organisations
• Research and men's support of votes for women

Key dates

1866		J.S. Mill presented women's suffrage to Parliament
1867		Mill's amendment to include women in the Second Reform Bill defeated
1903		Liberal/Labour electoral agreement
1906		Liberal landslide election victory
		The word 'suffragette' used for the first time
1907		Men's League for Women's Suffrage founded
1908		Men's League for Opposing Women's Suffrage founded
1909	July	First hunger strike
	September	First forcible feeding
1910	January	General election
		Conciliation Committee founded
	June	First Conciliation Bill passed second reading
		Men's Political Union founded
	November	Black Friday
	December	General election
1911	May	Second Conciliation Bill passed second reading

1912	March	Third Conciliation Bill failed second reading
		Christabel Pankhurst fled to France
		George Lansbury resigned seat
		Election fighting fund established
		Labour Party gave support to votes for women
1913		Amendment to manhood suffrage bill ruled out of order
	April	Cat and Mouse Act
	June	Asquith met NUWSS deputation
1914	June	Asquith met ELFS deputation
	August	War declared

1 | Introduction

It is tempting to classify the struggle for votes for women as a battle of the sexes; but, in fact, the lines of engagement between women and men were not so clearly drawn. At first, it appears that men generally disagreed with votes for women – certainly no government was prepared to enfranchise them. Indeed, mention of female suffrage within Parliament was often greeted by ribald laughter and antagonistic speeches. However, men, just like women, were not a homogeneous group, but were made up of individuals from diverse economic and social backgrounds who held a variety of political views. As a consequence, there emerged several different male perspectives on women's suffrage, and it is worth exploring the extent to which men either opposed or championed the suffrage movement. Despite setbacks, by 1914 suffrage had certainly become the foremost political question for women and was firmly on the national agenda of male politics.

2 | The Political Parties

Even though suffrage eventually became headline news, no party before 1918 was prepared to adopt women's suffrage as their official policy. Why was women's suffrage so unsuccessful in gaining wholesale party approval? It has been argued that Conservatives disliked any extension of democracy because they believed that voters should be part of the traditional ruling class, whereas the Liberals, fearful of the property-based qualification for the vote, were convinced that women would support the Conservatives. There was certainly a historical precedent for this fear because, when the Liberals passed the Third Reform Bill in 1884, many of the agricultural labourers who were enfranchised voted Conservative. The newly formed Labour Party of the twentieth century, of course, much preferred universal franchise to what was perceived to be a middle-class female vote for propertied women. However, such a clear-cut party interpretation underestimates the variety of opinions that existed within the parties concerned.

Key question
What were the similarities and differences between the political parties on the issue of votes for women?

As a result of party reluctance to support votes for women, all the suffrage bills in Parliament were put forward by sympathetic MPs as private member's bills, which had little chance of success since they did not have majority party backing. Between 1860 and 1914 no bill for women's suffrage ever got beyond its second reading. When women's suffrage was first debated, in 1867, there were 71 votes for and 123 against, but most MPs abstained from voting. Practically every year for the next 40 years a women's franchise bill was introduced – and ultimately failed.

Not only did each bill fail, but the debates surrounding them were usually characterised by facetious or hostile speeches from honourable members. In 1905 MPs debated for hours, with mock seriousness, a measure to compel carts on the road to carry rear lights – to avoid giving time to a bill on women's suffrage.

Conciliation bills and parliamentary reform

Eventually, in 1910, a group of MPs from all sides of the House of Commons formed a Conciliation Committee, which consisted of 25 Liberals, 17 Conservative, six Labour and six Irish Nationalists, to marshal support across party lines for votes for women. The Committee drafted a private member's bill to extend the parliamentary franchise to women householders. This meant, of course, that married women were excluded because husband and wife could not both be householders. Even though the bill was likely to favour the Conservative Party, since only widows and single women of property qualified, both the Liberals and Labour MPs on the Committee agreed with it because they preferred a few women to be given the vote rather than none at all. In their view, women's suffrage, as with men's suffrage, could only be won by instalments.

First Conciliation Bill

The first Conciliation Bill was introduced by a Labour MP, David Shackleton, on 14 June 1910, shortly after the death of Edward VII. This Bill passed its second reading with a large majority, but when Parliament dissolved in November women's suffrage had not been granted.

Second Conciliation Bill

When the Liberals returned to government a second Conciliation Bill was put forward by Sir George Kemp, Liberal MP for North-West Manchester, and passed its first and second readings with a larger majority than in 1910. On 29 May 1911, just a few weeks after the second reading, the Chancellor of the Exchequer Lloyd George announced that the government could not allot further time to the Bill that **session**. In an effort to conciliate, he promised that the government would allot time for the Bill in the next session, provided that it passed another second reading.

Third Conciliation Bill

When the new Parliamentary session opened in September 1911 hopes were high for the third Conciliation Bill. However, in November, to the surprise and consternation of suffragists and suffragettes, Asquith stated that his government would introduce a manhood suffrage bill which might be amended to include women's suffrage. The Conciliation Bill had, in the words of both Lloyd George and Christabel Pankhurst, been 'torpedoed'. It limped on to a second reading in March 1912, but it was doomed to fail, and it did.

Meanwhile, the promised manhood suffrage bill passed through the Commons. It too failed. The **Speaker of the House of Commons** ruled that the proposed women's suffrage amendments would change the nature of the Bill and therefore could not be accepted. It seemed to the suffragists and suffragettes that votes for women were unlikely before the next general election, due to be held in 1915. The Conciliation Committee which had worked hard to promote three bills and which had championed votes for women in Parliament was at a loss as to what to do. It seemed that reform could only take place with the support of a political party and political parties were unwilling to give that support.

The Conservative Party

Conservative MPs disagreed over whether women should gain the vote. Many leading Conservatives, including a number of prime ministers, supported the enfranchisement of women. However, it never became a party issue because of the generally antagonistic attitude of backbench MPs. The predominantly Conservative House of Lords was generally opposed to women's suffrage, but there were notable exceptions. **Lord Lytton**, President of the Men's League for Women's Suffrage, was in favour of votes for women and systematically promoted the cause within the House of Lords. However, most shared the views of Lord Curzon, who was antagonistic towards female suffrage. As Vice-President of the Men's League for Opposing Women's Suffrage (see page 63), he actively campaigned against votes for women, believing that militancy resulted from the mental instability of women. Many Conservatives agreed with Curzon's sentiments and were convinced that madness would ensue once women were enfranchised. Even so, the number of Conservatives who opposed votes for women decreased year by year.

Those in favour of votes for women

Votes for women found favour within some sections of the Conservative Party. Women's suffrage resolutions were passed at Conservative Party Annual Conferences in England on at least three occasions and by Scottish Annual Conferences more regularly. Many Conservative Party leaders seemed well disposed

---

Key dates

Third Conciliation Bill failed second reading: March 1912

Amendment to manhood suffrage bill ruled out of order: 1913

Key term

Speaker of the House of Commons An elected, impartial representative who enforces parliamentary rules, and liaises between the Crown, the Lords and the Commons. The Speaker can allow or prohibit motions and amendments to be put forward in Parliament.

Key question
Why did the Conservative Party disagree over votes for women?

Key figure

Lord Lytton 1859–1925; the son of a Viceroy of India and the brother of the suffragette Constance Lytton and the suffragist Betty Balfour. An avid supporter of votes for women, he never condemned the militants. He chaired the Conciliation Committee.

Key figures

Lord Salisbury
1830–1902; became leader of the Conservative Party in 1878 and was Prime Minister in 1885, 1886–92 and 1895–1902.

Arthur Balfour
1848–1930; his uncle, Lord Salisbury, appointed Balfour as Chief Secretary of Ireland, First Lord of the Treasury and Leader of the House of Commons. He replaced Salisbury as Conservative Prime Minister in 1902.

towards votes for women: Prime Ministers Benjamin Disraeli, **Lord Salisbury** and **Arthur Balfour**, for example, all spoke in support.

In 1866 Disraeli stated that 'I do not see … on what reasons … she has not a right to vote'; in 1888, Lord Salisbury believed 'that the day is not far distant when women will also bear their share in voting for members of Parliament and in determining the policy of the country'; and in 1892 Balfour pointed out the contradiction in giving 'a vote to a man who contributes nothing to taxation but what he pays on his beer, while you refuse enfranchisement to a woman whatever her contribution to the state may be'. However, no Conservative Prime Minister initiated any franchise reform for women.

Nonetheless, the fact that Conservative leaders sympathised with the principle of votes for women made it easier, and politically respectable, for MPs to introduce their own private member's bills in favour of women's suffrage. Several women's suffrage bills were put forward by the following Conservative MPs as private member's bills: in 1874 by Forsyth, in 1888 by Dimsdale, in 1892 by Rollit, in 1895 by Madona, in 1896 by Begg, and in 1903 by Denny. In 1912, the Conservative Agg-Gardner proposed a Conciliation Bill by stating that arguments against giving women the vote 'are both out of date and out of place. They might have been correct and proper two or three centuries ago, when the duties of women were restricted to weaving tapestries and looking after the children, but not in the twentieth century, when women have for years, by common consent, taken an active part in public affairs, when they are members of town councils, boards of guardians and Royal Commissions.'

These bills may not have succeeded, but they kept votes for women in the parliamentary, and the public, eye. During the 1870s a number of Conservatives began to realise that there might be some party advantage if the vote was granted to propertied women. 'It was not so much a question of the rights of women, as of the rights of property', said one MP. From the 1890s until 1908 there was a significant shift among Conservatives with the majority of their MPs supporting the women's suffrage bills put forward. By 1900, most MPs recognised the inevitability of votes for women and many worked hard for the Conciliation Committee. Nonetheless, women's suffrage never became party policy largely because Conservatives had an inherent dislike of progress.

Those against votes for women

As the historian Constance Rover points out, there was no evidence of any great commitment by Conservative prime ministers to implement women's suffrage when they were in office. When John Stuart Mill proposed a women's suffrage amendment to the 1867 Reform Bill, Disraeli (who was prepared to take a 'leap in the dark' to extend the franchise to working-class men) offered no help towards its safe passage. Similarly, Lord Salisbury did little to further the cause of women's suffrage and even voted against a second reading of a women's suffrage Bill in 1891. His nephew, Arthur Balfour, considered sympathetic to women's suffrage, again did little. When Balfour was succeeded as Conservative leader by **Andrew Bonar Law** the suffrage movement fared no better: in 1913 Bonar Law declined to support an amendment to a franchise reform bill that would have given women the vote. These Conservative leaders feared they would lose support from backbench MPs and their constituents if they gave active support to the enfranchisement of women.

Many Conservative MPs shared the view of Harold Baker, who in the debate on the 1912 Conciliation Bill argued that the vote was 'a badge, not of superiority but of difference, a difference of masculine character and coercive power, a difference which is adapted for the governance of alien races and for the safeguarding of our Empire'. In their view, there were two separate spheres for women and men: the public sphere of politics, naturally, was the province of men, whereas the private sphere of the home was where women should remain. Moreover, as another Conservative MP argued in the 1912 debate, 'the mental equilibrium of the female sex is not as stable as the mental equilibrium of the male sex'. This MP believed that 'normal' women did not want the vote and pointed to an informal census of women's opinions on female suffrage which showed 42,793 against and only 22,176 in favour.

The Liberal Party

In the early years, the campaign to enfranchise women was undoubtedly endorsed by the Liberals, but the party soon became split over the question. In the 1860s the suffrage campaign had been launched by leading Liberal intellectuals who saw women's enfranchisement as a basic human right. However, the more traditional wing of the Liberal Party did not hold these views, sharing the view of **William Gladstone** that women's role was in the home, not the House of Commons.

In the 1880s women's suffrage was submerged by the debate over Home Rule within the Liberal Party and when the party split over the Irish question in 1886 into the **Gladstonian Liberals** and the Liberal Unionists the sympathy for votes for women virtually disappeared. The leaders of the newly formed Liberal Unionists tended to be antagonistic to women's suffrage, whereas the Gladstone wing was more sympathetic. Gradually, as **New Liberalism** emerged from the Gladstonian section, support for women's suffrage increased and votes for women once more became a Liberal issue.

Those in favour of votes for women

Women's suffrage drew support from leading Liberal MPs, but this support, as with the Conservatives, was sometimes faint-hearted. Both Lloyd George and Churchill advocated women's suffrage at various meetings, but opposed the first Conciliation Bill of 1910 (see page 101) because it offered too limited a female franchise that might favour the Conservatives. In 1912, when a

Key figures

Andrew Bonar Law 1858–1923; made Secretary to the Board of Trade in 1902. In 1911 he became the leader of the Conservative Party, which was then in opposition. In 1916 Lloyd George appointed him Chancellor of the Exchequer. He became Prime Minister in 1922.

William Gladstone 1809–98; Liberal Prime Minister (1868–74, 1880–5, 1886 and 1892–94).

Key question
Why did some Liberals support and some oppose votes for women?

Key terms

Gladstonian Liberals
A name for a group of MPs who were associated with Gladstone who, although a reformer in many areas, believed in low taxation.

New Liberalism
A twentieth-century term for the doctrines of those Liberals who believed that reforms in education and health care should be paid for by higher taxation.

Key dates

J.S. Mill presented women's suffrage to Parliament: 1866

J.S. Mill's amendment to include women in Second Reform Bill defeated: 1867

Key figures

Charles Dilke 1843–1911; a leading Liberal MP who lost his parliamentary seat in the 1880s after a divorce scandal.

James Stansfeld 1820–98; a Liberal MP who led the campaign for the repeal of the Contagious Diseases Acts in Parliament.

Sir Francis Vane 1861–1934; an army officer, scout leader, Liberal MP and later baronet who advocated reform of the House of Lords.

further Conciliation Bill was being debated in Parliament, both Lloyd George and Churchill were associated with a rumour that Herbert Asquith would resign if the Bill were passed. However, when he was Prime Minister, Lloyd George was responsible for the safe passage of the 1918 Reform Bill, which enfranchised women over the age of 30.

Despite the antagonism from prime ministers and the feeble support of many leading Liberals, a number of individuals gave generously of their time, money and energies to promote votes for women. In the nineteenth century the MPs Jacob Bright, **Charles Dilke**, Henry Fawcett, **James Stansfeld** and John Stuart Mill and the barrister Richard Pankhurst were just some of many men who supported votes for women, often at the expense of other commitments. Between 1867 and 1886, when there were 15 women's suffrage proposals, the Liberals accounted for more than two-thirds of the yes votes.

In the twentieth century, the newer breed of Liberal MPs continued to support women's suffrage.

- William Barton (MP for Oldham) and Henry Harben (MP for Barnstaple) both resigned from Parliament because of the Liberal government's reluctance to enfranchise women.
- The leading Liberal Sir John Simon accepted the Vice-Presidency of the Manchester Men's League (for women's suffrage), which could have damaged his parliamentary career.
- **Sir Francis Vane** supported the suffragette movement. He helped to train Sylvia Pankhurst's East End Army.
- There is little doubt that the 25 Liberal MPs who worked hard for the Conciliation Committee were deeply committed to female suffrage.

Those against votes for women

As a general rule, Liberal prime ministers refused to support votes for women. In the nineteenth century, Prime Minister Gladstone was ambivalent over the idea of women's suffrage, sometimes raising women's hopes by speaking in favour of female suffrage yet later letting it be known that he, and any government he formed, would oppose any amendment to enfranchise women. Indeed, when he was in office, Gladstone opposed a women's suffrage amendment to the 1884 Reform Bill on the grounds that it might endanger its successful passing. He also feared that women would lose their femininity if they became involved in politics.

From this time on, as historian David Rubinstein points out, women were on their own since it was highly unlikely that any government would pass an Act that would enfranchise women. Indeed, between 1884 and 1907 there were few parliamentary votes on women's suffrage. In the early twentieth century, when he was Prime Minister, Henry Campbell-Bannerman privately expressed approval of votes for women but publicly blocked its progress in the House of Commons.

Asquith and votes for women

Historians have pinpointed the entrenched position of Asquith, Prime Minister at the height of suffragette militancy, who obstructed every move towards accepting votes for women and persistently refused to see women's suffrage deputations. Asquith, although married to a very shrewd political operator, appeared unchanging in his implacable opposition to votes for women. In his first major speech on suffrage in 1892 he gave four main reasons why he was against women's suffrage:

- The vast majority of women did not want the vote.
- Women were not fit for the franchise.
- Women operated best by personal influence.
- It would upset the natural order of things.

Asquith believed that woman's place was in the home, rather than in what he termed the 'dust and turmoil' of political life. Indeed, it is commonly accepted that it was Asquith more than any other person who prevented the Liberal Party from becoming the party to enfranchise women.

In the debate on the Conciliation Bill, 1912, Asquith argued that men and women were biologically different: 'The question "Why should you deny to a woman of genius the vote, which you would give to her gardener?" is answered in this way. You are dealing, not with individuals, but with the masses and the gain which might result through the admission of gifted and well-qualified women would be more than neutralised by the injurious consequences which would follow from women as a whole.' It was Asquith's opposition to votes for women that made the various women's suffrage reform bills fail to be enacted.

By 1913, Asquith seemed to bow to the inevitable. He met a deputation of the National Union of Women's Suffrage Societies (NUWSS) in June 1913, shortly after their women's pilgrimage. On 20 June 1914 he met a working-class delegation from Sylvia Pankhurst's East London Federation of Suffragettes (ELFS) and stated that he had come round to the idea of votes for women on the same terms as men. It is not unreasonable to suppose that Asquith, who knew that his statement would be widely publicised, had changed his mind. Of course, he had promised support before, so his words may just have been rhetoric.

The Labour Party

The Labour Party, which emerged from the 1900 **Labour Representation Committee**, was created in 1906 – the same year that the Liberals swept to power. In the 1900 election only two MPs were elected, but in the 1906 election, largely because of an electoral agreement with the Liberals, this increased to 29 MPs. The leadership of the Liberal and Labour parties agreed to avoid Liberal/Labour contests in elections so that the Conservative candidate would not win by a split vote. In 1910, 40 MPs were elected.

Key dates

Asquith met NUWSS deputation: June 1913

Asquith met ELFS deputation: June 1914

Liberal/Labour electoral agreement: 1903

Key term

Labour Representation Committee
A committee established to help socialist MPs get elected.

Key question
Why did members of the Labour Party disagree over women's suffrage?

Adult suffrage versus women's suffrage

Initially, the Labour Party's support for votes for women was somewhat muted as the party was split over whether to champion women's suffrage at the expense of universal suffrage. Even in 1900, roughly 60 per cent of working-class men were excluded from the franchise as the right to vote was still based on the ownership or occupation of property. Because women demanded the vote on the same terms as men, many Labour Party members (who saw universal suffrage as being of greater importance) were unsympathetic towards such an élitist measure. In addition, they feared that a limited franchise would be detrimental to the Labour Party as it would increase the political power of the propertied class. Not surprisingly, socialists preferred to campaign for full adult suffrage rather than a female suffrage that would enfranchise propertied women.

The militancy of the Women's Social and Political Union (WSPU) did not help. By 1907, as the historian June Hanham points out, 'it had become more difficult to combine labour and suffrage politics', particularly when suffragettes disrupted the speeches of Labour Party candidates.

A future leader of the Labour Party, Ramsay MacDonald, was certainly equivocal in his support of women's suffrage. Although MacDonald sympathised with women's suffrage and believed that it was a vital part of a socialist programme, he was overtly critical of the methods of the suffragettes:

> I have no objection to revolution, if it is necessary, but I have the very strongest objection to childishness masquerading as revolution, and all I can say of these window-breaking expeditions is that they are simply silly and provocative. I wish the working women of the country who really care for the vote … would come to London and tell these pettifogging middle-class damsels who are going out with little hammers in their muffs that if they do not go home they will get their heads broken.

Those in support of women's suffrage

In contrast, at least three key Labour MPs, Keir Hardie, **George Lansbury** and **Philip Snowden**, took a pragmatic view of reform. They argued that it was crucial to fight one step at a time and preferred to campaign for votes for women rather than wait for universal suffrage.

- Hardie worked hard for women's suffrage both in and outside Parliament. Although he was often ridiculed in the House of Commons his commitment never wavered. According to Sylvia Pankhurst, he collected funds, wrote leaflets, taught the suffragettes parliamentary procedure, introduced them to influential people, visited them in prison and even condoned their violent tactics.
- Similarly Snowden, vice-president of the Men's League for Women's Suffrage, promoted WSPU policies at least until 1912 when suffragette militancy reached a new height (see page 86).

Key figures

George Lansbury 1859–1940; joined the Independent Labour Party in 1903 and was elected MP for Bow and Bromley in 1906. He helped to found the *Daily Herald*.

Philip Snowden 1864–1937; was elected as Labour MP in 1906. Married to a suffragist, he supported votes for women. He was a pacifist in the First World War. In the two minority Labour governments of 1924 and 1929 he was appointed Chancellor of the Exchequer.

- Lansbury dedicated much of his political life to women's suffrage. He condoned suffragette violence, justifying it as a response to government duplicity. On one occasion he rushed across the House of Commons floor, shook his fist at Asquith and shouted 'You'll go down in history as the man who tortured innocent women' in objection to the force-feeding of suffragettes. Moreover, Lansbury demanded that all Labour MPs vote against all Liberal government proposals, even when they benefited the working class, until women were granted the vote. In 1912 he resigned his seat and sought re-election as an independent MP in protest against the Labour Party's half-hearted commitment to women's suffrage. This was an act of great generosity – or foolishness – because Lansbury failed to get elected. The social reformer Beatrice Webb described him as having a great heart but too little intellect.

Key dates

George Lansbury resigned his seat: 1912

Labour Party gave support to votes for women: 1912

Election fighting fund established: 1912

Relationships between the Labour Party and the suffrage movement

In 1912 the Labour Party became the first major political party to support votes for women as part of their official policy. However, relationships between the Labour Party as a whole and the suffrage movement were not always smooth.

At first the links between the two were strong, especially at a local level: after all, the Manchester-based WSPU was founded to improve the lives of working-class women. Certainly, the agitation for women's suffrage was seen to be inextricably bound up with Labour politics. Many radical suffragists, not just the Pankhursts, joined the Labour Party. In 1906 the Women's Labour League was founded to provide socialist women with an organisational base from which to raise the issue of votes for women within the movement. Local Labour groups often supported women's suffrage: the Woolwich Labour Party, for example, consistently supported the aims and methods of the WSPU because they realised that even a limited extension of the franchise would give a respectable number of working-class widows and spinsters the vote.

Not all local groups supported the suffrage movement. Lewisham Borough Council, for instance, laughingly declined to support women's suffrage when a motion was being debated at a council meeting. Moreover, the friendly relationship that existed between the WSPU and the Labour Party soured when the former engaged in violent behaviour and the latter refused to join George Lansbury in his opposition to the Liberal government.

Gradually, those in favour of votes for women won the day. From 1910 onwards all Labour MPs voted in support of women's suffrage and in 1912 the NUWSS broke with their Liberal past and turned instead to the Labour Party for support. In return for the Labour Party's official commitment to women's suffrage the NUWSS promised to raise funds to promote Labour candidates

Key question

Why did the relationship between the Labour Party and the suffrage movement change?

and to help to organise the Labour campaign. The election fighting fund that was set up was, according to historian Martin Pugh, the most important initiative of the final 3 years of the pre-war campaign. Nevertheless, support for female suffrage from such a minority party (the Labour Party only had 42 MPs at the time, and even this small number was as a result of the electoral pact with the Liberals) did not guarantee success in Parliament.

The Irish Nationalists

Key question
Why did Irish Nationalists change their minds about votes for women?

For much of the time, votes for women was far enough away to be an abstraction, a land of fantasy rather than political reality. Irish Nationalist MPs, who traditionally supported female suffrage, could pledge their suffrage allegiance without the fear of the dream coming true. However, the new twentieth-century political world had changed since the Liberal Party swept to power in 1906. Home Rule, the defining mark of the Irish nationalists, suddenly seemed a possibility.

- One of the main barriers to Irish independence, the House of Lords, had seen its power curtailed in 1911, and this brought the prospect of Irish Home Rule closer.
- Moreover, the government came to be dependent on Irish MPs to remain in government. In 1910 Asquith fought two general elections, holding on to power by forming political alliances with the Labour Party and the Irish Nationalists. (In the first election the Liberals won 275 seats, the Conservatives 273, the Irish Nationalists 82 and Labour 40. The second election produced a similar result.) In exchange for supporting the Liberals, the Irish Nationalists wanted something: Home Rule.

Key dates
General election: January 1910

General election: December 1910

There were problems: the Liberal Party was being harassed by women. Irish MPs were anxious that votes for women might lead to the resignation of Asquith, the break-up of the Cabinet and the defeat of the government, thus imperilling the prospects of Home Rule. It was also feared that if women's suffrage took place while Ireland remained under British rule it would simply provide more English with a say in a Parliament whose legitimacy they questioned. In 1912 Irish Nationalists voted against the Conciliation Bill, reneging on their previous commitment to female suffrage.

When the Irish Party MPs helped to defeat the Conciliation Bill they provoked a reaction from the 1000 or so members of the Irish Women's Franchise League, who embarked on a 2-year programme of heckling and window-breaking.

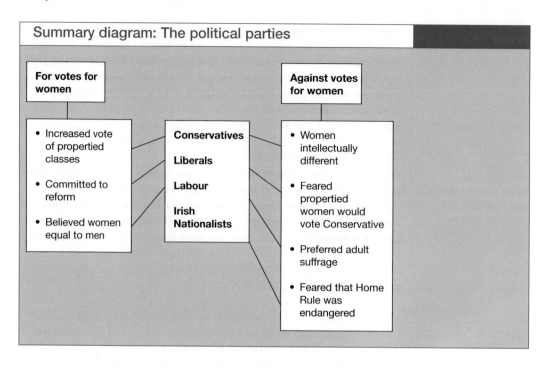

Summary diagram: The political parties

For votes for women
- Increased vote of propertied classes
- Committed to reform
- Believed women equal to men

Conservatives

Liberals

Labour

Irish Nationalists

Against votes for women
- Women intellectually different
- Feared propertied women would vote Conservative
- Preferred adult suffrage
- Feared that Home Rule was endangered

3 | The Liberal Government 1906–14

The sweeping electoral victory of the Liberal Party in 1906 heralded a new dawn of reform politics. It broke the power of the House of Lords and laid the foundations of a modern welfare state by introducing old age pensions, National Insurance and a host of other benefits. Suddenly women's suffrage seemed likely. After the election, the Liberals had 400 MPs and enjoyed an overall majority of 130. Between 1906 and 1910 the Liberal government held on to this large majority. Given the fact that votes for women was largely a Liberal cause, it might have been expected that the government would give women the vote. Unfortunately, the Liberal government proved no more willing than its Conservative predecessors to give votes to women. Historians have suggested that the Liberals were reluctant to do so for a number of reasons:

- First, Asquith, who was Prime Minister from 1908, was hostile to votes for women (see page 106).
- Secondly, its majority was gradually whittled down by two elections and from 1910 it relied on the Irish Nationalists and the Labour Party to stay in office. It was unwilling to jeopardise its term of government for the sake of votes for women.
- Thirdly, the Liberals had other, more pressing, problems with which to grapple. They faced insurrection in Ireland, rebellion by the House of Lords and widespread strike action by trade unionists. It was a period characterised as 'revolutionary'. This turbulent state of affairs perhaps explains the unwillingness of a Liberal government to put time aside for a women's suffrage bill.

Key question
Why did the Liberal government refuse to give votes to women?

Liberal landslide election victory: 1906

Key date

- Fourthly, the Liberals did not wish to cave into suffragette violence.
- Finally, of course, the Liberals feared that if they gave women the vote on the same terms as men it might help the Conservatives to win office because only wealthier women would be enfranchised.

However, these suggestions can be considered excuses rather than explanations. As we have seen previously, the Liberals were ambivalent about women's suffrage and refused to promote it as party policy. Constantly, and with consummate skill, the government undermined the efforts of the advocates of women's suffrage. The following catalogue of failed bills tends to support this argument:

THE LIBERAL GOVERNMENT AND VOTES FOR WOMEN

1906	Government refused to support an amendment to a Plural Voting Bill that would have enfranchised a number of propertied women
1907	Women's Suffrage Bill rejected
1908	Women's Suffrage Bill passed first reading
1909	Second Reading of Women's Suffrage Bill carried but Asquith failed to give support so the Bill failed
1910	First Conciliation Bill passed its second reading but ultimately failed because the government refused to grant it parliamentary time
1911	Second Conciliation Bill passed its second reading but Asquith announced that he preferred to support manhood suffrage. A new bill could include an amendment for the enfranchisement of women
1912	Third Conciliation Bill failed
1913	Government Franchise Bill introduced universal male suffrage but an amendment to enfranchise women failed to be accepted

---

Time after time, women were led to believe that votes for women were achievable, only to be let down and humiliated by what they quickly perceived to be a duplicitous government. Ultimately, of course, the Liberal government was considered by the suffragettes not just equivocal in its response to votes for women but oppositional. This can be seen in the response to various reform bills, the curtailing of suffragette freedom and the forcible feeding of those who broke the law.

Key question
Did the Liberal government treat the suffragettes unfairly?

Curtailing suffragette freedom

The response of the Liberal government towards women who broke the law certainly suggests that it was hostile to votes for women. The WSPU leaders pointed to the decided contrast between the treatment meted out to the law-breaking Ulster Unionists (who preached sedition in Belfast and smuggled guns to help a rebellion against the forthcoming partition of Ireland) and the law-breaking suffragettes. A blind eye was turned to the gun-smuggling of the Ulster rebels, who remained immune from arrest and were consulted over Ireland, whereas the suffragettes were first ignored and then harassed, arrested, imprisoned and force-fed.

When the WSPU began its militant activities, the Liberal government reacted by restricting suffragette activity. In an attempt to stop potential disruption, women were forbidden to attend Liberal meetings unless they held a signed ticket. The government refused to meet deputations or accept petitions, banned meetings in public places and censored the press in an attempt to silence the WSPU. The Commissioner of Police, directed by the Home Office, refused to allow suffragettes to hold meetings in any of the London parks and persuaded the management at the Albert Hall not to let it out to suffragettes. When the WSPU managed to hire a different venue, the owner of the hall was threatened with the withdrawal of his licence. The government also prosecuted the printers of *The Suffragette*, periodically raided the offices and homes of the WSPU members and in 1912 forced Christabel Pankhurst to flee to Paris, where she directed the movement from exile.

Christabel Pankhurst fled to France: March 1912 **Key date**

The cartoon below illustrates the fear of politicians, harassed by WSPU militants. The kicking horse symbolises the uncontrollable suffragette who had already kicked Churchill out as MP in Manchester and was in danger of doing so again. In fact,

THE COURIER, SATURDAY, MAY 9, 1908.

ANOTHER MANCHESTER?

DEAR WINSTON (thinking)—" Looks a bit fresh—not so safe a seat as I expected. I doubt that reversed saddle is to worry him."

A newspaper cartoon showing Winston Churchill's election prospects, Dundee 1908

Churchill was elected as MP for Dundee in 1908 despite suffragette activity.

'Black Friday'

Key question
How did the
government respond
to suffragette protest?

On numerous occasions the government acted even more harshly towards the suffragettes. As Home Secretary in charge of civil order, Winston Churchill was held responsible for the notorious police violence towards women on Friday 18 November 1910 – later termed 'Black Friday' by the suffragettes. On this day approximately 300 suffragettes marched to the House of Commons in protest at the failure of the first Conciliation Bill. When they tried to enter Parliament the police behaved with unexpected brutality. The police, instructed not to arrest the suffragettes, forced the women back, kicked them, twisted their breasts, punched their noses and thrust knees between their legs. All the 135 statements made by the suffragettes testify to the violence: 'I was seized by several policemen. One twisted my right arm behind my back with such brutal force, that I really thought he would break it … Another policemen gave me a terrible blow in my back, which sent me whirling among the crowd', said one 60-year-old woman, and 29 women testified to some form of sexual assault.

Historians offer different interpretations of this event:

- Andrew Rosen, a historian writing in the 1970s, excuses police cruelty by suggesting that the men brought in for this day had lacked experience of handling suffragette demonstrations. In the past, he argues, they had been used to policing the rough and tough working class of London's East End rather than young, genteel, middle-class women: they were at a loss to know what the correct procedure might be. In addition, women, by their very femininity, were seen to provoke police violence. 'By attempting to rush through or past police lines, these women were bringing themselves repeatedly into abrupt physical contact with the police. That the police found in the youthful femininity of many of their assailants an invitation to licence, does not seem, all in all, completely surprising'.
- In contrast, the feminist historians Susan Kingsley Kent and Martha Vicinus writing in the 1980s argue that the violence directed at the suffragettes was in fact sexual abuse. The cruelty meted out by the police is seen by such historians to be a direct result of the domestic ideology of Victorian and Edwardian Britain, whereby respectable women remained in the private sphere of home while only men and prostitutes entered the public sphere of the streets. Hence, when suffragettes demonstrated outside the male Parliament they were perceived to be no better than prostitutes. Because of this, and in order to protect their public space, men were willing to permit, even encourage, 'the violation of woman's most intimate space – her body'.

The Liberal government defended the actions of the police. Churchill, who was Home Secretary at the time, argued that:

> it was my intention, on 18th November, to have these women removed from the scene of disorder as soon as possible, and then to prosecute only those who had committed personal assaults on the police or other serious offences.
>
> I believe that the Metropolitan Police behaved on 18th November with the patience and humanity for which they are well known. I reject the unsupported allegations which come from that overflowing fountain of falsehood, the Women's Social and Political Union.

Imprisonment

Between 1906 and 1914 the Liberal government imprisoned approximately 1085 suffragettes who broke the law. At first women were given 'First Division' treatment, that is, they were awarded the status of political prisoners, and so allowed to wear their own clothes and receive food parcels. After 1908, however, women were placed in the 'Second Division' because the government regarded them as criminals rather than political dissidents. Consequently, the privileges they had once enjoyed were taken away and they were treated just like ordinary prisoners.

Suffrage historian June Purvis argues that the prison authorities hoped to undermine suffragettes by making them endure ritualistic humiliation that took away their sense of self. Prisoners had to remain silent, were locked in separate cells, forced to wear prison clothes and were referred to by their prison number rather than their name. Daily life was well regulated and equally demeaning. Prisoners were woken at 5:30a.m., ate a breakfast of tea, brown bread and butter; at 7a.m. they had to empty the slops, scrub the cell floor and clean their tin utensils and fold their bedclothes. Baths were taken weekly and books borrowed twice a week. Each prisoner was expected to do prison work such as making nightgowns or knitting socks. At 8p.m. the cell light was switched off. Contact with the outside world was limited – and censored. All correspondence was read by the prison authorities, which once more served to humiliate the suffragette prisoner because it invaded her privacy.

Eventually, in March 1910 the new Home Secretary, Winston Churchill introduced Rule 243A, which alleviated some of the conditions faced by suffragette prisoners. Under this rule, prisoners could receive visitors and letters, wear their own clothes, exercise twice a day and eat First Division food, and were allowed a supply of books. Even so, they were not given the status of political prisoners.

Key question
How were suffragettes treated in prison?

Key question
Why did the Liberal government introduce forcible feeding?

Key dates

First hunger strike:
July 1909

First forcible feeding:
September 1909

Key figure

Reginald McKenna
1863–1943; held a number of Liberal government posts including Secretary to the Treasury, President of the Board of Education and First Lord of the Admiralty. He was Home Secretary from 1911 to 1915 and therefore responsible for law and order.

Forcible feeding

When women responded to their imprisonment by going on hunger-strike the Home Secretary, **Reginald McKenna**, in a debate in the House of Commons on 11 June 1914, suggested four solutions to this problem:

> So far as I am aware these are four, and four only in number. I have had unlimited correspondence from every section of the public who have been good enough to advise me as to what I ought to do, and among them all I have not been able to discover more than four alternative methods. The first, is to let them die. That is, I should say, at the present moment, the most popular, judging by the number of letters I have received. The second is to deport them. The third is to treat them as lunatic, and the fourth is to give them the franchise … I think we should not adopt any of them.

At first, hunger-strikers were released from prison, but soon the government introduced force-feeding, which they called 'artificial' feeding, for women who consistently refused to eat.

Once again, historians are divided over the significance of this course of action. Some historians justify the force-feeding of suffragettes because it saved the lives of those on hunger strike.

- Roger Fulford, writing in the 1950s, dismisses the force-feeding by the Liberal government as a harmless procedure that had been in use for years with 'lunatics'. Historians writing in the 1970s tended to agree with these interpretations. In particular, suffragist historians, often antagonistic to the suffragettes, underplay the brutality of the government towards women.
- In stark contrast, much of the pictorial propaganda of the suffragettes represented force-feeding as oral rape, as the image on page 116 shows. Here a suffragette is being held down, and her legs tied up so that the doctor can pour liquid food down a tube in her nose. Feminist historians writing in the 1980s subscribed to this image, arguing that the 'instrumental invasion of the body, accompanied by overpowering physical force, great suffering and humiliation was akin to it'. Over 1000 women endured what the historian Jane Marcus calls the public violation of their bodies as they were force-fed through the nostril, the mouth and, albeit very rarely, even the rectum and vagina. Sometimes the tubes used were not sterile and had been used before, which increased the sense of outrage of those who had been force-fed. On 12 August 1912, a medical journal, *The Lancet*, disgusted by the practice of forcible feeding, described it as follows:

> Prisoners were held down by force, flung on the floor, tied to chairs and iron bedsteads … while the tube was forced up the nostrils. After each feeding the nasal pain gets worse. The wardress endeavoured to make the prisoner open her mouth by sawing the edge of the cup along the gums … the broken edge caused laceration and severe pain. Food into the lung of one unresisting

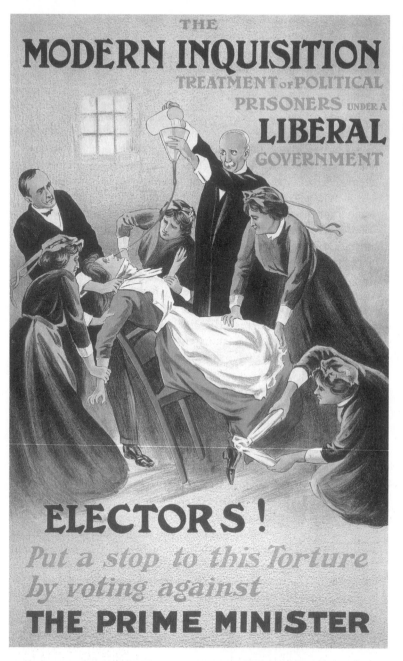

A poster published in 1910 by the WPSU showing a suffragette being force-fed. How useful is this poster to a historian studying government response to suffragette activities?

prisoner immediately caused severe choking, vomiting … persistent coughing. She was hurriedly released next day suffering from pneumonia and pleurisy. We cannot believe that any of our colleagues will agree that this form of prison treatment is justly described in Mr McKenna's words as necessary medical treatment.

Force-feeding, and the association of hunger strikers with lunatics, certainly seems to suggest that the government was deeply hostile to suffragette prisoners. But it could equally suggest that the Liberal government chose this method because it was alarmed at the prospect of women dying in prison. Nevertheless, the government chose its victims with care. On the one hand, influential women like Lady Constance Lytton and Mrs Brailsford (wife of an important Liberal journalist) were released from prison when they went on hunger strike, whereas working-class women received quite different treatment (see page 90). Emmeline Pankhurst too was never forcibly fed.

Key question
What were the effects of the Cat and Mouse Act?

Key date

Cat and Mouse Act: April 1913

Cat and Mouse Act

On 25 April 1913, as a result of adverse publicity, the Prisoners' Temporary Discharge for Ill-Health Act became law. The force-feeding of suffragettes on hunger strike stopped. Instead, prison

Poster showing the Cat and Mouse Act 1913 published by the WSPU.

authorities were given the power to temporarily release persistent hunger-strikers from prison to give them time to recover. But, as soon as they were better suffragettes were required to return to prison. The suffragettes called it the 'Cat and Mouse Act'.

Not surprisingly, no woman went back to prison voluntarily. Instead, they went to be nursed in suffragette nursing homes and then went into hiding. Consequently, the police kept released prisoners under surveillance, arrested them and imprisoned them without trial for the same offence once they were deemed to be fit enough to serve their sentence.

The suffragette poster on page 117 graphically portrays the Cat and Mouse Act. The large, bloody-toothed cat represents the police, the prison authorities and Home Secretary McKenna, who was responsible for the Act. The mouse is portrayed as a small and injured suffragette.

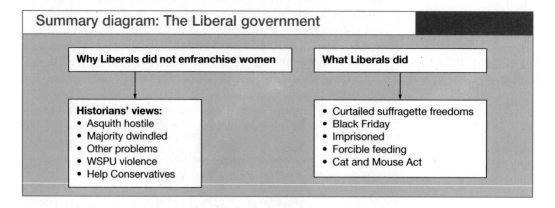

Summary diagram: The Liberal government

Why Liberals did not enfranchise women

What Liberals did

Historians' views:
• Asquith hostile
• Majority dwindled
• Other problems
• WSPU violence
• Help Conservatives

• Curtailed suffragette freedoms
• Black Friday
• Imprisoned
• Forcible feeding
• Cat and Mouse Act

4 | The Alternative Establishment

The male 'alternative establishment', that is the trade unions, religious groups and the press, was as divided as the political parties over the question of votes for women. Although the leadership of the majority of trade unions seemed to be indifferent to women's suffrage, a number of them supported it. Similarly, whereas the official church was unresponsive to votes for women, some committed individual clergy campaigned vigorously for the cause. The press, depending on its political allegiances, also responded in a variety of ways. However, there is still a lot of research needed in these areas and so it is impossible to reach any definite conclusion.

Trade unions

The trade union movement as a whole was divided over the question of votes for women. John Burns, a notable trade unionist, was implacably opposed to women's suffrage, whereas others agreed with it. According to suffrage historians Liddington and Norris, the official union response ranged from 'benign indifference to downright hostility'. Although the

Key question
What was the attitude of the trade union movement towards votes for women?

Key terms

Trades Union Congress
An association that represents the vast majority of trade unions.

Nonconformists
People who belong to a Christian church that does not conform to Church of England beliefs and practices.

Quakers
Members of the Society of Friends, a Christian organisation founded in the mid-seventeenth century, which is committed to pacifism and social equality.

Trades Union Congress (TUC) had passed a resolution in 1884 in favour of votes for women, little had been done to promote women's suffrage in practice. What is more, when the issue was raised in 1901 at another TUC conference (where there were only four women delegates), it provoked a decidedly hostile response, possibly because men favoured full adult suffrage rather than votes for women. Indeed, the National Union of Miners (NUM), which controlled a large block of votes, opposed a resolution on women's suffrage at the 1912 Labour Party Conference.

However, not all the trade union movement was antagonistic as, like the Labour Party, it responded differently at individual and local levels in the late nineteenth and early twentieth centuries:

- One of the miners' leaders, Robert Smillie, advocated strike action in support of women's suffrage.
- A member of the National Transport Workers' Federation was arrested and imprisoned for 2 months for breaking windows as a protest against the unjust imprisonment of suffragettes.
- In Lancashire, a textile area with a history of women's active participation in the trade union movement, several weavers' unions sent petitions to Parliament and encouraged Labour MPs to introduce women's suffrage into the House of Commons.
- In the East End of London, Sylvia Pankhurst's ELFS drew support from large sections of the male working class – dockers, seamen, gas workers, labourers, firemen and post office workers – many of whom came on demonstrations and protected the ELFS members from gangs of unruly local youths. Indeed, one prizefighter from the East End became Sylvia Pankhurst's personal bodyguard.

Key question
How did religious groups respond to women's suffrage?

Religious groups

Historians have virtually ignored the response of official religion to women's suffrage, even though church-going was much more central to people's lives in the nineteenth and early twentieth centuries. Despite this lack of research, it seems safe to say that religious groups responded to women's suffrage in diverse ways. The Church of England was somewhat ambivalent, whereas **Nonconformists** and **Quakers** in particular, sometimes gave unqualified support.

Roman Catholics

A number of Catholic clergy supported votes for women, but they were in the minority since most believed that women should stay at home and look after their husbands and children rather than engage in politics. Catholic congregations seemed even less enthusiastic than their clergy, if the experience of the ELFS was common: when a group tried to pray for women's suffrage in a Roman Catholic Church in Poplar they were beaten up by the people attending. Nonetheless, men did join the Catholic Women's Suffrage Society founded in 1911 to bring together Catholics of both sexes in order to gain votes for women. This was never a large organisation: in 1913 there were only 1000 members.

Church of England

Throughout this period, the Church of England maintained a discreet silence over the question of women's suffrage and was later criticised by the suffragettes for doing so. In a leaflet printed in 1912, the WSPU condemned the Church for being 'shamefully and obsequiously compliant' and for being 'degraded into the position of hanger-on and lackey of the Government'. The Church of England, acting through bishops in the House of Lords, was also censured for helping the government to pass the Cat and Mouse Act. Indeed, the Church of England was thought to disapprove more of militancy than forcible feeding, and this prompted the WSPU's blistering attack on the Church in its 1914 Annual Report for

> having aided and abetted the State in robbing women of the vote. The Church is thus held guilty of the subjection of women and all the vice, suffering and social degradation that result from that subjection. Whereas it is the duty of the Church to insist on the political enfranchisement of women – not only as a political reform, but as a moral and even a religious reform – the Church has actually boycotted this great question and has condoned the torture of the women who are fighting for their liberty.

Nevertheless individual clergy responded positively to women's suffrage. Significant leaders of Anglican religious thought in the early twentieth century – the Archbishop of Canterbury, the Lord Bishop of Exeter, the Lord Bishop of Hereford, the Lord Bishop of Liverpool and the Right Reverend Bishop of Edinburgh – favoured votes for women. The Rector of Whitburn, for example, said that the

> extension of the Suffrage to women seems to me a logical sequence of Christian principle. In the Christian society there is no superior sex, the equality of each member is recognised, the individuality of each person is sacred. St Paul asserted this when he wrote: 'in baptism there is neither male nor female'. The rights of each are equal, therefore women are entitled to express their convictions and assert their individuality by voting if they choose to do so.

Similarly, the Vicar at Kirkby Lonsdale believed that because Jesus Christ encouraged a certain freedom and independence in the conduct of women then it followed that Christians should support women's suffrage. Others believed women to be the moral guardians of the nation and the family who, once enfranchised, would exercise a beneficial influence on these areas.

Key terms

Labour churches
Set up in the late nineteenth century. Members generally supported the emerging Labour Party and believed that the labour movement could help to obtain the Kingdom of Heaven on Earth.

Yom Kippur
The Day of Atonement. It is a day set aside to make amends for the sins of the past year.

Stamp duty
In June 1855 the final penny of newspaper tax, called stamp duty, was removed. This opened the way for cheap mass-circulation papers. For example, the *Daily Telegraph* was founded a few months afterwards and cost just one penny.

When forcible feeding was introduced, a large number of these clergy protested against it.

A number of clergy, who argued that women's suffrage harmonised with essential Christian principles of equality, established a Church League for Women's Suffrage to promote the cause. By the end of 1913 the League had 103 branches and 5080 members, including the Bishop of Worcester.

Nonconformists

The connections between suffrage and nonconformism appear much stronger. This may have been because nonconformist women, unlike those in the Church of England, played a leading role. For example, the **Labour churches**, founded in Manchester in the latter part of the nineteenth century, encouraged women to participate on equal terms and invited suffragettes like Hannah Mitchell to speak to their congregations about votes for women. Similarly, the Quakers were sympathetic to women's suffrage. Quaker women enjoyed equal rights with male Quakers, having the opportunity both to speak at religious meetings and to participate in political events. Quakers were especially motivated by a sense of moral purpose and took a leading role in many reform movements such as anti-slavery, education for women and opposition to the Contagious Diseases Acts.

Jews

The Chief Rabbi supported votes for women and many leading activists such as Hugh Franklin were of Jewish origin. Hugh Franklin was a member of the Men's League for Women's Suffrage and later the Men's Political Union. He was imprisoned several times for militancy and went on hunger strike. In one imprisonment he was forcibly fed over 100 times. In 1912 a Jewish League for Woman Suffrage was founded which recruited both men and women. Not all religious Jews were sympathetic: two Jewish members of the Cabinet who had supported forcible feeding were confronted by three women at a **Yom Kippur** service in 1913.

Key question
How did the press respond to votes for women?

The press

The attitude of the press has been largely ignored by suffrage scholars, but there are a few general points one can make. In the second half of the nineteenth century the number of newspapers published increased largely because the government abolished **stamp duty** and more people could read. Many of these newer newspapers were sympathetic to Liberalism but, apart from the *Manchester Guardian*, none campaigned for women's suffrage. Indeed, before the illegal activities of the WSPU provided headline-catching news, most newspapers frankly ignored the women's suffrage movement. After 1905, when Christabel Pankhurst and Annie Kenney were arrested, newspapers took more notice of suffragette activity.

Newspapers hostile to votes for women

The press often reported militancy in ways that were condemnatory rather than complimentary or neutral. Once the militant campaign escalated, the response to the suffragettes grew even more hostile, with the press describing the suffragettes as mad, unladylike and misguided. *The Times*, in particular, remained unsympathetic to women's suffrage for over 50 years. In 1912 it viewed the suffragettes as 'regrettable by-products of our civilisation, out with their hammers and their bags full of stones because of dreary, empty lives and high-strung, over-excitable natures'. Letters to *The Times* suggest a deep antagonism towards women's suffrage, especially when comparisons were drawn between suffragette militancy and 'the explosive fury of epileptics'. In a similar fashion the *London Standard* condemned militancy as the act of deranged lunatics and a 'form of hysteria of a highly dangerous type'.

   Some reports merely wanted to shock, and of course to sell more papers. Both the *Daily Mirror* and the *Illustrated London News* carried full pages of photographs of suffragettes being assaulted on Black Friday that, because of their sexually suggestive nature, were guaranteed to appeal to the prurient. In 1906, the *Daily Mail* coined the word 'suffragette' to use as a term for militant suffragists.

The term 'suffragette' used for the first time: 1906

Key date

Newspapers in favour of votes for women

Not all newspapers were unsympathetic. At the other end of the political spectrum, *The Workman's Times* supported votes for women. Nevertheless, it shared more than a name in common with the 'official' *Times*, as it too believed that women's place was in the home not the workplace. The Liberal paper, the *Manchester Guardian*, supported votes for women, but often condemned the violence of the suffragettes. The *Daily Herald*, co-founded by George Lansbury in 1912, gave prominent coverage of women's suffrage and, not surprisingly, excused suffragette violence. Some men even published their own newspapers in support of votes for women: in 1907 J. Francis began a weekly paper, *Women's Franchise*. A few local newspapers gave qualified approval to votes for women: the *Lewisham Borough News*, for example, was sympathetic to women's suffrage, but criticised suffragette militancy.

Class, culture and votes for women

Historians claim that many aristocratic and upper-class men were opposed to votes for women. London's male clubland generally opposed female suffrage, as did the Oxford Union. The royal family was also opposed: Edward VII was quite definitely against giving the vote to women. One famous upper-class doctor remarked in 1912 that 'there is mixed up with the women's movement much mental disorder'. However, once again, these are just impressions based on a few individual comments and cannot be taken as representative of a whole social class.

Key question
How popular was votes for women among various classes?

Henry Nevinson
1856–1908; a leading journalist who wrote on a number of social issues including exposing continuing African slavery. He was a supporter of the WSPU and helped to found the Men's League for Women's Suffrage.

Henry N. Brailsford
1873–1958; a radical writer who supported liberation movements abroad and made friends with a number of exiled foreign revolutionaries. In 1907, disillusioned with the Liberals, he joined the Labour Party. He was a founding member of the Men's League for Women's Suffrage.

John Masefield
1878–1967; Poet Laureate between 1930 and 1967.

Individual men, from all social classes, continued to give support. In 1909 the journalists **Henry Nevinson** and **Henry N. Brailsford** both resigned their jobs at the *Daily News* in protest against the government's use of forcible feeding. The cricketer Jack Hobbs, an East End prizefighter Kosher Hunt, and many middle-class intellectuals including Gilbert Murray, **John Masefield** and John Galsworthy all gave their support to the suffrage campaign.

Music hall songs and suffragettes
Music hall songs and cartoons offer entertaining insights into the minds of some men. The following popular songs are affectionate in tone, but suggest that public opinion was negative:

> Put me upon an island where the girls are few
> Put me among the most ferocious lions in the zoo
> Put me in a prison and I'll never never fret
> But for pity's sake don't put me near a suffering-gette

Or

> I'm suffering from a suffragette
> Suffering all you can see
> Since my wife joined the suffragettes
> I have become a suffragee

Not all music hall artists were unsympathetic. After a short verse, one popular entertainer used to deliver a lengthy speech on the wrongs of women, urging them to stand up for their rights.

Museums and suffragettes
Fear of militancy closed many of the country's art galleries and museums to the public completely or sometimes to women only. The rule of 'No muffs, wrist bags or sticks' was widespread: the Royal Academy and the Tate Gallery were closed to women and the British Museum announced that it was open to all men, but only open to women if accompanied by men who were willing to vouch for their good behaviour. Unaccompanied women, they said, 'were only allowed in on presentation of a letter of introduction from a responsible person vouching for the bearer's good behaviour and accepting responsibility for her acts' (see the cartoon on page 124). Again, this response may be evidence of justifiable anxiety about the prospect of suffragette violence rather than of an unfriendly attitude.

Shops and suffragettes
Suffragists and suffragettes may have received an antagonistic response from some men, but they drew support from unexpected quarters. Diane Atkinson, a social historian, has noted that many leading department stores, both in London and in the provinces, displayed the WSPU colours in their windows. Selfridges, the large London department store, offered an elegant array of suffragette clothing, advertised regularly in the *Suffragette*, featured the colours in its windows and even donated a white uniform to Flora

A cartoon showing a satirical look at the response of museums to female visitors, published in the *Daily Mirror*, 13 March 1914.

Drummond to wear in the processions. In 1908 in Lewisham, one large department store employed a WSPU speaker to address one of their sports day events, while Sainsbury's exhibited clothes of green, purple and white in their windows. Many other retail stores stocked clothes and other items in the suffragette colours. In 1910 the Votes for Women slogan was even printed on the wrappers of Allison's bread. This, of course, may have been just good business sense – the suffragettes were seen to be wealthy customers – but the displaying of suffragette colours may have antagonised more people than it attracted.

Assaults on suffragettes

Recent research indicates that many suffragettes were violently and indecently assaulted when they participated in demonstrations, campaigned at by-elections or heckled politicians. The occasions on which women had to put up with violent sexual harassment were numerous: they were often

> **Key question**
> How were suffragettes treated by some men opposed to votes for women?

Key terms

Men's Committee for Justice to Women
Founded in 1909 to monitor cases where suffragettes were prosecuted for militancy.

Men's Declaration Committee
Founded in 1909 to collect signatures of professional men who supported votes for women.

Male Electors' League for Women's Suffrage
Founded in the 1890s. One of its members became the first man to go to prison for the cause.

Key question
How did men make their support for the suffrage movement visible?

Key term

Rebels' Social and Political Union
Founded in about 1913 to give support to the East London Federation of Suffragettes. George Lansbury's son, Willie, was a leading member.

intimidated, attacked, and the victims of anti-suffrage rioting. Antagonistic men indecently assaulted women on demonstrations, ripping their clothes and whispering obscenities in their ears. Andrew Rosen has told of the number of men who came expressly to suffragette demonstrations to bully and sexually abuse women. Some examples include:

- Gangs of 'roughs' used to lay in wait for suffragettes who tried to get into the House of Commons.
- In Glasgow in March 1912, 200 men broke up the WSPU shop by throwing iron bolts and weights through the windows.
- In Wales in 1912, suffragettes who dared to heckle the local hero, Lloyd George, were seriously assaulted, their hair pulled and their clothing ripped – one woman was stripped to the waist.
- In 1914 a crowd tried to push some suffragettes into the sea at Worthing. Their WSPU banner was torn and a cod's head was thrown at them.

Time and time again the suffragettes were subjected to brutal and sometimes sexual assault so that it became impossible for the WSPU to hold outdoor meetings because they feared violence by the crowd gathered to watch. Even Emmeline Pankhurst was not immune. When she opposed the Liberal candidate at Newton Abbot, Devon, Emmeline and her colleague were roughly handled and savagely assaulted by Liberal sympathisers. However, men who assaulted women were still very much in the minority, and so this type of harassment cannot be taken to indicate widespread male hostility to female suffrage.

5 | Male Organisations

A significant number of middle-class professional men, writers, artists, lawyers, academics, journalists, scientists, clergymen, medics and politicians gave active support to women's suffrage. Over 1000 men joined the various men's societies and many, many more joined the various mixed-sex organisations.

Men could be members of the NUWSS but were not eligible to join the WSPU – the Pankhursts believed that the suffrage struggle was a women's movement that could only be conducted by women. Thus, men founded their own organisations to support the suffragettes: the Men's League for Women's Suffrage and the Men's Federation for Women's Suffrage (this later became the Men's Political Union) were two of the most important. Others included the **Men's Committee for Justice to Women**, the **Men's Declaration Committee**, the **Male Electors' League for Women's Suffrage** and the Liberal Men's Association for Women's Suffrage. There were also local men's organisations such as the **Rebels' Social and Political Union** active in the East End of

London, the **Cambridge University Men's League** and the **Northern Men's Federation for Women's Suffrage**.

Men's League for Women's Suffrage

The first male-only organisation, the Men's League for Women's Suffrage, was established in 1907 and attracted men from all shades of political and religious opinion. By 1910 it had ten branches in Britain: a branch was even formed as far north as Inverness. Although the League was founded by Emmeline Pethwick-Lawrence's brother-in-law and had Lord Lytton as President, it appeared to have more in common with the NUWSS and the WFL rather than the WSPU. Both Fawcett and Despard (notably not the Pankhursts) attended its first public meeting. Furthermore, the League favoured the law-abiding, peaceful methods of the NUWSS, rather than the law-breaking confrontational style of the WSPU, as the leaflet advertising their first public meeting in 1907 demonstrates: 'We do not proceed by any uproarious methods; we content ourselves with appealing to the thoughtfulness of men.' Members of the league participated in demonstrations, wrote leaflets and pamphlets, organised petitions, lobbied MPs in support of women's suffrage and acted as a conduit between the suffragists and the government. In 1909 a declaration issued by the league contained a list of important men, including influential MPs, Church leaders, high-ranking army officers, academics and writers, in favour of votes for women. It published its own paper, *The Men's League Monthly Paper*.

Men's Political Union

The second major organisation, the Men's Federation for Women's Suffrage, which was later renamed the Men's Political Union, was formally constituted in 1910. By 1912 it had branches in Birmingham, Bristol, Glasgow, Hull, Leeds, London, Manchester, Newcastle, Norwich, Oxford and other places. The federation, which advocated militancy, stated that:

> Firstly, the policy of this Union is action, entirely independent of political parties; secondly, opposition to whatever government is in power, until such time as the franchise is granted; thirdly, participation in parliamentary elections in opposition to the government candidate, and independently of all other candidates; and lastly, vigorous agitation and the education of public opinion by all the usual methods, such as public meetings, demonstrations, debates, distribution of literature, newspaper correspondence and deputations to public representatives.

The Federation identified more with the WSPU, using the same suffragette colours of purple, white and green, than with the NUWSS. It believed that if men were really anxious to help women achieve the vote they should sever all connections with party politics and devote their energies to the suffrage cause. There is no doubt that many men who belonged to the Federation gave much time and commitment to women's suffrage, combining traditional forms of protest with militant ones. For example:

- It helped the ELFS to organise a march from the East End of London to Trafalgar Square.
- When women were shut out of Liberal meetings, members of the Federation went in to represent them.
- It heckled Liberal ministers: one man had his leg fractured in two places when he was thrown out of a meeting in Bradford.
- One man attacked Winston Churchill with a whip; two more threw mouse traps at the MPs in Parliament from the Strangers' Gallery in protest at the Cat and Mouse Act.
- Some broke windows.
- Some attempted arson; **Harold Laski**, for example, tried (unsuccessfully) to destroy a railway station in 1913.

Harold Laski 1893–1950; married to a militant suffragette, Laski was a committed socialist who formed the Left Book Club to spread socialist ideas. He later became chair of the Labour Party.

As a result of these protests, men were imprisoned and, like women, went on hunger strike and were either released under the Cat and Mouse Act or forcibly fed. One man who had set fire to a railway carriage was convicted, imprisoned and force-fed 114 times. Altogether 40 men were imprisoned for suffragette activities.

The response of the WSPU to male support

The WSPU initially welcomed this kind of male support, but by 1912 the Federation found itself out of favour with the WSPU. Indeed, Emmeline Pethick-Lawrence stated that 'Men in prison only embarrass us'. As suffrage historian Sandra Holton points out, male violence was different from women's:

- Female violence could be justified because women were excluded from traditional peaceful forms of political protest: because they had the vote, men could make their voices heard within the constitution. They had no need to resort to violence. Hence, Holton argues, male violence was seen by the WSPU to 'threaten the legitimacy of militant protest'.
- Suffragette militancy was justified by the suffragettes as part of a sex war with heroic, freedom-fighting women pitted against intransigent and violent men. The men who fought so hard for women's suffrage undermined this particular narrative because, as men, they were the enemy but, as members of the Federation, they were friends. Nevertheless, although exact figures are unknown, the number of men who joined the federation was extremely small so the suffragettes were able to maintain their general beliefs about men.

Key question
How successful was the Men's League?

Men's League for Opposing Women's Suffrage

Men also formed organisations to oppose women's suffrage. In 1908 a Men's League for Opposing Women's Suffrage was formed, but it was short-lived and in 1910 it amalgamated with the Ladies' League. The new League depended on Conservatives and Liberal Unionists for their support. It used similar tactics to the suffragists: they campaigned across the country, held meetings, collected signatures, raised funds and published their own paper, the *Anti-Suffrage Review*. However, most of the members of the

Men's League for Opposing Women's Suffrage founded: 1908

newly amalgamated league were women, and it was they who did most of the work. Men helped to fund-raise, placed their names on the headed notepaper and spoke on platforms, but it was women who kept the organisation running on a daily basis.

In some respects the opposition did rather better than those supportive of votes for women. During 1908 it collected 337,018 signatures against votes for women, whereas the suffragists only managed to obtain 288,736 in support of votes for women a year later. This group, which had a membership of approximately 9000, was significantly larger than the combined numbers of those organisations in favour of women's suffrage. Of course, the fact that an opposition group was formed was an indication that votes for women was considered an important question. Until the early years of the twentieth century those opposed to votes for women thought it unnecessary to organise because women's suffrage was just so ridiculous that it could not be taken seriously.

6 | Research and Men's Support of Votes for Women

Key question
What are the research problems associated with men and female suffrage?

The suffrage movement may have received a mixed response from those men who belonged to formal organisations, but it was hopelessly unsuccessful in convincing the majority of British men. The evidence that is available – from famous individuals, from popular music hall songs, from the banning of women from certain places, and from the increasing level of violence in the crowds that gathered around women's demonstrations – points to a generally hostile reaction. However, it is difficult, if not impossible, to measure the extent to which these particular groups were representative of male opinion as a whole. In addition, research on the history of men and the suffrage movement remains sparse, making it hard to assess the level of either sympathy or hostility from men in general. It is tempting to suppose that the majority of men were apathetic and impartial rather than antagonistic, but the evidence so far suggests that historians cannot make any very definite worthwhile judgements either way.

The research bias of historians

There is still much more research needed on the relation of men to the women's suffrage movement, but the history written so far has been affected by distinct social trends. At first, women's suffrage was subsumed under men's history: for example, George Dangerfield's book written in the 1950s examines the suffrage movement as part of a general Liberal political decline. With the rise of a separate women's history in the 1970s, women's suffrage became part of that history with the result that men were ignored.

In a curious twist of historiography, suffrage history came to be built around the ultimately victorious female, with men largely eliminated from the story except as the implacable opposition. Just as women used to be hidden from men's history, so men were hidden from women's suffrage history.

Until 1997, when *The Men's Sphere* was published, there had virtually been no research on organised male support of suffrage, or the responses of religious organisations, or of newspaper coverage. Of course, histories that exclude these topics – like histories that exclude women – are not only inadequate, but inaccurate, because they portray only a partial view of the world. Historians must therefore question the *female* bias in suffrage history and *men's* invisibility, and argue for a reappraisal of history based on the experiences of both sexes.

Nonetheless, it is odd to write about men's involvement in what was essentially a women's movement. Men's support of the suffrage campaign certainly raises important questions about the traditional role of men and women. Men who supported the female franchise usually behaved in a supportive capacity to women. This, of course, is an interesting reversal of customary practice as it is usually women who take a back seat in political movements. What is more, even the men who opposed women's suffrage reacted to events rather than initiated them, a role reversal that, paradoxically, must have ultimately undermined their beliefs about women's role in society.

Men and votes for women in 1914

Historians agree that by the outbreak of the First World War in 1914 the suffrage movement had reached an impasse. Although there were considerable numbers of men across the class, political and religious spectrum who supported women's suffrage, there were also considerable numbers who opposed it. Nevertheless, there was still a clear trend towards greater acceptance of the female vote. Parliament appeared little different from the nation at large in that MPs held a variety of opinions towards women's suffrage, ranging from sympathetic and indifferent to hostile. Liberal commitment to votes for women was muted, largely because of the intransigence of Asquith. But he too was changing his mind and had agreed to include women's suffrage as part of a new electoral system. Conservative opinion was generally opposed, while Labour was too insignificant a party to have much effect at all. It would take the trauma of war to break this particular deadlock.

Summary diagram: Men and votes for women

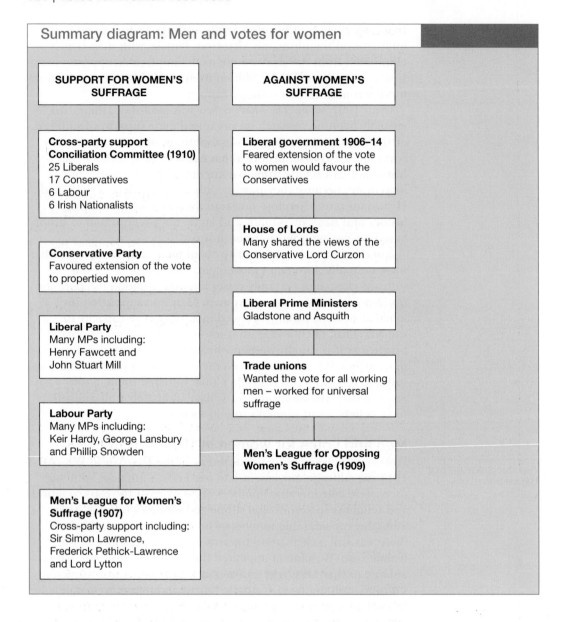

SUPPORT FOR WOMEN'S SUFFRAGE

AGAINST WOMEN'S SUFFRAGE

Cross-party support Conciliation Committee (1910)
25 Liberals
17 Conservatives
6 Labour
6 Irish Nationalists

Conservative Party
Favoured extension of the vote to propertied women

Liberal Party
Many MPs including:
Henry Fawcett and
John Stuart Mill

Labour Party
Many MPs including:
Keir Hardy, George Lansbury and Phillip Snowden

Men's League for Women's Suffrage (1907)
Cross-party support including:
Sir Simon Lawrence,
Frederick Pethick-Lawrence and Lord Lytton

Liberal government 1906–14
Feared extension of the vote to women would favour the Conservatives

House of Lords
Many shared the views of the Conservative Lord Curzon

Liberal Prime Ministers
Gladstone and Asquith

Trade unions
Wanted the vote for all working men – worked for universal suffrage

Men's League for Opposing Women's Suffrage (1909)

Study Guide: AS Questions

In the style of Edexcel

Study Sources 1, 2 and 3 below and then answer the question that follows.

Source 1

The Prime Minister, Herbert Asquith, gives his views on female suffrage to representatives of the National League for Opposing Women's Suffrage, on 12 December 1912.

I occupy a somewhat peculiar position in regard to this question. As an individual, I am in entire agreement with you that the grant of the parliamentary franchise to women in this country would be a political mistake of a very disastrous kind. On the other hand, I am the head of the Government in which a majority of my colleagues are of a different opinion.

However, I hope that if the case against female suffrage were clearly put to the country, then public opinion would declare that it is not fair to make this gigantic experiment of giving women the vote.

Source 2

From The March of the Women *by Martin Pugh, published in 2000.*

There is a traditional view that comes from the suffragettes and suffragists themselves. It is that female suffrage was a good cause, well explained to the public. However, the tradition goes, it was frustrated by trickery and weakness on the part of dishonourable politicians. However, despite the skill and determination of its supporters, the cause had some serious flaws.

Source 3

From Viscount Ullswater, A Speaker's Commentaries, 1925. James Lowther (later Viscount Ullswater) comments on the effects of suffragette violence on Parliament's attitude to the women's cause. Lowther was the Speaker of the House of Commons during the period of suffragette militancy. He had been a Conservative MP and was personally opposed to women's suffrage.

By 1913, the activities of the militant suffragettes had reached a stage at which nothing was safe from their attacks. The feeling in the House of Commons, caused by these lawless actions, hardened the opposition to the demands of the suffragettes. As a result, on 6 May the private member's bill that would have given women the vote, for which the Government had promised parliamentary time so that it could become law, was rejected by the House of Commons by a majority of forty seven.

Study Sources 1, 2 and 3
Do you agree with the view that, in the years 1903–14, giving women the right to vote was delayed by 'trickery and weakness' on the part of politicians? Use the sources and your own knowledge to answer the question. (40 marks)

Source: adapted from Edexcel, January 2004

Exam tips

The cross-references are intended to take you straight to the material that will help you to answer the question.

In planning your response to this question you will first need to establish the issues the selection of sources raises. Here you will be using your skills of making inferences from the sources to work out the implications of what is being said. You will also be using your skills of cross-referencing – comparing the sources to see where there are points of difference or corroboration. You will also be using skills of evaluation of the evidence provided by the contemporary figures in Sources 1 and 3. When you have identified the issues the source selection raises, you should integrate your own knowledge into the plan. Aim to develop further the points that you have raised from the sources. Then ask yourself whether there are there new points the sources don't raise but which are important to the answer. For example, the issue of the Irish Nationalists (see below) is not given in the sources.

Note that you are being asked whether the vote was delayed by 'trickery' and 'weakness' on the part of politicians so you need to address both aspects of this. In Asquith's speech to the National League he affirms his implacable opposition to votes for women, believing that 'the grant of the parliamentary franchise to women in this country would be a political mistake of a very disastrous kind'. Here was no trickery or weakness but genuine political belief. Yet, as Asquith pointed out, the majority of his colleagues disagreed with him. You will therefore need to be aware of the attitudes and actions of politicians beyond those of Asquith (see pages 104–6). How did MPs in the Conservative, Liberal and Labour parties react? Don't forget too about the Conciliation Committee and its work – you should be able to offer appropriate knowledge of the Conciliation and other Bills in this period (see pages 101–2).

From 1910 the Liberal government was hampered by being beholden to the Irish Nationalists. You need to show why it was such an issue (Liberals did not enjoy an overall majority and were dependent on the Irish Nationalists) and what its relationship was to female suffrage (Irish Nationalists were opposed), and explore the role of the Irish Nationalists after 1910 (wanted time allocated to Home Rule and did not want unpopular measures to undermine this). Avoiding the question of votes for women at such a sensitive period could be construed as political acumen rather than either trickery or weakness on the part of the Liberal government. Here you might argue that women's suffrage was only one of a number of issues facing the government (see pages 110–11).

Of course, you also need to examine the role of the suffragists and the suffragettes in gaining the vote. As Pugh notes, the cause had some serious flaws. You need to offer clear evidence of the effect of militancy on politicians and whether or not it was a factor in delaying women's suffrage. You can also use Source 3 here to show that the activities of the militant suffragettes hardened opposition within the House of Commons. It is also important to use the information about the author to help you think about what weight to place on what Viscount Ullswater says. He's certainly in an excellent position to comment on events and attitudes within the House of Commons. Do you think his own attitude to women's suffrage makes a difference here? You may conclude that it doesn't, but examiners will want to see that you have considered this, and to see your reasons for your decision.

Another issue you can develop from Pugh's account is: was female suffrage well explained to the public? To what extent did votes for women gain widespread support? In conclusion, the sources indicate that neither trickery nor weakness can explain the delay in achieving votes for women since there were so many other factors, including opposition by the Prime Minister, methods used by the suffragettes and wider political issues facing a government with declining electoral support.

In the style of AQA

(a) Explain why the Liberal government was reluctant to grant votes to women in the years 1906–10. (12 marks)

(b) 'During the period 1908–14, the suffragette campaigns harmed their cause.' Explain why you agree or disagree with this statement. (24 marks)

Exam tips

The cross-references are intended to take you straight to the material that will help you to answer the questions.

(a) You will find a list of suggestions as to why the Liberal government was reluctant to give women the vote on pages 110–11, but don't forget you must not simply list these factors, you must also explain them. You should think carefully about their relative importance and effect and consider how they interlink. To obtain top marks you need to show some personal evaluation of the reasons and provide a supported judgement.

(b) Look back at page 82 in Chapter 3. You will need to discuss the tactics used by the suffragettes in and after 1908 when suffragette militancy increased. You should try to assess whether such tactics, as a whole or individually, had any positive or negative effect, on the suffragette campaigns. The tactics would include tax and census evasion, window-smashing, arson, attacks in art galleries and elsewhere and the death of Emily Davison. You should also consider the impact of the hunger strikes and assess whether these increased or decreased public and government.

6 Women, Suffrage and the First World War

POINTS TO CONSIDER

The Great War (as the First World War was called) is often seen as a turning point in suffrage history. Shortly after war was declared on Germany in August 1914, most of the women's suffrage groups abandoned their campaign for the vote in favour of supporting the war effort. By the end of the chapter you should be able to decide the extent to which women achieved the vote as a result of their work in the First World War.

This chapter will examine:

• The suffrage movement and the war
• Women's war work and the vote
• War, suffrage and the government

Key dates

1914	August	First World War began
	September	WSPU abandoned campaign for the vote
		Amnesty for suffragettes granted
		Women's Volunteer Reserve (WVR) founded
1915	May	Asquith formed coalition government
	July	Right to Serve march
		National Register Bill
	October	Suffragettes of the Women's Social and Political Union founded
1916	March	Independent Women's Social and Political Union founded
		Speaker's Conference
	December	Lloyd George replaced Asquith as Prime Minister
1917		Women's Auxiliary Army Corps (WAACS) founded
		Women's Royal Naval Service (WRNS) founded
		Women's Land Army founded
1918	February	Representation of the People Act gave votes to women over the age of 30
		Women's Royal Air Force (WRAFS) founded
	November	End of war

1 | The Suffrage Movement and the War

The First World War had a profound effect on suffrage politics. In August 1914, as Britain was going to war against Germany, the Women's Social and Political Union (WSPU) declared peace with the Liberals – the sex war, as historian Martin Pugh has pointed out, was swamped by the Great War. Emmeline Pankhurst remarked that there was no point in continuing to fight for the vote when there might be no country to vote in. Most of the other suffrage societies agreed with her, discontinued their suffrage campaign and shifted their energies to support the war effort. In return, the government declared an **amnesty** for all imprisoned suffragettes on condition that they did not break the law again.

It may seem reasonable to suppose that both the suffragettes and the suffragists helped women to gain the vote by leading their organisations to support the war effort. Yet, while this is a plausible explanation, it is only partially valid, as the response of the women's suffrage movement to war was varied. Certainly, the WSPU led the way in patriotism, followed less enthusiastically by the National Union of Women's Suffrage Societies (NUWSS). However, not all women's suffrage groups supported the war: the Women's Freedom League and the East London Federation of Suffragettes (ELFS) were opposed to it. Nevertheless, war did bring militant suffragette activity to a sudden halt, thus making it easier for the government to concede votes for women at a later date.

The Women's Social and Political Union (WSPU)

When war was declared in August 1914 the WSPU and its members abandoned their violent methods and demonstrated a new patriotic loyalty. Emmeline Pankhurst and her daughter, Christabel, saw the war, just as they had the suffrage question, as the 'goodies' fighting the 'baddies', as a battle between a democratic Britain and an autocratic Germany. Germany – like their previous enemy the Liberal government – was depicted as the world's bully. In the view of the Pankhursts, Germany had provoked war. At a large meeting held in September 1914, Christabel Pankhurst pleaded for Britain to support the 'feminine' state of France that had been threatened by the 'over-masculine' state of Germany. God, according to the Pankhursts, was firmly on the British side.

The jingoism of the leaders of the WSPU matched that of the general public as the suffragettes became arch-patriots. In 1915 *The Suffragette* newspaper was renamed *Britannia* (taken from the nationalistic song **'Rule Britannia'**) and in November 1917 the name of the WSPU was changed to the Women's Party.

Activities of the WSPU

Within a few days of war, Emmeline Pankhurst threw herself into a vigorous campaign in which the defeat of Germany took priority over women's suffrage. Ironically, one of the Pankhursts'

Key question
How far did women's contributions to the war effort help women to gain the vote?

Key dates

First World War began: August 1914

Amnesty for suffragettes granted: 1914

WSPU abandoned campaign for the vote: September 1914

Key question
Why did the WSPU abandon its campaign for votes for women?

Key terms

Amnesty
A general pardon for political offences.

'Rule Britannia'
A nationalistic song written in the mid-eighteenth century. The words of the chorus are 'Rule, Britannia! Britannia, rule the waves; Britons never will be slaves'.

Key dates

National Register Bill:
July 1915

Right to Serve march:
July 1915

greatest principles, that of the unity of women, disappeared at a stroke. The fight against Germany, Emmeline Pankhurst declared, 'was a very much bigger thing than the vote itself … what we are asking for and working for and longing for is to preserve those institutions which would admit of women having the Vote. If we lose this war then … not only is the possibility of women voting going to disappear, but votes for men will be a thing of the past'.

With somewhat alarming alacrity, the WSPU placed its organisation, and its funds, at the disposal of the government. From 1915 onwards there was a great shortage of labour: two million men had joined the armed forces at a time of pressing demand for increased munitions production. To encourage women to join the workforce, Lloyd George, now Minister of Munitions, liaised with the WSPU. Enmities between the two were quickly overcome. Demonstrations, largely financed by Lloyd George and co-ordinated by the WSPU, were organised to publicise the need for women to join the labour force. For example, the WSPU was given £2000 to stage a 'women's right to serve' march (known as the Great Procession of Women), on 17 July 1915. It was the Pankhursts who persuaded Lloyd George to establish training schools for women in munitions, it was they who first put forward the idea of a women's Land Army (see page 145) and it was they who helped to set up a National Register of women workers. Eventually in July 1915 a National Register Bill was passed under which all people, male or female, between the ages of 15 and 65 had to register.

Emmeline and Christabel Pankhurst once again travelled around the country, this time to encourage men to work hard for the war effort and to recruit women for the munitions factories. They set about promoting the war effort world-wide: visiting Russia to encourage them to keep fighting and touring the USA and Canada to speak on women and war service. At home, they called for **military conscription** for men, **industrial conscription** for women and the abolition of trade unions for the duration of the war. Furthermore, the WSPU demanded that **conscientious objectors** and Germans living in Britain be interned.

Both Pankhursts worked closely with Lloyd George to prevent strike action and the influence of trade unions. In February 1915, for example, Emmeline Pankhurst visited a factory and shipyard in Newcastle to thwart an expected strike. While there she found out the names of the ring-leaders and promptly sent them to Lloyd George. Some time later she enquired what had happened to the ring-leaders and was informed that they had been sent to the front. We do not know her response, or whether the trade union leaders were really sent to the trenches, but it is safe to say that Emmeline Pankhurst's patriotism knew no bounds.

Votes for women and the WSPU

Nevertheless, neither Emmeline nor Christabel Pankhurst lost sight of women's suffrage. They may not have campaigned for votes for women, but during the war years they used their new

Key terms

Military conscription
Compulsory enlistment for the armed forces.

Industrial conscription
Compulsory work for the government.

Conscientious objector
Someone who refuses to fight for their country on the grounds that war is wrong.

friendship with Lloyd George to promote it wherever possible. Emmeline Pankhurst continuously claimed that women's efforts in the war had shown that they were ready for the franchise. 'When the clash of arms ceases', she insisted 'the demand will again be made. If it is not quickly granted, then once more the women will take up the arms they today generously lay down.' On Thursday, 29 March 1917, Emmeline Pankhurst accompanied Millicent Fawcett and others to 10 Downing Street to meet Lloyd George and **William Astor**. At the meeting the suffragette leader reminded the two men that she and the WSPU had abandoned all suffrage work to help with the war effort and urged Lloyd George to lead Parliament in giving votes to women.

Splits in the WSPU

Not all WSPU members agreed with the Pankhurst pronouncements and their use of WSPU funds to promote the war effort. As a consequence, two different groups split from the WSPU to form their own suffrage organisations: the Suffragettes of the Women's Social and Political Union (SWSPU) in October 1915 and the Independent Women's Social and Political Union (IWSPU) in March 1916. Unfortunately, apart from a brief mention in a few books, these groups have largely been ignored by historians. However, each group produced its own paper, the *Suffragette News Sheet* and *The Independent Suffragette*, which provide some opportunities for historical research.

The East London Federation of Suffragettes (ELFS)

In marked contrast to her flag-waving relatives, Sylvia Pankhurst condemned the war, supported conscientious objection and stuck to her socialist principles. At times the ELFS even preached treason: 'We believe that the conscientious objector who refuses to become a soldier, the soldiers who establish a truce in the trenches, and the people which forces its government to make peace, are all fighting the same fight.' In the midst of war the ELFS published a letter from a German politician urging suffragettes to fight both for the vote and for peace. Sylvia Pankhurst participated in a Women's Peace Conference at The Hague in the Netherlands, and was elected to the Executive Committee of the **Women's International League for Peace and Freedom**.

By the end of the war Sylvia Pankhurst believed that only a complete change in society could bring equality to women. She, and her organisation, applauded the **Bolshevik revolution** in Russia because 'the capitalist system of society is irreconcilable with the freedom and the just demands of the workers'. In her view, capitalism should be got rid of and socialism put in its place. It is therefore not surprising that in 1916 the ELFS first changed its name to the Workers' Suffrage Federation and later in 1918 to the Workers' Socialist Federation, with a corresponding change in their newspaper title from *The Women's Dreadnought* to *The Workers' Dreadnought* in 1917. This paper became an influential socialist newspaper of the war: Siegfried Sassoon first published his famous anti-war 'Soldier's Declaration' in the *Dreadnought*.

Activities of the ELFS

Throughout the war Sylvia Pankhurst and the ELFS campaigned for **civil liberties**, for the control of food prices and profits, and for the **nationalisation** of the food supply. Towards the end of the war they demanded the abolition of private profit and even suggested that food be supplied free, paid for by council tax. The plight of working-class women concerned the ELFS and much of its effort revolved around improving their lives. For example:

- The ELFS campaigned for better rates of pay in charitable organisations such as Queen Mary's Workshops, a factory set up by **Queen Mary** to employ women during the war. Sylvia Pankhurst criticised this charity for not paying its workers enough to live on.
- The ELFS organised petitions, demonstrations and deputations about the pay and conditions in munitions factories to Lloyd George, and campaigned for equal pay for equal work, arguing that it was 'vitally important that every woman shall refuse to do a man's work unless she gets a man's pay'.
- The war brought distress to soldiers' wives and dependants and so the ELFS campaigned widely on their behalf. In 1914 it protested against the threat to discontinue the allowances of women found guilty of misconduct, immorality or child neglect. In 1915, along with the Labour MP George Lansbury, the ELFS also formed the League of Rights for Soldiers and Sailors' Wives and Relatives to fight for an increase in the separation allowances paid to women whose husbands were away fighting.
- Sylvia Pankhurst, and her organisation, opened an unemployment bureau and set up a toy and boot factory to help the unemployed. The ELFS set up five centres in the East End of London, which offered free milk to mothers and a nurse to advise on the health of their babies; it converted an old pub called the Gunmakers' Arms into a nursery and renamed it the Mothers' Arms; and it opened a cost-price restaurant that offered dinner at well below the price charged by local restaurants.
- When the government introduced **Regulation 40D** in March 1918 the ELFS, along with other feminist groups, opposed it.

Sylvia Pankhurst continually argued for women's suffrage and adult suffrage. Along with members from her East End group, she lobbied MPs not to support a limited franchise for women. She set up and was a member of various suffrage organisations that she left when they ceased to be as radical as she wished. All were very small indeed; for example:

Key terms

Civil liberties
Freedom of action and speech.

Nationalisation
The government takeover of an industry or business from private ownership.

Regulation 40D
A law passed in 1918 that made it a crime for women with a sexually transmitted disease to have, or even suggest to have, sexual intercourse with anyone in the armed forces.

Key figure

Queen Mary
1867–1953; the wife of George V, who ascended the British throne in 1910.

- the National Council for Adult Suffrage founded to pressurise MPs to support full adult suffrage
- the Labour Council for Adult Suffrage founded to campaign for adult suffrage.

Certainly, Sylvia Pankhurst lost her plea for universal adult suffrage when only women over the age of 30 gained the vote in 1918. From the evidence charted above, and the fact that it was a tiny organisation, it is difficult to believe that the government wished to reward the ELFS for their emphatically negative reaction to the war. However, in much of its practice, the ELFS mirrored the work of other suffrage organisations by focusing on relief work. For much of the time Sylvia Pankhurst acted as social worker rather than working socialist.

Women's Freedom League (WFL)

Charlotte Despard, leader of the Women's Freedom League (WFL), shared Sylvia Pankhurst's belief that the war was an imperialist venture. These two ardent socialists rejected the overwhelming, and to their eyes, unthinking patriotism of their former colleagues. The fact that Despard's brother was Chief of Staff of the British Army did not deter her from becoming active in the peace campaign. In her view the British government had not done enough to avoid war so she supported the campaign of the Women's Peace Council for a negotiated peace.

Unfortunately the members of the WFL disagreed with her politics, disassociated themselves from her position and declared that Despard's pacifism was in no way representative of their organisation. During the war it suspended its militant activity and continued, in a somewhat limited way, to campaign for women's suffrage. In 1916 it lobbied MPs to support votes for women. For the most part it concentrated on ameliorating the conditions of war for women. The WFL, for example:

- set up the Women's Police Volunteers in 1914 (see page 141)
- founded the Woman's Suffrage National Aid Corps, which helped women who were suffering economically because of the war
- founded a settlement which supplied about 200 vegetarian meals a day
- opened the Despard Arms, a public house which served soft drinks only
- ran a children's play club.

The National Union of Women's Suffrage Societies (NUWSS)

Meanwhile the NUWSS was bitterly divided over the war. While there were some members who wholeheartedly supported the war effort, there were others who were ambivalent and still others who were unwilling to support it at all. Millicent Fawcett had signed an appeal for peace at the beginning of August 1914, but she changed her mind a few days later when war broke out and

Key question
How did the Women's Freedom League respond to war?

Key question
In what ways did the NUWSS help the suffrage cause in the war?

declared: 'Women, your country needs you'. War, she believed, was the gravest crisis facing Britain, for if Germany won it would destroy the democratic institutions of Parliament. Nonetheless, as Brian Harrison points out, Fawcett 'was no flag-waving jingoist; she opposed the idea of giving **white feathers** ... regretted the need for conscription and repudiated vulgar anti-German feeling'. Nevertheless, she felt it unwise to link suffrage with the controversy over pacifism versus patriotism.

Not all members of the NUWSS agreed with Fawcett, preferring to retain their identity as suffragists rather than be swept away by a wave of **chauvinism**. Eventually these disagreements led to a division in the NUWSS, especially when it did not support the international Women's Peace Conference held at The Hague. Fawcett, in particular, refused to associate the NUWSS with the conference because she feared that its reputation would be damaged if it was associated with pacifism. In 1915 all the national officers, apart from Millicent Fawcett and the Treasurer, resigned and helped to form the Women's International League for Peace and Freedom.

Wartime relief work

Whatever their attitude towards the war almost all of the suffragists were active in wartime relief work. Indeed, relief work served to heal some of the divisions within the NUWSS and strengthened the bonds between the remaining membership. One of the first tasks of the NUWSS was to establish a register of voluntary workers, who would in turn find suitable work for the unemployed. When war broke out there was a dramatic increase in female unemployment as many of the industries such as dressmaking, which employed large numbers of women, virtually collapsed as richer women cut back on their purchase of luxury goods. Other industries failed as well, leaving many women out of work; for example, cotton, when the German market ended, and fisheries, when the North Sea was closed to shipping. By September 1914 over 44 per cent of women were unemployed.

In response to this high female unemployment, members of the NUWSS set to work organising the unemployed. In Birmingham, it opened a clothes factory and a dining room for pregnant and nursing mothers as well as establishing **women patrols** to 'protect the honour of young girls' and guard against prostitution. At the outbreak of war the Dundee branch offered to help the city council to alleviate poverty and distress caused by war; in London, the NUWSS established a Women's Service Bureau that worked with Belgian refugees, War Relief Committees, Red Cross Units, Hospital Stores and Canteens.

By 1915, as men were called to the front, there was a shortage of workers so the NUWSS, as with the other suffrage organisations, set up an employment register and interviewed women to replace the men sent to the front. It supplied:

- women for munitions work. Indeed, the first 80 munitions workers at the Woolwich Arsenal were recruited by the London

Society, as were supervisors and workers for munitions factories all over Britain
* the first 100 female bus conductors to the London General Omnibus Company.

It also trained women in welding, dentistry, glass-blowing and other occupations.

Votes for women and the NUWSS
The NUWSS remained committed to women's suffrage. Unlike the WSPU it left its organisational structure intact so that it would be in a position to recommence suffrage activities when the time was right. Indeed, the NUWSS used the same staff and organising facilities for its charitable work as it had for the vote. Some branches, such as Birmingham's, never lost sight of the suffrage cause and held meetings and demonstrations and drafted petitions to promote votes for women. This was significant, for whenever the franchise question was raised in the House of Commons the NUWSS was well placed to lobby trade unions, municipal authorities, the press and the government in support of women's suffrage.

Advertisement for a recruitment rally in Glasgow. How useful is this poster to a historian researching into women's war effort and the vote?

Certainly, the hard work of both the suffragettes and the suffragists during the war ended the spectre of militancy and conferred respectability on the suffrage cause. It was thought that the women involved in the suffrage movement had shown themselves to be responsible and mature beings who were more than capable of taking part in the democracy that they had worked hard to defend.

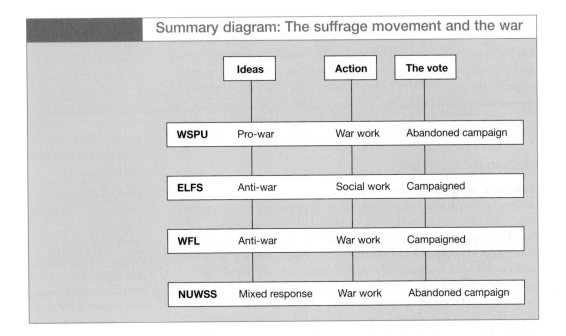

Summary diagram: The suffrage movement and the war

	Ideas	Action	The vote
WSPU	Pro-war	War work	Abandoned campaign
ELFS	Anti-war	Social work	Campaigned
WFL	Anti-war	War work	Campaigned
NUWSS	Mixed response	War work	Abandoned campaign

2 | Women's War Work and the Vote

Key question
To what extent did women gain the vote because of their war work?

When women were enfranchised in 1918 billboards announced that 'The Nation Thanks the Women'. It seemed as if a grateful nation, overwhelmed by the sacrifices of munitions workers in particular, was now granting them suffrage as reward for their efforts. Is this true? Or was it that women were now being enfranchised because the war had changed masculine perceptions about women's role in society? Now, for the first time, women were accepted in the public world of work, and this acceptance led, ultimately, to their participation in the public world of politics.

From the outset, women of all social classes were absorbed into the war effort and played a crucial part on the home front. Many upper- and middle-class women experienced their first taste of paid work during the war, entering occupations that would have been deemed unsuitable in peacetime. Working-class women joined the workforce in unprecedented numbers, taking on jobs that had once been thought of as men's. Women who had been active in the suffrage campaign did not disappear but became involved in wartime activities.

Middle-class women and work

Helping the wounded

Former suffragettes like **Dr Louisa Garrett Anderson** helped to form the Women's Hospital Corps (WHC), which organised military hospitals in Paris, London and northern France. The WHC recruited many other former suffragettes, most of whom wore purple, white and green ribbons pinned to their hospital uniforms. Others established field hospitals. One of the most important initiatives of the NUWSS was the setting up and financing of Scottish Women's Hospitals Units. Led by **Dr Elsie Inglis**, these units employed all-female teams of doctors, nurses and ambulance drivers to work on the front lines of the war in some of the worst of the fighting zones. By 1918 there were 14 medical units operating in Corsica, France, Salonika, Serbia and elsewhere. The NUWSS also provided medical help for civilians whose lives had been disrupted by the war.

Nursing the wounded

Voluntary Aid Detachment (VAD)

A significant number of middle- and upper-class women joined the Voluntary Aid Detachment (VAD). This was formed in 1909, but was greatly expanded during the war, to nurse injured soldiers both at home and at the front. These women have often been portrayed romantically as heroines who sacrificed their privileged upbringing to nurse the sick and wounded. Vera Brittain (a famous writer and mother of former MP Shirley Williams), who was about to go to Oxford University when war was declared, wrote about her experiences as a young VAD gazing 'half-hypnotized, at the dishevelled beds, the stretchers on the floor, the scattered boots and piles of muddy khaki, the brown blankets turned back from smashed limbs bound to splints by filthy blood-stained bandages. Beneath each stinking wad of sodden wool and gauze an obscene horror waited for me.' Criticism was sometimes made of these middle- and upper-class girls who perhaps spent a morning at the hospital while domestic servants cleaned their homes. Nevertheless, these nurses generally received a sympathetic press and were seen to deserve the vote.

First Aid Nursing Yeomanry (FANY)

Others joined the First Aid Nursing Yeomanry (FANY), founded in 1907, whose 'aim was to assist the Military and Civilian authorities in times of emergency'. Its members drove ambulances to the front to collect the wounded, ran field hospitals and set up canteens for the troops. By the end of the war members of FANY had been awarded a number of military distinctions, including 17 military medals, one Legion D'Honneur and 27 Croix de Guerre for their work in dangerous circumstances.

Key question
How did former suffragettes and suffragists contribute to wartime medical care?

Key figures

Dr Louisa Garrett Anderson
1873–1943; daughter of Elisabeth Garrett Anderson, Louisa trained at the London School of Medicine for Women. She was imprisoned in 1912 for militancy.

Dr Elsie Inglis
1864–1917; born in India, studied medicine in Edinburgh and founded her own medical college. She was a suffragist who helped to found the Scottish Women's Suffrage Federation. In Serbia she was taken prisoner of war. After her repatriation, she travelled to Russia, but left after the Bolshevik revolution.

A Voluntary Aid Detachment (VAD) worker starting up the engine of a motor ambulance, probably in northern France. This photograph was taken in June 1917 by Ernest Brooks, the first British official war photographer to be assigned to the front. Do you think doing this type of work convinced the government to give women the vote?

Key question
What role did women play in the armed forces?

Women's armed forces

Women joined the various women's services set up during the war:

- Women's Volunteer Reserve (WVR) 1914 – later renamed the Women's Legion
- Women's Auxiliary Army Corps (WAACS) 1917
- Women's Royal Naval Service (WRNS) 1917
- Women's Land Army 1917
- Women's Royal Air Force (WRAFS) 1918.

Most women who joined the auxiliary armed forces worked in a supportive capacity, as drivers, messengers, typists, telephonists, storekeepers and cooks, although some received technical training. A few WRAFS were employed as welders and carpenters to work on aeroplanes, but none actually piloted a plane, so they were called penguins: birds who cannot fly. Women from upper- and middle-class backgrounds joined the Land Army as agricultural workers. (Selection boards usually turned down working-class women who volunteered for the Land Army because they were believed to lack the high moral fibre needed for farm life.) On the farm, women were expected to do a wide variety of jobs such as ploughing, planting and harvesting, as well as look after the sheep and other animals. At the very least, the war disposed of one old argument against votes for women: the one that women were incapable of taking part in the defence of the country. Undoubtedly women did play a large part in the nation's defence – at least on the home front – and were certainly entitled to benefit from the consequences.

Working-class women and work

Unlike most of their upper- and middle-class colleagues, working-class women did not go out to work because of the war: they had to work anyway. However, war did change the nature of their occupation. War offered an alternative to grossly exploitative jobs in domestic service or small factories. In fact, domestic service diminished by 400,000 during the war, reducing from 1,658,000 to 1,258,000. At railway stations there were women porters, ticket collectors and guards. Women replaced men as bus drivers, window cleaners, chimney sweeps, coal deliverers, street sweepers, electricians and fire-fighters. By 1917, bus conductresses had gone up from a half a dozen to about 2500 and female transport workers increased from 18,000 in 1914 to 117,000 in 1918. Munitions obviously showed the biggest increase. In 1914, Woolwich Arsenal employed 125 women, whereas by 1917 over 25,000 women worked there.

Key question
How did working-class women help the war effort?

Munitions workers

It was the munitions worker who captured the imagination of the press and the general public. Munitions workers performed a variety of jobs, ranging from filling shells and making bullets to assembling detonators. Their hours were long – sometimes 14 hours a day for weeks on end – and their conditions of work dangerous because they worked with high explosives such as TNT. This explosive also turned the colour of the skin to yellow, so munitions workers were given the nickname of 'Canary Girls'. In Woolwich Arsenal about 37 per cent of the women suffered from stomach pain, nausea and constipation as a result of TNT poisoning. Other symptoms included skin rashes, giddiness, drowsiness and swelling of hands and feet. In 1916 the first deaths from toxic jaundice were reported, but little was done.

Working in a munitions factory was highly dangerous because of the risk of explosion. Safety measures were taken to avoid accidents: each woman had to hand over all personal belongings such as matches, cigarettes, wedding rings and other jewellery before they entered the shell-filling section. Women wore protective clothes without any metal zips in them, garters rather than suspender belts and caps to tie up long hair as metal hair-grips were banned. In spite of these precautions, accidents were common. The most notorious was at Silvertown in the East End of London in 1917, where a number of women were killed in a horrific explosion.

Furthermore, it was the women workers, and the munitions workers more than any other, who disposed of the physical force argument that women were 'by nature incapable of taking part in the defence of the country against foreign enemies'. Each shell packed with TNT, each ambulance driven to the front and each soldier nursed at a field hospital undermined the theory that women were incapable of bearing a share in the national defence.

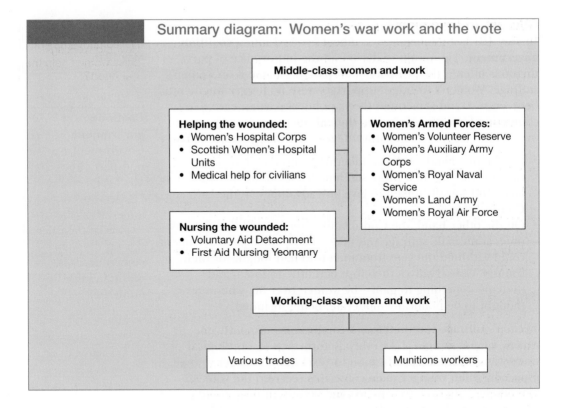

Summary diagram: Women's war work and the vote

Middle-class women and work

Helping the wounded:
- Women's Hospital Corps
- Scottish Women's Hospital Units
- Medical help for civilians

Women's Armed Forces:
- Women's Volunteer Reserve
- Women's Auxiliary Army Corps
- Women's Royal Naval Service
- Women's Land Army
- Women's Royal Air Force

Nursing the wounded:
- Voluntary Aid Detachment
- First Aid Nursing Yeomanry

Working-class women and work

Various trades

Munitions workers

3 | War, Suffrage and the Government

It is important, of course, to examine women's suffrage and war from the perspective of parliamentary politics. For over 50 years before the war an all-male Parliament had been reluctant to enfranchise women, and yet, by the close of war politicians had changed their minds. The reasons for the shifts that took place in government thinking between 1914 and 1918 therefore need consideration. Was it because of women's work in the war? Or did other factors play a part?

Key changes in Parliament

During the war, Parliament witnessed a number of changes with regard to votes for women, most notably in its leadership and its attitude. International changes too helped to convince the government that votes for women were essential if they were to retain their view of Britain as the leader of freedom and democracy.

Key question
How important were parliamentary changes for women's suffrage?

Changes in government

In May 1915, the Liberal government evolved into a **coalition government**. The resulting decline in the importance of party divisions offered the prospect of all-party agreement on women's suffrage. Women's suffrage supporters were no longer fragmented between two, and sometimes three, political parties, each competing for votes. Moreover, the enfranchisement of women over 30 did not present an advantage to any one political party.

- On the one hand, both the Liberals and the Labour Party thought that the new proposed female electorate was much too large and socially mixed to give any advantage to the Conservatives.
- On the other hand, the Conservatives recognised that, by this time, adult male suffrage was unavoidable since no government could withhold the vote from men who had fought for their country. Conservatives therefore had little to lose – and perhaps something to gain – by women over 30, who were thought to be politically moderate, being included.

Women's suffrage was therefore a compromise: no party got exactly what it wanted. Like other Reform Acts it was illogical – there was no rational justification for excluding younger women, especially when younger male conscripts received the vote. Nonetheless, the compromise worked because it maximised support where the more radical proposal of universal suffrage might not. And, of course, men would still be in the majority.

Changes in leadership

There were a number of key changes in Parliament that altered the balance between those who opposed and those who were in favour of votes for women. The appointment of several suffragist MPs to government posts augured well for the success of any women's suffrage amendment. More importantly Lloyd George, who was (more or less) sympathetic to women's suffrage, replaced Asquith as Prime Minister in December 1916. Lloyd George encouraged the previously unsympathetic newspaper *The Times* to carry glowing articles on women war workers to add weight to women's suffrage and influence wavering and antagonistic MPs. And, of course, he worked closely with Christabel and Emmeline Pankhurst during the war to prevent strike action and to minimise the influence of trade unions (see page 137). This new relationship between old adversaries undoubtedly helped when the question of votes for women re-emerged at the end of the war.

Changes in attitude

The war allowed a number of hostile MPs the excuse to climb down from their, now untenable, position of opposing votes for women. These MPs, although not fully converted to women's suffrage, realised that reform was inevitable and so used women's war work as a pretext to recant and save face. Women, so they rationalised, had demonstrated that they were mature and sensible enough to be rewarded with the vote by their significant

Key date — Asquith formed coalition government: May 1915

Key term — **Coalition government** Government run on non-party lines. In 1915 the Conservatives joined the Liberals to govern together during the war emergency. The coalition lasted until 1922.

Key date — Lloyd George replaced Asquith as Prime Minister: December 1916

contribution towards the war effort. Before the war and again in May 1915 Asquith had demonstrated a change of heart over votes for women (see page 106). In his speech on the Speaker's Report in March 1917 he argued that women's war efforts had convinced him that they now deserved the vote.

But his private remarks concerning the female electorate of Paisley in 1920 suggest that he still resented women's involvement in parliamentary politics:

> There are about fifteen thousand women on the Register – a dim, impenetrable lot, for the most part hopelessly ignorant of politics, credulous to the last degree, and flickering with gusts of sentiment like a candle in the wind.

The cartoon below suggests that it might be unchivalrous to enfranchise men and not women. It alludes to the fact that women as well as men helped in the war effort and calls for votes for heroines as well as heroes. Chivalry holds a wreath commemorating the women nurses who died as well as the wounded soldiers. The picture implies the inevitability of an enlarged franchise and a belief that the battle for votes for women had been won: the man seated at the desk is the Prime Minister, Herbert Asquith, who is seen ready to sign his consent. The cartoon is positive in tone about the effect of the vote, indicating that men and women would be able to protect each other in the future.

Front cover of *Votes for Women*, edited by the Pethick-Lawrences, who left the WSPU in 1912.

VOTES FOR HEROINES AS WELL AS HEROES

CHIVALRY: "Men and women protect one another in the hour of death. With the addition of the woman's vote, they would be able to protect one another in life as well."

Changes internationally

Finally, Britain was merely reflecting an international trend towards full democracy. Women in New Zealand, Australia, Finland, Denmark and Norway had already been enfranchised. Canada (except Quebec) had granted votes for women in 1917, as had four US states. And just as the debate was taking place on women's suffrage in Britain, the US House of Representatives carried votes for women by a two-thirds majority (even though it was not ratified until August 1920). It would have been a peculiar political embarrassment if Britain – the 'mother of democracy' – had lagged behind those offspring countries.

Need for franchise reform: the Speaker's Conference

Perhaps most importantly, there was a need for franchise reform in general. The existing franchise law required men who qualified as householders to have occupied a dwelling for at least a year prior to an election. Large numbers of the armed forces were thus ineligible to vote because they no longer held or had never held a 12-month residency. And a significant minority of men, who had risked their lives fighting in the front lines, had never ever been enfranchised. This, of course, would not do.

In 1916, an all-party conference, composed of MPs from both the House of Commons and the House of Lords presided over by the Speaker of the House of Commons, was appointed to draft a proposal on the franchise and registration. The **Speaker's Conference**, as it was known, took place behind closed doors, no evidence was gathered and no lobbying accepted. The debate was conducted without any contribution from women – at least officially. Fortunately, there were many supporters of women's suffrage within the Speaker's Conference, so arguments in favour of votes for women were assured of a sympathetic hearing.

Eventually, a new Representation of the People Act was framed. Under the terms of the Act practically all men over the age of 21 and a limited number of women would be granted the vote, i.e. women over the age of 30 who were either on the local government register or married to men on the local government register. It was feared that if women were given the vote on exactly the same terms as men they might swamp the male electorate by their numbers, so in introducing an age restriction, the conference had avoided this perceived calamity. Men would therefore still comprise 60 per cent of the electorate, but over eight million women were likely to be enfranchised.

The MPs who took part in the debate, as you can see from the quotations on page 151, were generally supportive of votes for women. So when the division bell sounded in the House of Commons, 385 MPs voted in favour and 55 against the clause in the Representation of the People Bill supporting votes for women. The Bill then passed smoothly through the Lords largely because Lord Curzon, a member of the coalition government and President of the League for Opposing Woman Suffrage, encouraged peers to abstain from voting if they could not support it. And so, on 6 February 1918, votes for women – after more

Key question
What was the importance of the Speaker's Conference for votes for women?

Key term

Speaker's Conference
A formal inquiry into elections. It is chaired by the Speaker and its membership is drawn from across the political parties.

Key dates

Speaker's Conference: 1916

Representation of the People Act gave votes to women over the age of 30: February 1918

than 60 years of campaigning and a war to end all wars – was at last achieved.

Extracts from the Debate on the Representation of the People Bill (22–23 May 1917) to enfranchise all men, and women voters over the age of 30

Mr Cochrane: In my opinion the case for the extension of the franchise to women has been enormously strengthened during the last three years. In the first place, it is due to the conspicuous service that women have given to the nation during the War ... it would have been impossible to carry on the War without them. The second cause which has contributed to this change of feeling, I suggest, is the total abstinence from those militant methods which, I believe, did far more damage to their cause than their strongest opponents ever realised.

Mr Ramsay MacDonald: From my point of view I do not believe that the War has contributed one single new argument in favour of women's suffrage ... So far as service to the nation is concerned, what would our nation have been without the service that women were giving long before War broke out?

Captain O'Neil: I was opposed to women's suffrage previous to the War ... because of the most unfortunate and disgraceful campaign with which it was urged ... I must confess that the general conduct of women during the War ... have caused me to change my view.

Col. Lord H. Cavendish-Bentinck: I do not base the claims for women on the work which they have done during the War. I base the claims for women on higher grounds than that. ... women have a right equally with men to co-operate in the framing of society ... I feel very strongly that they have a right to be treated as citizens.

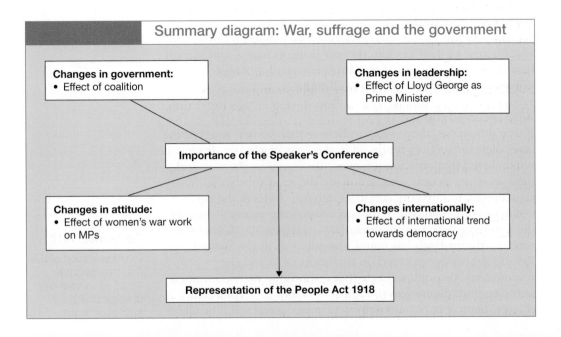

Summary diagram: War, suffrage and the government

Changes in government:
• Effect of coalition

Changes in leadership:
• Effect of Lloyd George as Prime Minister

Importance of the Speaker's Conference

Changes in attitude:
• Effect of women's war work on MPs

Changes internationally:
• Effect of international trend towards democracy

Representation of the People Act 1918

4 | The Key Debate

A question which continues to interest historians is:

Did women gain the vote because of their war work?

Arguments for

It has been argued that the greatest effect of the war on women's suffrage was that women were granted the vote towards the end of it. On 6 February 1918, eight million women, out of an electorate of 21 million, were given the opportunity to vote. Until fairly recently, historians generally agreed that women were awarded the vote as a token of gratitude for their war work.

Constance Rover, writing in 1967, argues that it is frequently said that women were given the vote because of the war. In her view the war changed the situation in more ways than are obvious at first sight. 'The obvious effect', she believes 'was that women's contribution to the war effort was seen and appreciated … Surely a land fit for heroes to live in might include a place for a few heroines as well?'

Her views are shared by Gifford Lewis, writing in 1988, who believes that the highly skilled and dangerous work done by women during the war in the armament and munitions factories and in auxiliary and nursing service at the front was probably the greatest factor in the granting of the vote to women at the end of the war.

Importantly too, the spectre of militancy was dead. Suffragettes had proved themselves worthy of the vote by working with the government in its fight to win the war. Moreover, the government could not be accused of giving in to violence and intimidation by a group of militant females. Instead, they could be seen as rewarding responsible patriotic citizens.

Arguments against

Yet the evidence for the interpretation that women received the vote because of their work in the war is inconclusive, and several historians have questioned the direct correlation between women's war work and women's suffrage.

Who received the vote?

It would be naïve, they argue, to believe that women received the vote solely for services rendered in the First World War. It must be remembered that only women over 30 were given the vote and these were not people who had made the most substantial contribution towards the country's defence. Indeed, the very women who had helped in the war effort – the young women of the munitions factories in particular – were actually denied the vote. As Martin Pugh has noted, the vote – as in the Second Reform Act – was conferred on the respectable and the responsible. It was felt unlikely that responsible married women would commit themselves to radical demands or revolutionary change, but instead would help to promote social stability. Older women, it was felt, might help to stave off the riots and revolutions that were seen to menace the country, by being a steadying voice in the political arena.

Pre-war suffrage campaign

A number of historians argue that the emphasis placed on women's economic contribution to the war discounts the groundwork put in by the pre-war suffrage campaign. Women, they argue, might well not have been granted the vote if the suffragists and suffragettes had not campaigned so effectively before the war. Undoubtedly, the pre-war suffrage movement did much to prepare the ground for votes for women. French women, by contrast, were not enfranchised despite their participation in the war effort, largely because there had been no women's suffrage movement pre-war.

War delayed votes for women

In the 1980s, Sandra Holton suggested that war delayed women's suffrage. Just before the outbreak of war, she argues, the efforts of the suffragists (rather than the suffragettes) had convinced government of the need to enfranchise women. Certainly, there were conciliatory gestures by key MPs:

- Asquith received deputations from the NUWSS and the ELFS.
- Sir John Simon, an influential member of the cabinet, came out in support.
- Lloyd George offered a place on his platform to suffrage speakers.

There was also evidence that the Liberal Party was pressurising prospective MPs to support women's suffrage and replacing those unsympathetic to the suffrage cause with those who agreed with it. Women's suffrage was on the verge of being granted just before the war broke out. Sandra Holton argues that 'only two weeks before the outbreak of war, negotiations between suffragists and government were taking place'. In addition, the Liberal leadership seemed ready to make women's suffrage part of its party programme.

These, of course, must remain tentative speculations. Negotiations between the government and women's suffragists had taken place many times before, but had never provided votes for women. There was no guarantee that it would have been the case this time. It is also important to remember that the coalition government which awarded votes for women was remarkably different from the pre-war Liberal government which feared a limited female franchise and which was preoccupied with other pressing domestic problems.

War obstructed votes for women

To complicate matters, some have even suggested that the war, far from facilitating votes for women, actually obstructed it because it brought to the fore the old argument of fighting for one's country and the right to vote. Brian Harrison, in 1993, states that 'first, the war seemed to confirm the Antis' physical force argument – the idea that men and women had separate roles because women are, on average, physically weaker than men. Although many women serving in the Armed Forces were extremely brave, they did not experience the horrors of the front line ... Second, the war weakened the suffragist movement. It pushed all peacetime problems down the political agenda.'

Fear of post-war militancy

Furthermore, it seemed likely that the women's suffrage movement would recommence once the war had ended with perhaps a renewal of the militancy that had plagued previous governments. As Emmeline Pankhurst commented in 1916, 'We're like a dog that has buried a bone. They think we have forgotten all about it. But we've got the place marked.' One can only assume that, because the political climate was very different in 1918 than it had been in 1914, it would be inconceivable for the government to imprison those self-same women who had so publicly participated in the war effort. As David Morgan suggests, 'It was clear that the killing of Suffrage by any method would lead to a dangerous reversion to massive dissatisfaction among thousands of women whom publicly politicians were praising for their war efforts.' Unrest was a real fear since post-war Britain was threatened by widespread strike action, even by the police force. There were mutinies in the army and even an organisation that mirrored the Bolsheviks: the Leeds Soviet Convention, which called for the creation of workers' and soldiers' councils.

> **Key date**
>
> End of the war: November 1918

Conclusion

Clearly, neither the view that women achieved the vote entirely because of their pre-war campaigns nor the view that women achieved the vote solely because of the war is ultimately sustainable. As with most historical judgements, there are a number of reasons for such a significant event and historians much prefer a synthesis of causes to crude over-simplification. It must also be remembered that the vote was still not entirely won: full adult universal suffrage was not achieved until 1928.

Key books in the debate

Brian Harrison, 'The First World War and feminism in Britain', *History Review*, 1993.

Sandra Holton, *Feminism and Democracy* (Cambridge, 1986).

Gifford Lewis, *Eva Gore Booth and Esther Roper* (Pandora, 1988).

David Morgan, *'Suffragists and Liberals': The Politics of Woman Suffrage in Britain* (Rowman and Littlefield, 1975).

Martin Pugh, *Electoral Reform in War and Peace* (Routledge & Kegan Paul, 1978).

Constance Rover, *Women's Suffrage and Party Politics in Britain, 1866–1914* (Routledge & Kegan Paul, 1967).

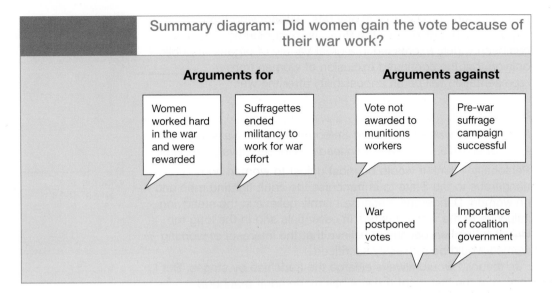

Summary diagram: Did women gain the vote because of their war work?

Arguments for

Women worked hard in the war and were rewarded

Suffragettes ended militancy to work for war effort

Arguments against

Vote not awarded to munitions workers

Pre-war suffrage campaign successful

War postponed votes

Importance of coalition government

Study Guide: AS Questions

In the style of Edexcel

Study Sources 1–4 and then answer the questions that follow.

Source 1

From a speech made by Lloyd George to a meeting composed entirely of women, quoted in the Daily Sketch*, 10 December 1918.*

In replying to a vote of thanks, Mr Lloyd George paid a well-deserved tribute to the chairman, Mrs Fawcett.

The Premier began by stating that nothing had given him greater satisfaction than to assist women being granted the vote. Women, by their deeds, had confuted the old argument of anti-feminists, that a woman was all right in times of peace, but would have to be ruled out in the days of war. How magnificently they responded in the manufacture of munitions of war, which enabled our armies not only to hold their own, but to beat the foe. It was quite impossible to keep up the production of food, let alone increase it, unless we had the help of women. If it had not been for the direct assistance of women, often in spheres from which they had hitherto been ruled out we could not have won through in this war.

The big gathering was obviously one of voters. It was an over-thirty crowd, and for the most part so well-dressed and matronly as to have either a husband or a property qualification.

Source 2

From a letter written by Millicent Fawcett to the Prime Minister, Herbert Asquith, in May 1916.

Our movement has received very great increases of strength during recent months, former opponents now declaring themselves on our side, or at any rate, withdrawing their opposition. The change in the Press is most marked. The view has been widely expressed in a great variety of organs of public opinion that the continued exclusion of women from representation will be an impossibility after the war.

Source 3

From a letter written from Lord Selbourne to Lord Salisbury on 25 August 1916. They were two leading Conservative politicians.

Personally, I think it would be most unjust to women and dangerous to the State to enfranchise the adult fighting men and no women. Dangerous, because I firmly believe in the steadying influence of the women voters in essentials and in the long run. Unjust to women because I believe that the interests of working women would be ruthlessly sacrificed.

In theory, I would always enlarge the franchise by stages. But I think that the history of the war has made adult manhood suffrage inevitable; we shall have to do in one stage what I should have preferred to do in several.

Source 4

From Arthur Marwick, Women at War, 1914–1918, *published in 1977.*

To say that war brought votes for women is to make a very crude generalisation, yet one which contains an essential truth. One must see the question of women's rights not in isolation, but as part of a wider context of social relationships and political change. A broad liberal-democratic movement starting in the late nineteenth century had come near to achieving votes for women before 1914. Yet the political advance of women in 1914 was still blocked by the vigorous hostility of men, and the often fearful reluctance and opposition of many women. The war brought a new confidence to women, removed apathy, silenced the female anti-suffragists. Asquith was only the most prominent of the converts among men. Undoubtedly the replacement of militant suffragette activity by frantic patriotic endeavour played its part as well.

(a) **Read Sources 1, 2 and 3**

How far do these three sources support the view that votes for women was universally welcome? (20 marks)

(b) **Read Sources 2, 3 and 4**

Do you agree with Arthur Marwick in Source 4 that it was essentially true that 'war brought votes for women'? Explain your answer, using these two sources and your own knowledge. (40 marks)

Source: Question (b) adapted from Edexcel

Exam tips

The cross-references are intended to take you straight to the material that will help you to answer the questions.

(a) This question asks you to cross-reference sources in order to make a judgement. You are not required to use your own knowledge but must focus on the material available. At first glance it seems that all the sources support the view that votes for women was universally welcome. War, according to Lloyd George, had 'confuted the old argument of anti-feminists', a view confirmed by Millicent Fawcett who writes that old opponents had withdrawn their opposition to female suffrage. However, as Source 3 hints at, some believed that votes for women was an inevitability which should come in stages rather than be granted all at once. Indeed, the hidden message of the last sentence in Source 1 suggests that there was still some hostility to votes for women in 1918 since the franchise was limited to women over 30.

When coming to your overall judgement, don't forget to take into account the origin and purpose of the sources. What difference does that make to the weight you will place upon what is said? For example, Lloyd George was talking to an audience of largely prospective voters after the vote had been won, so his words may have emphasised his support for female suffrage. Fawcett was writing privately to Asquith during the war and may have overstated public support in an attempt to persuade the Prime Minister to grant votes for women.

(b) This question requires analysis and judgement based on sources and knowledge. It is important to remember that students who address only one assessment objective will lose marks. All the sources clearly show awareness of the changed situation from 1914: Selbourne believes it to be unjust not to give votes for women and change after 1914 is central to Marwick's argument. As Marwick suggests, the war 'brought new confidence to women, removed apathy, silenced the female anti-suffragists'. Here you can show your knowledge of how war gave new opportunities, and perhaps new impetus, to a long-running campaign. Militant suffragette activity also stopped in favour of 'patriotic endeavour'. How did women's patriotism help? Source 2 provides evidence of changed opinions. However, you should be aware of the relative importance of the war. Marwick argues that votes for women had 'come near' before 1914 largely because of women's actions. You could perhaps show awareness of the specific debates between historians on this point as some historians argue that votes for women had been won in theory before the war began (see page 153). Examiners want to see a reasoned conclusion which balances the various explanations.

In the style of AQA

Read the following sources and then answer the questions that follow.

Source A

From a speech by Herbert Asquith, 1917.

Why, and in what sense, the House may ask, have I changed my views? ... My opposition to woman suffrage has always been based, and based solely, on considerations of public expediency. I think that some years ago I ventured to use the expression 'Let the women work out their own salvation'. Well, Sir, they have ... How could we have carried on the War without them? There is hardly a service in which women have not been at least as active as men ... But what moves me more in this matter is the problem of reconstruction when the war is over. The questions which will arise with regard to women's labour and women's functions are questions in which I find it impossible to withhold from women, the power and the right of making their voices heard. And let me add that, since the War began, now nearly three years ago, we have had no recurrence of that detestable campaign which disfigured the annals of political agitation in this country, and no one can now contend that we are yielding to violence what we refused to concede to argument.

Source B

From an article by Brian Harrison, 'The First World War and feminism in Britain', published in History Review *in 1993.*

In some ways, the war actually obstructed votes for women. First, the war seemed to confirm the Antis' physical force argument – the idea that men and women had separate roles because women are, on average, physically weaker than men. Although many women serving in the Armed Forces were extremely brave, they did not experience the horrors of the front line. The separation of role was also reinforced by geography, with many men across the Channel while most women stayed at home. Second, the war weakened the suffragist movement. It pushed all peacetime problems down the political agenda.

Source C

Col. Lord H. Cavendish-Bentinck's speech from the Debate on the Representation of the People Bill (22–23 May 1917) to enfranchise all men, and women voters over the age of 30.

I do not base the claims for women on the work which they have done during the War. I base the claims for women on higher grounds than that. ... women have a right equally with men to co-operate in the framing of society ... I feel very strongly that they have a right to be treated as citizens.

(a) Explain how far the views in Source B differ from those in Source A in relation to attitudes in Parliament to the granting of a women's vote in 1917. (12 marks)

(b) Use Sources A, B and C and your own knowledge. How important was war work to the granting of a female suffrage in 1918? (24 marks)

Exam tips

The cross-references are intended to take you straight to the material that will help you to answer the questions.

(a) There is a clear difference of opinion here between Source B, which believes that war obstructed votes for women and Source A which credits the war with a change of attitude, making the House of Commons favourable to women's suffrage. You should try to identify some useful phrases from the sources to contrast and should also try to show your broad understanding of the context of the speeches. In order to assess 'how far' you will need to look for similarities. Source B does begin with 'in some ways' suggesting the war was not wholly obstructive, and both sources refer to women's work in the war and the abandonment of campaigns during the war.

(b) You will need to look at the ways in which war work contributed to the 1918 female suffrage and ways in which it did not. The debate is outlined on pages 152–4, so it would be worth re-reading these before you make your plan. You will need to decide what your argument will be before you begin and don't forget to support each idea with a specific example, using both the sources and your own knowledge as evidence. Source A obviously credits war work as most important while Sources B and C do not. You might like to argue that Source B's belief that the war obstructed votes for women has little validity, even though the war once more raised arguments about the separation of spheres. Indeed, the view expressed in Source B negates the valuable work done by women throughout the war years. Women, Source A suggests, were as active as men. Certainly, the work done by women, such as that of farm labourer, ambulance driver and mechanic, had previously been performed by men, thus undermining the separate spheres argument.

You could also argue that the claim in Source B that war pushed all social problems down the political agenda is flawed because it underestimates the entrenched opposition to votes for women before the war. As Asquith confirms in his speech, he was very much against votes for women before the war and blocked the Conciliation Bills and other political reforms between 1908 and 1914. You must remember that it was a wartime coalition government, headed by Lloyd George who replaced Asquith as prime minister, which eventually gave women the vote as part of a wider franchise reform. Indeed, women may have been granted the vote because their war work convinced government of their respectability and worthiness.

Source C provides additional support for the view that women did not simply gain the vote because of their war work, although it does not agree with Source B that the war actually impeded their position. Overall, it is your choice whether you argue that the pre-war suffrage campaign or another factor was more important than war work, but whatever you decide, your answer should be balanced and lead to a convincing conclusion.

7 Life after Suffrage

POINTS TO CONSIDER

So was it all worth it? Did the vote bring about the changes that the suffragists and suffragettes yearned for? This final chapter will consider the extent to which women benefited from the vote. It will examine:

- Effects on Parliament
- Effects on the women's movement
- Effects on women's work
- Effects on marriage and the family
- Effects on sexual morality

Key dates

1918	Women over the age of 30 gained the vote
	Constance Markiewicz elected to Parliament, but did not take up her seat
1919	Nancy Astor became the first woman MP to sit in Parliament
	Sex Disqualification Removal Act
	NUSEC formed
1922	Married Women's Maintenance Act
	Infanticide Act
	Criminal Law Amendment Act
1923	Matrimonial Causes Act
1925	Guardianship of Infants Act
	Widows, Orphans and Old Age Pensioners' Bill
1928	Equal Franchise Act
1929	Age of marriage raised to 16
1979	Margaret Thatcher became first female Prime Minister
1992	Betty Boothroyd became first female Speaker of the House of Commons

1 | Introduction

In her book *Unshackled: The Story of How We Won the Vote*, published in 1959, Christabel Pankhurst wrote, 'The World War was over. The peace was signed. The women's war was over. The vote was won. A new chapter was opening.' But did the vote augur a new world for women? Many certainly hoped so.

At first, suffragists, elated at the prospect of voting, insisted that the vote had a tremendous significance for women's rights. To their minds, the enfranchisement of women would revolutionise government thinking as the voting power of the new electorate could not be ignored. Ray Strachey, suffragist and writer, said that:

> The Representation of the People Act had not been on the Statute Book a fortnight before the House of Commons discovered that every Bill which came before it had a 'woman's side', and the Party Whips began eagerly to ask 'what the women thought'. The ... House of Commons, which had been firmly closed to all women since the early days of the militant agitation, was now opened, and access to Members became wonderfully easy. Letters from women constituents no longer went straight into waste-paper baskets but received elaborate answers, and ... women's societies were positively welcomed at Westminster.

Historians, of course, are more circumspect than suffrage activists because, with hindsight, they are able to evaluate the causes and consequences of significant historical events more clearly. From this vantage point you too can make a judgement about the extent to which the franchise accomplished what those who energetically campaigned for it had desired. However, controversy is also at the heart of history and so, not surprisingly, historians differ on the effect that the vote had on women's lives, especially since the consequences of votes for women are, in many ways, still working themselves out.

Historians Martin Pugh and Olive Banks share the optimism of the suffragists and claim that, because of their newly acquired voting power, women achieved considerable gains. According to Pugh, there were 21 pieces of legislation between 1918 and 1929 that concerned women. Given these achievements, it is tempting to represent women's advancements as an inevitable evolutionary process. History, however, is more like a roller-coaster than a straight railway track: women did not always achieve what they believed the franchise promised.

2 | Effects on Parliament

In 1918 the Representation of the People Act was passed and for the first time in legal and political history a significant number of women had the opportunity to participate in the democratic process. Britain could now claim that she had a representative government as electoral democracy was no longer the preserve of men. After many years of struggle, Britain allegedly had a just and balanced government as the majority of the population was now enfranchised. But these views must be approached with some caution, as women aged between 21 and 29 and even some women over the age of 30 were still denied the vote. Not until 1928 did women receive the vote on the same terms as men, thus

Key question
What effect did female suffrage have on Parliament?

Key date
Women over the age of 30 gained the vote: 1918

properly marking the beginning of modern democracy in Britain (see page 2).

Becoming an MP

Key question
Why was it so difficult for women to become MPs?

Women may well have voted, but they were slow in taking their places in the House of Commons. In the first election, in December 1918, 17 women, including a number of suffragists and suffragettes, stood for Parliament. All but one of the female candidates were defeated at the polls, including Christabel Pankhurst (Smethwick) who stood as **Women's Party** candidate, Emmeline Pethick-Lawrence (Manchester) and Charlotte Despard (Battersea North), both of whom stood as Labour candidates. The only woman to be elected was Constance Markievicz who, because she stood as a member of **Sinn Fein** (who did not recognise the authority of the British Parliament over Ireland), refused to take her seat. Female parliamentary candidates, despite the enthusiastic help they received from ex-suffrage activists, were in a weak position:

Key dates

Constance Markiewicz elected to Parliament, but did not take up her seat: 1918

Nancy Astor became first woman MP to sit in Parliament: 1919

Key terms

Women's Party
This was a party founded by Christabel Pankhurst and open to women of all classes.

Sinn Fein
Founded in 1907 as an Irish nationalist organisation.

- Women had no separate party machinery of their own with which to contest seats.
- They had limited financial resources with which to fight their seats, were inexperienced in fighting elections and were generally allocated unwinnable seats by the political parties because the parties did not wish to give women any of their safer seats. For example, Emmeline Pethick-Lawrence was supported by the very small Labour Party in a predominantly Liberal stronghold.
- The country's electorate were not ready to vote for women MPs. Ironically, the first woman MP to take her seat in the House of Commons (Nancy Astor) got there in 1919 when her husband, who had been Conservative MP for Plymouth, was elevated to the peerage.

Female MPs and nominations

Nancy Astor was the exception rather than the rule. In 1922 only 33 women were nominated as Parliamentary candidates out of a possible 615. By 1929 this had risen to 69, but it was hardly a significant figure especially when four out of five women stood in constituencies known to be hopeless for their particular parties and therefore had little chance of winning. Moreover, ten out of the 36 women who actually became MPs in this period gained their seats at by-elections rather than general elections, which suggests that their success may have as much to do with arbitrary factors such as voter dissatisfaction as with support for specifically female candidates. Furthermore, several Conservative women MPs owed their success, like Nancy Astor, to family connections rather than to feminist pressure.

Social convention and female MPs

Most women had the legal right to become MPs but social convention generally denied them the opportunity. Until August

1917 women had to listen to debates behind a grille in the Ladies' Gallery so that the male MPs would not be distracted by the female form and the women would be protected from male glances. The grille was removed, but women's role in 1920 was still perceived to be in their own house looking after their family, not in the House of Commons looking after the country. As a consequence, the predominantly all-male selection committees feared that women might alienate the electorate and were unwilling to accept them as prospective MPs. Indeed, Conservative Selection Committees looked for husband and wife teams where the men would be MPs and the women (naturally!) would act in a supportive capacity, organising fêtes and bazaars to raise money and entertaining the party faithful.

Women in Parliament

Once in Parliament, women fought hard to make their mark in a masculine political world. As Martin Pugh points out, the House of Commons was an uncomfortable and unwelcoming place for its female members. Certainly, they were swamped by men – there were never more than 15 female MPs among over 600 men. One

◄
Key question
Why was it difficult for women to influence the House of Commons?

Women were able to stand for Parliament and be elected at the age of 21, but were unable to vote until they were aged 30. This cartoon from the *Daily Mirror* in 1923 shows a 'flapper', a 1920s term for an unconventional young woman who wore both her hair and her skirts short, elected to the House of Commons. How were women thought to 'feminise' Parliament?

newly elected Conservative MP, Thelma Cazalet, remarked that 'there was still something slightly freakish about a woman MP, and I frequently saw male colleagues point me out to their friends as though I were a sort of giant panda'.

When Nancy Astor made her first entrance in the House of Commons she made quite a stir. 'I was', she said later, 'deeply conscious of representing a Cause'. Winston Churchill, who had often visited her home, ignored her and when challenged said he found her presence in the House of Commons as embarrassing as if she had entered his bathroom when he was naked. Nancy replied 'Nonsense, Winston, you are not good-looking enough to have fears of this sort'. Nancy Astor spoke often, and spoke well, but never forgot the basic principles of traditional femininity and always dressed as soberly as the men. She, along with the other female MPs, did not go into the bars, the smoking rooms or the members' cloakroom for fear of giving offence. And as the cartoon on page 164 shows, women's participation in Parliament was often ridiculed, so MPs like Nancy Astor were careful not to upset tradition too much.

The role of female MPs in the House of Commons

Once elected, female MPs worked extremely hard since, as Brian Harrison points out, they represented their sex as well as their constituency. Nancy Astor, for example, received between 1500 and 2000 letters a week from people outside her constituency. These new MPs also established links that cut across party lines and tried to promote legislation to advance women's rights. Party loyalty sometimes took second place as women MPs voted against their party. For example, when the Labour MP **Margaret Bondfield** introduced a private member's bill to provide shoes and boots for poor children every female backbencher supported it.

Female MPs and government posts

It was difficult for women to make much of an impact as most only sat for 1–3 years in Parliament. Only a few women like Nancy Astor were elected over several parliamentary terms, so women were rarely appointed to official Government posts. Nonetheless, in 1924, Margaret Bondfield was appointed **Parliamentary Secretary** at the Ministry of Labour in the short-lived Labour government. Not to be outdone, the Conservatives appointed Katherine Atholl as Parliamentary Secretary of State at the Board of Education when they replaced the Labour government in the same year.

The photograph on page 166 shows eight female MPs who were in the House of Commons in 1924:

- Dorothy Jewson (Labour), former member of the WSPU, a pacifist and trade union organiser, spent time promoting health and housing issues and helped to form the Workers' Birth Control Group, which tried to persuade the Labour Party to adopt a policy of free birth-control advice.

Key figure

Margaret Bondfield 1873–1963; a former trade union activist who campaigned for women's rights, supported adult suffrage and opposed the war. In 1929 she was appointed Minister of Labour and thus became the first woman Cabinet Minister.

Key date

Widows, Orphans and Old Age Pensioners' Bill: 1925

Key term

Parliamentary Secretary An MP who assists a Minister with government business.

- Susan Lawrence (Labour), a former trade union organiser, helped to guide the **Widows, Orphans and Old Age Pensioners' Bill** through Parliament in 1925.
- Nancy Astor (Conservative) became known for her commitment to the principles of equal franchise, pensions, better education and working conditions, marriage property reform, legislation to protect young children and temperance reform.
- Margaret Wintringham (Liberal), former NUWSS member, campaigned for an extension of women's suffrage, the right of women to sit in the House of Lords, provision of state scholarships for girls, equal pay and women-only railway carriages.
- Katherine Atholl (Conservative) spoke against genital mutilation in Africa.
- Mabel Philipson (Conservative) was active on the Select Committee that framed legislation to give married women rights over their own children.
- Vera Terrington (Liberal) was in Parliament for less than a year so had little effect.
- Margaret Bondfield (Labour).

Key term

Widows, Orphans and Old Age Pensioners' Bill 1925
A scheme that enabled workers to pay a weekly contribution so that they could receive a pension at the age of 65. If an insured worker died, benefits were paid to their widow and children.

Absent from the photograph is Ellen Wilkinson (Labour), who was elected for Middlesbrough East in 1924. Ellen Wilkinson, soon dubbed 'Red Ellen' both for her left-wing politics and the colour of her hair, had been an NUWSS district organiser, a pacifist during the war and a trade union official who was active in the 1926 General Strike. Virulently anti-Conservative and committed to left-wing policies, Ellen Wilkinson became a devoted friend of

Eight women MPs on the terrace of the House of Commons in 1924. How helpful is this photograph to a historian studying the effects of the vote?

Nancy Astor, thus illustrating the commitment of these new MPs to work across party lines in support of women's issues.

Women MPs and the nature of politics

It is safe to assume that neither the enfranchisement of women nor the election of female MPs changed the nature of parliamentary politics. Suffragists and suffragettes had hoped that, once women achieved the vote, they would make a distinctive contribution to the political arena by 'feminising' politics. It was believed that women would bring special skills to parliament that would make the confrontational style of party politics disappear in favour of politics based on principles. This wish was not fulfilled. The House of Commons remained essentially a man's institution led by men to deal with men's affairs in a man's way. Men dominated the House of Commons in sheer weight of numbers. The election of women MPs neither brought about a new age nor 'feminised' the political process, as women merely adapted to the masculine style of the House of Commons, learning debating skills and a willingness to be rude to the opposition. Overall, women MPs failed to make a distinctive stand over women's issues and some of the women MPs with feminist sympathies were forced to compromise their feminism or else become marginalised within party politics.

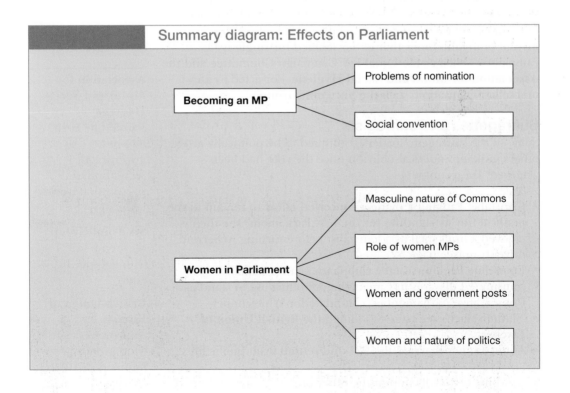

Summary diagram: Effects on Parliament

- Becoming an MP
  - Problems of nomination
  - Social convention
- Women in Parliament
  - Masculine nature of Commons
  - Role of women MPs
  - Women and government posts
  - Women and nature of politics

3 | Effects on the Women's Movement

Some historians claim that the women's movement declined after 1918 as few campaigners remained fully committed to extending votes for women on the same terms as men. However, this is not the case. Many women remained actively involved even though the suffrage movement was not as strong as it had been pre-war. Suffragists kept up a quiet pressure on the government throughout this time, continuously pointing out the illogicality of the 1918 decision. Yet their story is only just being written: most historians end their work in 1918 and ignore the 10 years after women gained a limited franchise. However, it is safe to say that further franchise reform was not a priority for either most feminists or the government. In many ways it was a 'tidying up' process. The Prime Minister, Stanley Baldwin, fearful that if the Conservatives did not reform the vote Labour would, gave his support to the Equal Franchise Bill which would give women over 21 the vote. And so approximately five million – younger – women were added to the voting register in 1928.

Key question
Did the women's movement disappear after a limited vote was achieved?

Equal Franchise Act: April 1928

Key date

New organisations

It is often argued that once women had achieved a limited franchise in 1918, feminism lost its vital spark. Without any political direction it degenerated into a small number of fragmented organisations. But, as feminist historian Sheila Jeffreys points out, this fails to give weight to the other concerns of feminists. Once the vote had been achieved, there were a myriad of organisations that either lobbied for single-issue campaigns – such as the Equal Pay Campaign Committee and the **Association for Moral and Social Hygiene** – or acted as an umbrella organisation, such the **Six Point Group**.

Suffragettes and suffragists

Some of the suffragette leaders continued to be politically active; others sank into political oblivion once the vote had been achieved. For example:

- Christabel Pankhurst made a concerted effort to remain in the political fray by standing for the first Parliament; she then enjoyed a brief spell as a journalist before turning to Second Adventism (see page 52).
- Emmeline Pankhurst led a campaign against sexually transmitted diseases in Canada before returning to stand as Conservative parliamentary candidate for Whitechapel.
- 'Slasher Mary' (see page 88) joined the **British Union of Fascists**.
- Annie Kenney married in 1921 and retired from public life.

Meanwhile, the leadership of the other organisations continued to press for universal suffrage and remained politically active in left-wing causes:

Association for Moral and Social Hygiene
Formed in 1915 to eliminate government regulation of prostitution world-wide.

Six Point Group
Formed in 1921 with six specific aims.

British Union of Fascists
An extreme right-wing group founded in 1932. It was sympathetic to the Nazis.

Key terms

- Sylvia Pankhurst helped to found the British Communist Party, championed an anti-Fascist crusade and emigrated to Ethiopia (see page 60).
- Charlotte Despard stood as parliamentary candidate for Battersea in the first election, but her major energy was directed to working for Irish independence. She remained committed to radical socialist policies throughout the rest of her life and, at the age of 91, addressed an anti-Nazi rally in Hyde Park in the 1930s.
- The Pethick-Lawrences both became Labour Party activists, with Fred even defeating Winston Churchill in the 1923 election.
- Millicent Fawcett, although no longer leader of the NUWSS, campaigned for greater work opportunities and legal justice for women.

Key term

Depression
A period in the 1930s when there was high unemployment.

Subsequent decades, Martin Pugh argues, actually saw the waning of the impact of women's enfranchisement as the leading figures of the suffrage movement grew old and faded from the political scene. Indeed, when women finally achieved equal suffrage with men this was not followed by any immediate advances in women's position – but maybe this was due to the fact that Britain was about to enter a **depression**.

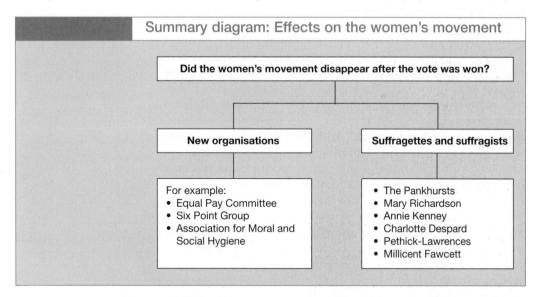

Summary diagram: Effects on the women's movement

Did the women's movement disappear after the vote was won?

New organisations

For example:
- Equal Pay Committee
- Six Point Group
- Association for Moral and Social Hygiene

Suffragettes and suffragists

- The Pankhursts
- Mary Richardson
- Annie Kenney
- Charlotte Despard
- Pethick-Lawrences
- Millicent Fawcett

Key question
How did the vote affect women's work?

4 | Effects on Women's Work

Suffragists and suffragettes had wanted the vote partly to widen women's employment opportunities, increase their pay and improve their working conditions. To some extent they had their wishes fulfilled, at least in the legal sense. In 1919, as a direct result of women's franchise, the Sex Disqualification Removal Act made it illegal to deny employment on grounds of marriage and enabled women to enter professions previously barred to them.

Key date

Sex Disqualification Removal Act: 1919

Women were able to take up civil service and judicial posts, become barristers or magistrates and serve on juries. The Act opened the legal profession to women like Christabel Pankhurst who had studied law but had not been allowed to practise it except in her own defence. It also allowed women to become chartered accountants and bankers.

Certainly in the 1920s there were a number of significant firsts:

- first female veterinary surgeon
- first female pilot to enter an air race
- first female British delegate to the League of Nations
- first female solicitor
- first female barrister
- first female jury member
- first female Justice of the Peace (JP)
- first female deacon in the Church of England
- and the first female cabinet minister.

Work for middle-class women

Despite the vote, most work was as much characterised by a sexual division of labour in 1928 as it had been over 60 years before. Many professions continued to be male dominated. In 1919 many of the London teaching hospitals still refused to train women doctors. In 1920 when the civil service was reorganised, women remained excluded from high positions. By 1927 only a small number of women had been appointed as JPs.

Greater opportunities emerged for middle-class women in the teaching and clerical professions, but women were rarely given the top jobs. Indeed, the President of the National Association of Schoolmasters declared in 1934 that 'only a nation heading for a madhouse would force upon men … such a position as service under a spinster headmistress'. And when the expansion of the white-blouse worker – the department store shop assistant, and the clerk – offered women employment opportunities this owed as much to technological and educational advances, such as the invention of the typewriter, as to the vote.

Moreover, employers often ignored the 1919 Sexual Disqualification Removal Act and obliged women to resign when they married. In the 1920s about three-quarters of all local authorities operated a marriage bar for women teachers and many public health authorities dismissed married female doctors and nurses; similarly, women civil servants were given a **dowry** and forced to leave once they married. The decision not to employ married women was justified because 'women could not service two masters', that is their husbands and their bosses, at the same time.

Dowry
Money brought by a bride to her husband.

Key term

Jobs for working-class women

Votes for women did little for working-class women as there continued to be a high degree of sexual segregation in working-class occupations. Domestic service or agricultural labour remained the only two options available to working-class rural women until well after the Second World War. Once again, even when women worked in the same areas as men, they were found in the lower grades of those occupations, being over-represented in unskilled rather than skilled jobs. New opportunities did occur for women in the new **light industries** where nimble fingers were needed on the assembly lines but these, like those of the white-blouse workers, were the effect of technological change rather than the effect of the vote.

Work and pay

Women remained a cheap and easily exploitable workforce as their work commanded lower rates of pay than men, whether they were middle class or working class. Despite a campaign to obtain equal pay, female teachers' salaries were set one-fifth lower than men's by the Standing Joint Committee on Teachers' Salaries. Similarly, women civil servants were paid 75 per cent of male salaries as a rule. In all-female middle-class occupations women were worse off. Nurses, for example, were thought to work for love rather than money, so they were paid low salaries. Working-class women fared little better, for they continued to receive wages roughly half those of men.

One is therefore led to believe that although women had gained political power through the ballot box, economic power was still held by men. The justification for this inequality can be traced to the idea that women were thought to be wives and mothers rather than workers. Indeed, Martin Pugh claims that it was commonly held that working women deprived men of jobs – one manufacturer even advocated the dismissal of women workers in order to solve the unemployment problem. Women's pay was not surprisingly viewed as 'pin-money', a supplement to the wages of husbands, rather than a living wage. As a consequence, women were denied both equal pay and equal opportunities.

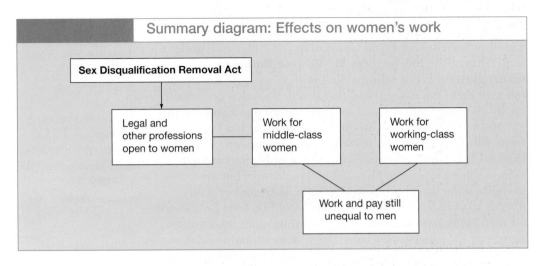

Summary diagram: Effects on women's work

5 | Effects on Marriage and the Family

Key question
To what extent did the vote help to promote marital equality?

Post-war politicians promised to create homes fit for heroes and feminists wanted no less themselves. High hopes were held that women's suffrage might not only act as a legal protection against husbands, but also help to promote equality in marriage. There were some notable successes in this area. For example:

- In 1922, a Married Women's Maintenance Act increased the level of maintenance for separated women and their children. Once divorced, however, women who wished to stay in the marital home found they had no claim to it even though they were not the 'guilty' party. Furthermore, courts (with male judges) generally examined the conduct of women, just as much as their financial needs, before assessing their claim to maintenance.
- In 1922, an Infanticide Act eliminated the charge of murder for women found guilty of killing an infant if suffering from the effects of childbirth.
- In 1923, the Matrimonial Causes Act allowed a wife to divorce her husband on grounds of adultery, thus ending a long history of double standards for men and women (see pages 5–6).
- In 1925, the Guardianship of Infants Act completed the work of nineteenth-century feminists by placing mothers and fathers in an equal position with regard to custody of their children.
- In 1929, the Age of Marriage Act raised the age of marriage to 16. It had previously been 12. The new law sent out the message that marriage was meant to be a union between two consenting adults.

Key dates

Married Women's Maintenance Act: 1922

Infanticide Act: 1922

Matrimonial Causes Act: 1923

Guardianship of Infants Act: 1925

Age of marriage raised to 16: 1929

NUSEC formed: 1919

The National Union of Societies for Equal Citizenship

In order to redress these economic and domestic inequalities, many feminists tried to improve the lives of married women with children. In 1919 the NUWSS changed its name to the National Union of Societies for Equal Citizenship (NUSEC) and, under the leadership of the Independent MP **Eleanor Rathbone**, campaigned for social reforms. Rather than struggle for equal pay with men, it was suggested that married women be given a family allowance if they cared for their children at home. In this way, women's unpaid work in the home would at last be financially recognised and rewarded. The leadership of NUSEC believed that family allowances would not only give married women some measure of financial independence, but also strengthen the position of single women. With money paid directly to women with children, there would be little justification for men being paid a 'family wage' and thus more than women. Equal pay for equal work would therefore be brought about.

Not surprisingly, many feminists disagreed with this approach to women's rights. This 'new' feminism, with its emphasis on welfare at the expense of equality, was seen, for a number of reasons, as a betrayal rather than a continuation of feminism:

Key figure

Eleanor Rathbone 1872–1946; a leading figure in the NUWSS, supported family allowances and eventually became an Independent MP in 1929. Her campaigns led to the 1945 Family Allowances Act, which provided every family with money to help support their children.

- First, feminists such as Millicent Fawcett disagreed with family allowances because they consolidated, rather than challenged, women's home-making and child-rearing roles.
- Secondly, family allowances diverted women from the struggle for equal pay in the public world by offering them a bribe to stay at home.
- Thirdly, family allowances might depress working-class wages in general because the state subsidised families with children and there was therefore little incentive for employers to raise salaries in line with the cost of living.

Summary diagram: Effects on marriage and the family

Legal changes:
- Maintenance Act 1922
- Infanticide Act 1922
- Matrimonial Causes Act 1923
- Guardianship of Infants Act 1925

Campaigns for family allowances:
- Importance of Eleanor Rathbone and NUSEC

Key question
What impact did the vote have on sexual morality?

Key date
Criminal Law Amendment Act: 1922

6 | Effects on Sexual Morality

Suffragists and suffragettes wanted the vote to protect young girls from sexual assault, to eliminate sexually transmitted diseases, to curb unfair legislation against prostitutes, and to ensure a single moral standard for both sexes. Once again, they enjoyed only a limited success, as the following evidence will show.

Feminists achieved a small victory when the 1922 Criminal Law Amendment Act abolished the 'reasonable cause to believe' clause. Under the old Act, men who had seduced a girl under 16 were able to claim that they had not realised that she was under age and thus avoided conviction. However, the new Act was limited in scope as it only applied to full sexual intercourse and not to indecent assault.

Propaganda and censorship

The extent of sexually transmitted disease continued to cause alarm. Emmeline Pankhurst spent a lot of time in North America lecturing on the dangers of sexually transmitted diseases, but the women's movement in Britain seemed to reserve judgement on the subject. However, the British Social Hygiene Council made strenuous efforts to curb its spread and several films were produced – *The Girl Who Doesn't Know, Damaged Goods, The Flaw* – to educate people on the disease itself. In the 1920s Manchester City Council opened clinics in public lavatories, but these were quickly closed as a result of feminist and other public disapproval. It was the discovery of penicillin rather than women's moral crusading that diminished the rate of sexually transmitted disease infection.

These female moral crusaders had friends in high places to help them to establish sexual moral standards: one film censor later became President of the National Vigilance Association (see page 47) and one Home Secretary in the 1920s undertook to improve public sexual morality. As a consequence, there was rigid sexual censorship: books such as Radclyffe Hall's *Well of Loneliness* about lesbianism either faced prosecution or were not distributed and thus quietly disappeared.

Nancy Astor and prostitution

In 1925 Nancy Astor introduced a bill to reform the law on **soliciting** and prostitution. At the time, women could be convicted of soliciting purely on the word of a police officer, and then fined or sent to prison. Soliciting – not prostitution – was an offence so men were never charged with trying to obtain a prostitute. Incensed at this injustice, Astor advocated equality between the sexes in relation to prostitution offences and the elimination of the term 'common' prostitute from the legal code. Her efforts led to a Department Committee of Inquiry on Street Offences 1927, but the parliamentary bills she put forward never reached the statute book.

The collapse of the sexual double standard

It could be argued that the sexual double standard, so criticised by both suffragists and suffragettes, was replaced by an even lower single standard in that there was a decline in female sexual morality rather than an improvement in male morality. Indeed, some feminists supported the Association for Moral and Social Hygiene, an organisation descended from Josephine Butler's Ladies' National Association, which campaigned to raise the age of consent to 18 years. Others criticised this and the moral puritanism of the pre-war suffragettes and instead advocated women's right to sexual pleasure. As a consequence, the campaigns they led were different ones. It was believed that women could not enjoy sex because of a fear of pregnancy, so the birth-control movement won favour among many new-wave feminists. Birth control, promoted by **Marie Stopes** who set up the first birth-control clinic in 1921 in Holloway, London, enabled women to take control of their own sexuality, or – as some like Nancy Astor feared – be as irresponsible as men.

Key term

Soliciting
Stopping someone and offering them sexual services if they pay money.

Key figure

Marie Stopes
1880–1958; daughter of a scientist father and feminist mother, Marie Stopes became Britain's youngest doctor of science. She joined the Women's Freedom League. Her best-selling books *Married Love* (1918) and *Wise Parenthood* (1918) were regarded as shocking because they were about sex and birth control.

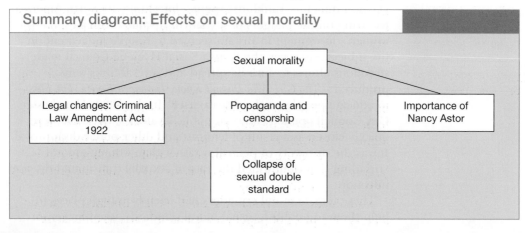

Summary diagram: Effects on sexual morality

Sexual morality

Legal changes: Criminal Law Amendment Act 1922

Propaganda and censorship

Importance of Nancy Astor

Collapse of sexual double standard

Profile: Nancy Astor 1879–1964

1897 – Married Robert Gould Shaw
1903 – Divorced
1904 – Married Waldorf Astor
1919 – First woman to take her seat in the Commons
1921 – Set up a Consultative Committee
1922 – Put forward Intoxicating Liquor Bill
1925 – Tried to reform the law on prostitution
1945 – Stood down as MP
1964 – Died

Nancy Astor, an American by birth, was the first woman to sit in the House of Commons. The Conservative Party chose her to represent Plymouth at a by-election when her husband, Waldorf Astor, was elevated to the peerage. She represented her constituency for 26 years.

Astor was a Conservative, but her Conservatism was mediated by her feminism and she quickly established a reputation for women's rights. She was a staunch champion of the Women's Cause in Parliament, promoting a great deal of legislation to improve the position of women. In pursuing her vision she looked after the new female MPs who joined her in the House of Commons, regardless of their party affiliations. Her aim was to unite all women MPs and get them to see themselves as women first and party members second. She set up a Consultative Committee to co-ordinate women's political activities.

Throughout her life Nancy Astor was concerned with maternal welfare, child protection and equal moral standards. She was committed to equal franchise, better education and working conditions, pensions, marriage and property law reform, the protection of young children and changing the laws on prostitution. Her feminism was informed by a strong moral stance: she was a firm adherent of temperance and supported strict controls on gambling.

A final thought

Key dates

Margaret Thatcher became first female Prime Minister: 1979

Betty Boothroyd became first female Speaker: 1992

In 1979 the Conservative MP Margaret Thatcher became the first female Prime Minister and in 1992 Betty Boothroyd became the first female Speaker of the House of Commons. The achievements of these two women were exceptional. Contemporary Britain is still characterised – to some extent – by male dominance within parliamentary politics and the economic inequalities that women suffer. In such a context it is all too easy to be cynical about the enfranchisement of women. Power, it is argued, no longer rests in Parliament, but in commerce and finance. The failure of the franchise to realise the hopes of the suffragists and the suffragettes, it is said, illustrates the limitations of the vote to effect change.

Nonetheless, the franchise should not be dismissed as 'marking a cross on a piece of paper', for it not only acts as a check on government and makes those in government answerable to the electorate, but also has the authority to change the economic framework of society. Governments may have failed to satisfy the demands of British feminists between the wars, but the position of women in Italy and Germany, where democracy collapsed, was calamitous. Furthermore, one only has to think of the nationalisation of the 1940s, the subsequent denationalisation of the 1980s and 1990s and the Labour landslide victory of 1997 to appreciate the immense power that Parliament still enjoys to change our lives, for good or ill. And women, who represent over 50 per cent of the electorate, certainly have the capability to change the composition of Parliament and with it the political direction of Britain.

Summary diagram: Life after suffrage

1918	Votes for women over 30
	Constance Markiewicz elected
1919	Nancy Astor elected
	Sex Disqualification Removal Act
	NUSEC founded
1920	Maintenance Act
1921	Six Point Group founded
	Birth control clinic opened
1922	Married Women's Maintenance Act
	Infanticide Act
	Criminal Law Amendment Act
1923	Matrimonial Causes Act
1925	Guardianship of Infants Act
	Widows, Orphans and Old Age Pensions Act
1926	General Strike
1928	Votes for women on same terms as men
1929	Age of Marriage Act
	First female cabinet minister

Study Guide: AS Questions

In the style of AQA

(a) Explain why few women entered Parliament in the 1920s.

(12 marks)

(b) 'The First World War had little impact on the position of women in the workplace, 1918–30.' Explain why you agree or disagree with this view. (24 marks)

Exam tips

The cross-references are intended to take you straight to the material that will help you to answer the questions.

(a) You will need to explain the various factors that placed women in a difficult position when it came to parliamentary election. Re-read page 163 and consider the suggestions given there. These ideas are developed further on pages 163–7. You need to think about them and comment on how they relate to one another. Try to pick out the most important factor and provide some judgement in your answer.

(b) To answer this question you will probably want to provide a brief outline of the sort of work women did in the First World War (see Chapter 6), but the focus of your answer should be on what happened after the war and whether or not women had changed their position as workers as a result of the war-time experience. Re-read pages 169–71. Try to be specific about which women were affected by any changes that took place, looking at both the middle and working classes. You should also consider whether it was the war or other factors that brought any changes about. You might, for example, wish to argue that the war had actually made little practical difference to most women and that any middle-class advances were more because of changes in types of employment and the spread of education. You must decide what your case will be and, for high marks, you should try to sustain and support a line of argument that leads to a convincing conclusion.

Glossary

Amnesty   A general pardon for political offences.

Anarchy   Disorder; lack of government.

Association for Moral and Social Hygiene   Formed in 1915 to eliminate government regulation of prostitution world-wide.

Autocratic   Dictatorial. Not allowing any discussion.

Bolshevik revolution   The seizure of power in Russia by the Bolshevik Party in October 1917.

Borough   A town represented by an MP in the House of Commons.

British Union of Fascists   An extreme right-wing group founded in 1932. It was sympathetic to the Nazis.

Cambridge University Men's League Founded in 1909 as a branch of the Men's League. Members, 'some in slouched hats and smoking pipes, some in cap and gown, some with their hands in their pockets and wearing a diffident air', walked in the 1910 suffrage procession.

Census enumerator   Someone who collects census information from householders.

Charity schools   Schools set up by individuals or religious groups.

Chastity for men   A view that men should be chaste, that is abstain from sex outside marriage.

Chauvinism   Over-patriotic, excessive support for one's country.

Civil disobedience   Disobeying the civil law, e.g. laws concerning taxes.

Civil liberties   Freedom of action and speech.

Civil war   A war between people of the same country.

Coalition government   Government run on non-party lines. In 1915 the Conservatives joined the Liberals to govern together during the war emergency. The coalition lasted until 1922.

Common Cause   Published between 1909 and 1920 as a journal of the NUWSS.

Common law   Law which is based on legal judgments made by judges hearing court cases, as opposed to statutory law which is made by Parliament.

Conscientious objector   Someone who refuses to fight for their country on the grounds that war is wrong.

Conservative Party   'Conservative' began to be used as a word for the Tory Party in the 1830s. They were against Home Rule and wanted the UK to remain united.

Constitution   Rules of an organisation that include its aims and objectives, policies and methods.

Corrupt Practices Act   This limited the use of people being paid to persuade others to vote for their candidate.

Criminal Law Amendment Act   Raised the age of sexual consent to 16. It also made homosexuality illegal and brought in stricter laws against prostitution.

Danger duty   Term used by the WSPU for illegal activities.

DBE   Dame Commander of the Order of the British Empire. Part of a British system whereby individuals are honoured for their bravery, achievement or service.

Defence of the realm   The protection of Britain from enemy forces.

Democracy An electoral system in which every adult has the vote.

Demonstrations Public marches for a political purpose.

Depression A period in the 1930s when there was high unemployment.

Dowry Money brought by a bride to her husband.

Education Act of 1870 This established School Boards that had the authority to build schools from money collected from local taxes. Women were allowed to vote for and serve on School Boards.

Education Act of 1902 Abolished School Boards and set up Local Education Authorities (LEAs), which were given the power to establish secondary schools. Women were not allowed to vote or serve on these.

Edwardian A term used to describe the reign of King Edward VII, who reigned between 1901 and 1910.

Enfranchised Given the vote.

Ephemera Everyday, seemingly unimportant items.

Factory schools From 1833 cotton manufacturers had to provide half-time schooling for children who worked in their factories.

Fascism An extreme right-wing nationalist movement that existed in Italy between 1922 and 1943. Its leader was Benito Mussolini.

Feminist Someone who believes that women and men should be treated equally.

Feminist historian A historian who believes that women are oppressed and must fight to end that oppression.

First and second readings The first reading announces the main parts of a proposed Parliamentary Bill. At the second reading, it is read out in full and discussed; amendments can be added. It then proceeds to the third reading and to

the House of Lords. If both Houses agree, the Bill is given to the monarch to sign.

Garrison towns Towns with an army stationed permanently.

Gladstonian Liberals A name for a group of MPs who were associated with Gladstone who, although a reformer in many areas, believed in low taxation.

Great Reform Act of 1832 This gave the vote to approximately one in seven men.

Home Rule Self-government for Ireland. At the time Ireland was part of the UK.

Household suffrage Male heads of households permitted to vote.

Householders Those who lived at a permanent address and paid taxes on their home.

Hunger strike A refusal to eat in order to increase sympathy for a cause.

Hustings Before 1872, parliamentary candidates stood on an open-air platform in a public place, 'on the hustings', and voters put up their hands to cast their vote for them.

Hysterical Today, the word means mad, wild, uncontrolled or frenzied. Derived from '*hystera*', the Greek word for womb.

Independent Labour Party Founded in 1893 to promote the interests of the working class. It had a women's section.

Industrial conscription Compulsory work for the government.

Labour churches Set up in the late nineteenth century. Members generally supported the emerging Labour Party and believed that the labour movement could help to obtain the Kingdom of Heaven on Earth.

Labour movement A term used to describe those who worked for improvements for the working class.

Labour Party Formed in 1906 as a socialist party committed to improving the lives of the working class.

Labour Representation Committee A committee established to help socialist MPs get elected.

Ladies' Gallery A separate place for women to sit in the House of Commons; protected by an iron rail, called a grille.

Ladies' National Association An organisation for women founded in 1869 to repeal unjust laws for prostitutes. Today it is known as the Josephine Butler Society and continues to campaign against the exploitation of prostitutes.

Laissez-faire The theory that governments should not interfere in business.

The Lancet A medical journal that was influential and esteemed at the time; still published today.

Liberal government The Liberals swept into power in 1906, fought two elections in 1910 and remained in power until 1922.

Liberal Party Founded in 1859. It believed in social reform. Under Gladstone it became committed to Home Rule for Ireland. In 1886 the Liberal Party split into Liberals and Liberal Unionists over this issue.

Liberal Unionists Formed in 1886 after a split with the Liberal Party. They wanted Ireland to remain part of the UK.

Light industries Industries manufacturing small or light articles such as shoes.

Lobbying An organised attempt by people to influence law-makers.

Male Electors' League for Women's Suffrage Founded in the 1890s. One of its members became the first man to go to prison for the cause.

Married Women's Property Acts The 1870 Act gave women the right to keep their earnings, their personal property, and money under £200 left to them in someone's will. The 1882 Act gave women control of the money they brought into marriage and acquired afterwards.

Men's Committee for Justice to Women Founded in 1909 to monitor cases where suffragettes were prosecuted for militancy.

Men's Declaration Committee Founded in 1909 to collect signatures of professional men who supported votes for women.

Military conscription Compulsory enlistment for the armed forces.

Munitions factories Factories that produced guns, bullets, shells and other weapons.

National Union of Women Workers Founded in 1895, mainly to support women who worked in charity organisations, this organisation was initially concerned with the elimination of prostitution. It is still in existence and is called the National Council of Women. One of its aims is to encourage women to take an active part in public life.

National Union of Women's Suffrage Societies Founded in 1897. Known as suffragists, they favoured peaceful methods.

National Vigilance Association Founded in 1885 to help to enforce the Criminal Law Amendment Act.

Nationalisation The government takeover of an industry or business from private ownership.

New Liberalism A twentieth-century term for the doctrines of those Liberals who believed that reforms in education and health care should be paid for by higher taxation.

Nonconformists People who belong to a Christian church that does not conform to Church of England beliefs and practices.

Northern Men's Federation for Women's Suffrage Founded in 1913 to co-ordinate the work of male supporters in northern England and in Scotland. It campaigned for women's suffrage during the war and folded in 1919.

Oligarchy   Government by a small group of people.

Oxford Union   Formed in 1823 as a debating society at the University of Oxford. It enjoys a reputation for the quality of its debate and has proved to be a training ground for many British politicians. It has always invited prestigious people to speak on behalf of a controversial issue.

Pacifism   A belief that war and violence are wrong and that all quarrels can be settled peacefully.

Parliamentary Secretary   An MP who assists a Minister with government business.

Pauper children   Children who had no family and lived in workhouses.

Peterloo   A demonstration held at St Peter's Field, Manchester, in 1812 in support of parliamentary reform. The demonstrators were attacked by soldiers wielding swords. The demonstration was ironically named Peterloo after a British victory over the French at Waterloo.

Pilgrimages   Journeys taken for religious, political or sentimental reasons.

Pit-brow women   Women who worked outside a coal mine, at the top of the pit (the pit-brow), sorting coal.

Plural Voting Bills   Men had the right to vote in their own constituency, as university graduates and as business owners. The Plural Voting Bills aimed to stop men from voting more than once.

Poor Law Amendment Act   Encouraged local authorities to build workhouses for their unemployed poor rather than to help in other ways.

Poor Law Guardian   A locally elected official who supervised the workhouses in the area.

Primrose League   Founded in 1883 to spread Conservative ideas. A woman's section was formed in 1885.

Private member's bill   A parliamentary bill put forward by an individual MP.

Proprietor of white slaves   A man who bought and sold women for prostitution.

Quakers   Members of the Society of Friends, a Christian organisation founded in the mid-seventeenth century, which is committed to pacifism and social equality.

Radical activist   Someone who campaigned for social and political reforms such as votes for women, improvements in working conditions and better housing for the working class.

Rate-paying   Paying local taxes.

Rebels' Social and Political Union   Founded in about 1913 to give support to the East London Federation of Suffragettes. George Lansbury's son, Willie, was a leading member.

Regulation 40D   A law passed in 1918 that made it a crime for women with a sexually transmitted disease to have, or even suggest to have, sexual intercourse with anyone in the armed forces.

'Rule Britannia'   A nationalistic song written in the mid-eighteenth century. The words of the chorus are 'Rule, Britannia! Britannia, rule the waves; Britons never will be slaves'.

Sanctuary   The most sacred part of the Christian Church where a fugitive from the law could take refuge against arrest.

Second Reform Act of 1867   This gave the vote to approximately one in three men.

Secret ballot   A system where the choice of voters is kept confidential. Until 1872 voters had to declare their vote in public.

Secretary   An official appointed by a society to keep its records and look after the business side of the organisation.

Separate spheres   An idea that there were two spheres in society. Men belonged to the public sphere whereas women belonged to the private sphere. Each sphere was seen to be different but equal.

Session A period of time when Parliament meets. Bills expire if they do not become law by the time the parliamentary session ends.

Sexual double standard The moral standard whereby it was acceptable for men, but not women, to have sex outside marriage.

Sinn Fein Founded in 1907 as an Irish nationalist organisation.

Six Point Group Formed in 1921 with six specific aims.

Socialism A theory that advocates that the state should own and control businesses, factories and industry in order to promote equality.

Soliciting Stopping someone and offering them sexual services if they pay money.

Speaker of the House of Commons An elected, impartial representative who enforces parliamentary rules, and liaises between the Crown, the Lords and the Commons. The Speaker can allow or prohibit motions and amendments to be put forward in Parliament.

Speaker's Conference A formal inquiry into elections. It is chaired by the Speaker and its membership is drawn from across the political parties.

Spinsters Unmarried women. Single women were the main spinners of cloth and the word spinster comes from this.

Stamp duty In June 1855 the final remaining penny of newspaper tax, called stamp duty, was removed. This opened the way for cheap mass-circulation papers. For example, the *Daily Telegraph* was founded a few months afterwards and cost just one penny.

Suffrage The vote.

Suffrage Atelier An organisation founded in 1909 to encourage artists to draw or paint material in support of votes for women.

The Suffragette A WSPU newspaper published between 1912 and 1915. Each issue of the paper sold about 17,000, but this fell to about 10,000 because of police persecution.

Suffragettes Women who sought the vote using violent methods.

Suffragists Women who sought the vote using peaceful methods.

Temperance reform Reform of the alcohol laws.

Third Reform Act of 1884 This gave the vote to approximately two in three men.

Trades Union Congress An association that represents the vast majority of trade unions.

Ulster Unionists A political organisation whose members wanted the northern province of Ulster in Ireland to remain British. When the Liberals introduced another Home Rule Bill in 1912 the Ulster Unionists threatened to rebel.

United Suffragists Founded in 1914 and open to men and women, militants and non-militants. In 1914 *Votes for Women* became its official paper, which it published until 1918.

Universal suffrage Votes for all adult men and women.

Viceroys Rulers of India who were appointed by the British government. Between 1858 and 1947 India was under the control of Britain.

Victorian A term used to describe things, people and events in the reign of Queen Victoria, who reigned between 1837 and 1901.

Votes for Women The official paper of the WSPU between 1907 and 1912. After 1912 it was edited by the Pethick-Lawrences. It had a circulation figure of over 30,000 in 1910, but after 1912, when the paper ceased to be linked to the WSPU, its editors found it difficult to keep the paper solvent.

Votes for Women Fellowship   Between 1912 and 1914 it promoted the newspaper *Votes for Women* as an independent suffrage paper not affiliated to any group.

White feathers   In August 1914 Admiral Fitzgerald founded the Order of the White Feather. This was an organisation that encouraged young women to give white feathers to men not in uniform in order to shame them into joining the armed forces.

Widows, Orphans and Old Age Pensioners' Bill 1925   A scheme that enabled workers to pay a weekly contribution so that they could receive a pension at the age of 65. If an insured worker died, benefits were paid to their widow and children.

Woman's Dreadnought   In 1917 it changed its name to the *Workers' Dreadnought* and after the First World War became the paper of the Communist Party of Great Britain. It was the only suffrage paper directed at working-class people.

Women patrols   At a meeting of the National Council of Women (a philanthropic organisation for women) it was decided to form patrols to look after the sexual welfare of young working-class women. At the same time a former Women's Freedom League organiser set up the Women Police Volunteers for the same purpose. This eventually led to the formation of the Women's Police.

Women's International League for Peace and Freedom   This league was founded at the Women's Peace Conference held between 28 April and 1 May 1915.

Women's Liberal Federation   Founded in 1886 by female Liberals to promote votes for women.

Women's liberation movement
A movement, which began in the 1960s, that wanted equal pay for equal work, free abortion on demand, educational opportunities and equal rights for lesbians.

Women's Party   This was a party founded by Christabel Pankhurst and open to women of all classes.

Women's Social and Political Union
Founded in 1903 by Emmeline Pankhurst to campaign for votes for women. Known as suffragettes, they used violent methods.

Women's Suffrage Journal   Published between 1870 and 1890 and edited by Lydia Becker. It enjoyed a small circulation: in 1875 the print order was for 400 copies.

Women's Tax Resistance League   An organisation that supported women who refused to pay taxes because they could not vote.

Workhouse schools   From 1834 workhouses had to provide schooling for the children who lived there.

Working class   A collective term for those people and their families who earned a living as manual workers.

Yom Kippur   The Day of Atonement. It is a day set aside to make amends for the sins of the past year.

Young Hot Bloods   A name given to the members of a WSPU group. Being a hot blood meant being passionate, possibly overzealous, about an issue.

Index

Actresses' Franchise League 34, 61–2, 73–4
Anderson, Elizabeth Garrett 1, 5, 36, 62, 76
Anti-suffragists 23–30, 32, 34, 36, 63, 150
Arson 68–9, 86–8
Artists' Suffrage League 61, 62
Asquith, Herbert 60, 69, 77, 79, 85, 92, 100,
    102, 105, 106, 110, 131–5, 147, 148–9,
    153, 156–60
Astor, Nancy 138, 161, 163, 165–7, 174–6

Balfour, Arthur 80, 103–4
Balfour, Lady Betty 44
Becker, Lydia 9, 19–20, 36, 37–40, 43, 69, 71,
    75, 77, 184
Bell, Gertrude 23
Billington-Greig, Teresa 58–9, 66–7
'Black Friday' 91, 99, 113–14
Blatch, Harriot Stanton 40, 42
Bodichon, Barbara 4, 36, 37
Bright, Jacob 40, 41, 105
Bright, Ursula 41
Butler, Josephine 7, 21, 40, 47, 174, 181
Burdett-Coutts, Angela 13

Campbell-Bannerman 77, 79, 105
'Cat and Mouse Act' 100, 117–18, 120,
    127
Catholic Women's Suffrage Society 61–2, 120
Census evasion 68, 84
Central Committee of the National Society for
    Women's Suffrage (CCWS) 36, 39
Churchill, Winston 79, 104–5, 112–14, 127,
    165, 169
Church League for women's Suffrage 61, 62,
    121
Clarke, Mary 50
Cobden, Jane 39
Common Cause 45, 74, 179
Conciliation Bills 77, 85, 89, 93–4, 99–101,
    106, 109, 111, 113, 134, 160
Conciliation Committee 77, 92, 99, 101–3, 105,
    132, 134
Conservative Party 44, 80, 100, 102–4, 106,
    109, 127, 131–2, 134, 148, 163–4, 166,
    179, 182
Conservative and Unionist Women's Suffrage
    Association 36, 44, 61, 62
Contagious Diseases 1, 2, 7, 18, 38–9, 121
Coronation procession 68, 71–3
Curzon, Lord 24, 102, 132, 150

Davies, Emily 36, 76
Davison, Emily 69, 86, 90–1
Despard, Charlotte 57, 58, 83, 126, 140, 163,
    169
Disraeli, Benjamin 27, 36, 103
Drummond, Flora 88, 123

East London Federation of Suffragettes (ELFS)
    36, 59–61, 99, 106, 119, 127, 136, 138–40,
    143, 153, 182
Elmy, Elizabeth Wolstenholme 6, 41

Fawcett, Millicent 19–21, 29, 36, 39, 40, 43–7,
    64, 70, 71, 77, 92–3, 95, 126, 138, 140–1,
    155–7, 169, 173
First Aid Yeomanry 144, 147
Forcible feeding 99, 115–17, 127
Friends' League for Women's Suffrage 61, 62

Gawthorpe, Mary 80
Gladstone, William 26, 27, 104–5, 132, 180, 181
Gore-Booth, Eva 44
Grey, Edward 79

Hardie, Keir 78, 107, 132
Hunger striking 68, 89–90, 99, 115–18

Imprisonment 114
Irish nationalists 109–10, 133–4
Irish Women's Franchise League (IWFL) 36, 63,
    109

Jewish League for Woman Suffrage 62, 121

Kenney, Annie 48, 54, 68, 79, 81, 121, 168–9
Kingsley, Mary 23

Labour Party 8, 44, 47–8, 65, 68, 78–80, 91,
    100, 106–10, 119, 123, 131–2, 134, 148,
    163, 166, 168, 180
Lancashire and Cheshire Women Textile and
    Other Workers' Representation Committee
    (LCWT) 36, 44, 46, 70
Lansbury, George 100, 107–8, 139, 182
Liberal Party 39–40, 43–4, 46–8, 50, 63, 76–80,
    82, 92, 100, 104–6, 108–18, 126, 133–4,
    148, 153, 163, 166, 179, 180, 181, 183
Lloyd George, David 31, 68, 69, 79, 86, 90, 92,
    101, 104–5, 125, 135–9, 147–8, 151, 153,
    155, 157, 160

London Graduates' Union for Women's Suffrage 61–2
London National Society for Woman Suffrage 35–7, 39
Lytton, Constance 44, 53, 68, 74, 90, 91, 102, 117
Lytton, Lord 102, 126

MacDonald, Ramsay 107, 151
Manchester National Society for Women's Suffrage 35–7
Married Women's Property Acts 1, 6, 19, 181
Men's Federation for Women's Suffrage 125–7
Men's League for Women's Suffrage 99, 102, 107, 121, 123, 125–6, 132
Men's League for Opposing Women's Suffrage 63, 99, 102, 127–8, 132–3
Men's Political Union 121, 125–7
Militancy 78–98
Mill, John Stuart 17–18, 36, 44, 47, 76, 77, 99, 103, 105, 132
Munition workers 143, 146

National Anti-Suffrage League 63
National League for Opposing Women's Suffrage 32, 133–4, 150
National Society for Women's Suffrage (NSWS) 35–9, 69
National Union of Societies for Equal Citizenship 172–3
National Union of Women's Suffrage Societies (NUWSS) 15, 20–1, 35, 42, 43–7, 53–4, 57–8, 62–6, 68–74, 76, 78, 84, 91, 93–4, 100, 106, 108, 125–6, 136, 140–4, 153, 166, 172, 179, 181
Nightingale, Florence 5, 13

Osler, Catherine 44

Pankhurst, Christabel 7, 15, 19, 20–2, 48–9, 51, 52, 57–60, 65, 68, 74, 78–81, 83, 85, 97, 100, 102, 112, 121, 131–8, 148, 154, 168, 173, 184
Pankhurst, Emmeline 9, 15, 19–20, 40–1, 42, 48–9, 61, 64, 71, 73–4, 77–80, 84–9, 91–4, 97–8, 117, 125, 136–8, 148, 154, 168, 173, 184
Pankhurst, Richard 15, 40, 41, 49, 54, 75, 80, 105
Pankhurst, Sylvia 36, 48–9, 51–8, 60, 77, 105–7, 119, 125, 138–40, 169
Parliamentary reform
  for men 11, 12, 16–17, 35, 150, 180, 182, 183
  for women 2, 10–11, 27, 135, 150, 152, 161–2, 168, 176

Pethick-Lawrence, Emmeline 36, 48, 52, 58, 72, 59, 93, 126–7, 149, 163, 169, 183
Pethick-Lawrence, Frederick 23, 36, 48, 52, 56–9, 149, 169, 183
Plural Voting Bills 78, 182
Prisoners' Temporary Discharge for Ill Health Act 117–18

Richardson, Mary 88, 168–9
Robins, Elizabeth 33, 73–4
Roper, Esther 44, 52

Secret ballot 11, 12
Smyth, Ethel 73, 89, 96
Speaker's Conference 135, 150–1, 159, 183
Suffrage Atelier 13, 183
Suffragette, The 49, 52, 55, 74, 112, 123, 136, 183
Suffragettes 2, 14–16, 18–20, 22, 25, 28–30, 51–3, 55–6, 58–60, 64–5, 68–70, 72–5, 77, 78–83, 86–9, 91–5, 98, 99, 102, 105–8, 111–18, 121–7, 133–6, 138, 143–4, 152–3, 156, 159–61, 163, 167–9, 173–5, 183, 184
Suffragists 2, 12–20, 22, 29–30, 39, 40, 43, 59, 64–5, 68–70, 72–3, 75–8, 81–2, 85, 91, 93–5, 102, 107, 115, 122, 124, 126, 133–4, 141, 143–4, 148, 152–4, 159–63, 167–9, 173–5, 183

Tax evasion 83–4
Taylor, Helen 44
Trade Unions 116–17
Trojan horse raid 68–9
Twining, Louisa 13

Voluntary Aid Detachment 144, 147
Votes for Women 49, 52, 56, 61, 65, 74, 89, 95, 183, 184

Ward, Mrs Humphrey 24, 26, 28, 63
Window smashing 68–9, 85, 86
Women's Anti-Suffrage League 24, 36, 63
Women's Franchise League 35, 40–2
Women's Freedom League (WFL) 36, 58, 68, 71, 73, 75, 79, 83–5, 106, 126, 136, 140, 177, 184
Women's International League for Peace and Freedom 138
Women's Social and Political Union (WSPU) 15, 17, 33–46, 48–59, 61–73, 75–8, 79–82, 84–5, 96–8, 107–8, 111–12, 114, 120–1, 123–6, 135–8, 143, 160, 165, 179, 183, 184
Women's Suffrage Journal 37–8, 74, 183
Women's Tax Resistance League 17, 68, 84, 184
Women Writers' Suffrage League 61, 62